D0221948

An Introduction to Artificial Intelligence

An Introduction to Artificial Intelligence

Janet Finlay and Alan Dix
University of Huddersfield

UCL
PRESS

First published in 1996 by UCL Press

UCL Press Limited
University College London
Gower Street
London WC1E 6BT

The name of University College London (UCL) is a registered
trade mark used by UCL Press with the consent of the owner.

British Library Cataloguing in Publication Data
A catalogue record for this book is available from the British Library.

ISBN: 1-85728-399-6 PB

This book has been typeset, proofed and passed for press by the authors.

Typeset in Palatino.
Printed and bound by
Biddles Ltd, Guildford and King's Lynn, England.

Contents

Preface

Why another AI text-book?

This book is based upon course material used by one of the authors on an introductory course in artificial intelligence (AI) at the University of York. The course was taught to MSc conversion course students who had little technical background and only basic level mathematics. Available text-books in AI either assumed too much technical knowledge or provided a very limited coverage of the subject. This book is an attempt to fill this gap. Its aim is to provide accessible coverage of the key areas of AI, in such a way that it will be understandable to those with only a basic knowledge of mathematics.

The book takes a pragmatic approach to AI, looking at how AI techniques are applied to various application areas. It is structured in two main sections. The first part introduces the key techniques used in AI in the areas of knowledge representation, search, reasoning and learning. The second part covers application areas including game playing, expert systems, natural language understanding, vision, robotics, agents and modelling cognition. The book concludes with a brief consideration of some of the philosophical and social issues relating to the subject.

It does not claim to be comprehensive: there are many books on the market which give more detailed coverage. Instead it is designed to be used to support a one-semester introductory module in AI (assuming a 12 week module with a lecture and practical session). Depending on the emphasis of the module, possible course structures include spending one week on each of the 12 main chapters or spending more time on techniques and selecting a subset of the application areas to consider.

The book does not attempt to teach any programming language. However, since it is useful to demonstrate techniques using a specific implementation we provide example PROLOG programs which are available from our WWW site (http://www.hud.ac.uk/schools/comp+maths/books/ai96). If you prefer to receive the programs on disk please send £8 to us at the address below and we will supply a disk.

Acknowledgements

As with any endeavour there are many people behind the scenes providing help and support. We would like to thank our families, friends and colleagues for their tolerance and understanding while we have been writing this book. In particular, thanks must go to Fiona for suggestions that have enhanced the readability of the book and to the anonymous reviewers for useful feedback.

Janet Finlay and Alan Dix
School of Computing and Mathematics
University of Huddersfield
Canalside, Huddersfield
HD1 3DH
UK

Introduction

What is artificial intelligence?

Artificial intelligence (AI) is many different things to different people. It is likely that everyone who picks up this book has their own, albeit perhaps vague, notion of what it is. As a concept, AI has long captured the attention and imagination of journalists and novelists alike, leading both to popular renditions of current AI developments and futuristic representations of what might be just around the corner. Television and film producers have followed suit, so that AI is rarely far from the public eye. Robots, computers that talk to us in our own language and intelligent computer "experts" are all part of the future as presented to us through the media, though there is some division as to whether these developments will provide us with benign servants or sinister and deadly opponents.

But outside the realm of futuristic fiction, what is AI all about? Unfortunately there is no single answer: just like in the media representation it very much depends upon who you talk to. On the one hand, there are those who view AI in high-level terms as the study of the nature of intelligence and, from there, how to reproduce it. Computers are therefore used to model intelligence in order to understand it. Within this group there are those who believe that human intelligence is essentially computational and, therefore, that cognitive states can be reproduced in a machine. Others use computers to test their theories of intelligence: they are interested less in replicating than in understanding human intelligence. For either of these groups, it is vital that the techniques proposed actually reflect human cognitive processes.

On the other hand, there are those who view AI in more "pragmatic" terms: it is a discipline that provides engineering techniques to solve difficult problems. Whether these techniques reflect human cognition or indicate actual intelligence is not important. To this group the success of an AI system is judged on its behaviour in the domain of interest. It is not necessary for the machine to exhibit general intelligence.

A third set of people, perhaps falling somewhere between the previous two, want to develop machines that not only exhibit intelligent behaviour but are able to learn and adapt to their environment in a way similar to humans. In striving towards this, it is inevitable that insights will be gained into the nature of human intelligence and learning, although it is not essential that these are accurately reproduced.

So can we derive a definition of AI that encompasses some of these ideas? A working definition may go something like this:

> AI is concerned with building machines that can act and react appropriately, adapting their response to the demands of the situation. Such machines should display behaviour comparable with that considered to require intelligence in humans.

Such a definition incorporates learning and adaptability as general characteristics of intelligence but stops short of insisting on the replication of *human* intelligence.

What types of behaviour would meet this definition and therefore fall under the umbrella of AI? Or, perhaps more importantly, what types of behaviour would not? It may be useful to think about some of the things we consider to require intelligence or thought in human beings. A list would usually include conscious cognitive activities: problem solving, decision making, reading, mathematics. Further consideration might add more creative activities: writing and art. We are less likely to think of our more fundamental skills – language, vision, motor skills and navigation – simply because, to us, these are automatic and do not require conscious attention. But consider for a moment what is involved in these "everyday" activities. For example, language understanding requires recognition and interpretation of words, spoken in many different accents and intonations, and knowledge of how words can be strung together. It involves resolution of ambiguity and understanding of context. Language production is even more complex. One only needs to take up a foreign language to appreciate the difficulties involved – even for humans.

On the other hand, some areas that may seem to us very difficult, such as mathematical calculation, are in fact much more formulaic and therefore require only the ability to follow steps accurately. Such behaviour is not inherently intelligent, and computers are traditionally excellent as calculators. However, this activity would not be classed as artificial intelligence. Of course, we would not want to suggest that mathematics does not require intelligence! For example, problem solving and interpretation are also important in mathematics and these aspects have been studied as domains for AI research.

From this we can see that there are a number of areas that are useful to explore in AI, among them language understanding, expert decision making, problem solving and planning. We will consider these and others in the course of this book.

However, it should be noted that there are also some "grey" areas, activities that require skill and strategy when performed by humans but that can, ultimately, be condensed to a search of possible options (albeit a huge number of them). Game playing is a prime example of such an activity. In the early days, chess and other complex games were very much within the domain of humans and not computers, and were considered a valid target for AI research. But today computers can play chess at grand master level, largely due to their huge memory capacity. Many would therefore say that these are not now part of AI. However, such games have played an important part in the development of several AI techniques, notably search techniques, and are therefore still worthy of consideration. It is for this reason that we include them in this book.

However, before we move on to look in more detail at the techniques and applications of AI, we should pause to consider how it has developed up to now.

History of artificial intelligence

AI is not a new concept. The idea of creating an intelligent being was proposed and discussed in various ways by writers and philosophers centuries before the computer was even invented. The earliest writers imagined their "artificial" beings created from stone: the Roman poet Ovid wrote a story of Pygmalion, the sculptor, whose statue of a beautiful woman was brought to life (the musical *My fair lady* is the more recent rendition of this fable). Much later, in the age of industrial machines, Mary Shelley had Doctor Frankenstein manufacture a man from separate components and bring him to life through electricity. By the 1960s, fiction was beginning to mirror the goals of the most ambitious AI researcher. In Arthur C. Clarke's *2001*, we find the computer HAL displaying all the attributes of human intelligence, including self-preservation. Other films, such as *Blade runner* and *Terminator*, present a vision of cyborg machines almost indistinguishable from humans.

Early philosophers also considered the question of whether human intelligence can be reproduced in a machine. In 1642, Descartes argued that, although machines (in the right guise) could pass as animals, they could never pass as humans. He went on to identify his reasons for this assertion, namely that machines lack the ability to use language and the ability to reason. Interestingly, although he was writing at a time when clocks and windmills were among the most sophisticated pieces of machinery, he had identified two areas that still occupy the attention of AI researchers today, and that are central to one of the first tests of machine intelligence proposed for computers, the Turing test.

Turing and the Turing test

To find the start of modern AI we have to go back to 1950, when computers were basically large numeric calculators. In that year, a British mathematician, Alan Turing, wrote a now famous paper entitled *Computing machinery and intelligence*, in which he posed the question "can machines think?" (Turing 1950). His answer to the question was to propose a game, the *Imitation game*, as the basis for a test for machine intelligence. His test is now known as the *Turing test*.

His proposal was as follows. Imagine you have a person able to communicate with two others, one male and one female, only through a teletype or computer link. This person must try to distinguish the male from the female simply by asking questions, while those being questioned try to fool the interrogator about their gender. In the Turing test, one of the human participants is replaced by a computer. If the computer is able to convince the interrogator it is the human, Turing argued, it can be said to be intelligent.

The Turing test has been widely criticized since it was proposed, and in Chapter 12 of this book we will look in detail at some of the objections to it. However, the main criticism is that it takes a behavioural rather than a psychological view of intelligence. Regardless of the criticisms the Turing test is significant as it provided the first concrete goal for AI research.

The development of AI

In 1956 about a dozen researchers met at Dartmouth College. They represented a number of academic disciplines including mathematics, electrical engineering and psychology but they had one interest in common: using the powerful tool of the computer to simulate human intelligence. It was here, at the Dartmouth Conference, that the name "Artificial Intelligence" was coined.

In the early days of AI, research concentrated on applications that were considered to involve intelligence and reasoning, mainly game playing and theorem proving. During the decade following the Dartmouth Conference there were significant developments in search techniques, pattern matching, heuristics and constraint satisfaction, which are still important today. However, these early applications proved to be solvable using rapid searches through all possible options, rather than the selection strategies and reasoning applied by humans, and attention turned to the problem of modelling and reproducing true understanding.

From the mid-1960s researchers concentrated on applications such as perception, language understanding and general problem solving. One such application, ELIZA (Weizenbaum 1966), was hailed by some as a breakthrough in language understanding. ELIZA appeared, on the surface, to understand and respond intelligently to human conversation, albeit in the slightly artificial context of Rogerian psychoanalysis. "Patients" would communicate with ELIZA via a keyboard and the program would respond in such a way that many patients believed that they were talking to a human. A conversation with ELIZA would run something like this (machine responses in upper case):

    TELL ME ABOUT YOUR PROBLEM
    men are all alike
    HOW DO YOU FEEL ABOUT MEN?
    none of them can be trusted
    NOT ANY?
    well very few
    COULD YOU BE MORE PRECISE PLEASE?

my grandfather was trustworthy
TELL ME ABOUT YOUR GRANDFATHER
he is dead
HOW LONG HAS HE BEEN DEAD?
a couple of years – he was my mother's father
TELL ME ABOUT YOUR MOTHER
she is very nice
CAN YOU THINK OF A SPECIFIC EXAMPLE?
she is always glad to see me
IS YOUR FATHER ALSO ALWAYS GLAD TO SEE YOU?
most of the time
HOW DID YOUR PARENTS TREAT YOU AS A CHILD?

Such a conversation may appear convincing but does ELIZA therefore pass the Turing test? In 1966, the program's developer, Joseph Weizenbaum, wrote a paper to dispel this notion (at the same time casting some doubt on the validity of the Turing test) (Weizenbaum 1966). ELIZA actually works on the basis of some clever tricks of substitution, pattern matching and random selection. The user's sentence is searched for key words that are then either substituted into a new sentence by ELIZA or used to fire an associated response. If more than one possible response is available, ELIZA chooses between them randomly. In spite of appearances, therefore, ELIZA embodies no *understanding* of the English language. As Weizenbaum says, it shows "how easy it is to create and maintain the illusion of understanding" (Weizenbaum 1966). Once these tricks are understood it is very easy to fool ELIZA:

HOW DID YOUR PARENTS TREAT YOU AS A CHILD?
they gave me my grandfather clock
TELL ME ABOUT YOUR GRANDFATHER ...

However, research continued into language understanding in the early 1970s and another significant system emerged: SHRDLU. SHRDLU (the name comes from six of the 12 most commonly used letters in English) was developed by Terry Winograd (Winograd 1972). The system can understand and comply with quite complex sentences but there is a catch: it is restricted to the domain of simulated blocks. Although this may seem limited, SHRDLU still far surpassed any other system of the time.

Consider an instruction such as "Find a block that is taller than the one you are holding and put it on top of the red box." What knowledge is required to interpret such a sentence? First you need to understand the concepts of relative sizes. Then you need to interpret the reference in the second clause: to what does "it" refer? Then you need to understand relative position and differentiate by colour. SHRDLU was able to interpret such instructions through the use of stored knowledge and was one of the applications of this period that led to the development of a number of methodologies for knowledge representation (discussed in Ch. 1).

The physical symbol system hypothesis

In 1976 Newell and Simon proposed a hypothesis that has become the basis of research and experimentation in AI: the *physical symbol system hypothesis* (Newell & Simon 1976). The hypothesis states that

> A physical symbol system has the necessary and sufficient means for general intelligent action.

So what does this mean? A *symbol* is a token that represents something else. For example, a word is a symbol representing an object or concept. The symbol is physical although the thing represented by it may be conceptual. Symbols are physically related to each other in *symbol structures* (for example, they may be adjacent). In addition to symbol structures, the system contains operators or processes that transform structures into other structures, for example copying, adding, removing them. A *physical symbol system* comprises an evolving set of symbol structures and the operators required to transform them. The hypothesis suggests that such a system is able to model intelligent behaviour. The only way to test this hypothesis is by experimentation: choose an activity that requires intelligence and devise a physical symbol system to solve it. Computers are a good means of simulating the physical symbol system and are therefore used in testing the hypothesis. It is not yet clear whether the physical symbol system hypothesis will hold in all areas of intelligence. It is certainly supported by work in areas such as game playing and decision making but in lower-level activities such as vision it is possible that subsymbolic approaches (such as neural networks) will prove to be more useful. However, this in itself does not disprove the physical symbol system hypothesis, since it is clearly possible to solve problems in alternative ways.

The physical symbol system hypothesis is important as the foundation for the belief that it is possible to create artifical intelligence. It also provides a useful model of human intelligence that can be simulated and therefore tested.

More recent developments

By the late 1970s, while the physical symbol system hypothesis provided fresh impetus to those examining the nature of intelligent behaviour, some research moved away from the "grand aim" of producing general machine understanding and concentrated instead upon developing effective techniques in restricted domains. Arguably this approach has had the most commercial success, producing, amongst other things, the expert system (see Ch. 6).

More recently the development of artificial neural networks, modelled on the human brain, has been hailed by some as the basis for genuine machine intelligence and learning. Neural networks, or "connectionist" systems, have proved effective in small applications but many have huge resource requirements.

Traditional AI researchers have been slow to welcome the connectionists, being sceptical of their claims and the premises underlying neural networks.

In one example, a recognition system used neural networks to learn the properties of a number of photographs taken in woodland. Its aim was to differentiate between those containing tanks and those without. After a number of test runs in which the system accurately picked out all the photographs of tanks, the developers were feeling suitably pleased with themselves. However, to confirm their findings they took another set of photographs. To their dismay the system proved completely unable to pick out the tanks. After further investigation it turned out that the first set of photographs of tanks had been taken on a sunny day while those without were cloudy. The network was not classifying the photographs according to the presence of tanks at all but according to prevailing weather conditions! Since the "reasoning" underlying the network is difficult to examine such mistakes can go unnoticed.

Neural networks will be discussed in more detail in Chapter 11.

The future for AI

In spite of a certain retreat from the early unbounded claims for AI, there are a number of areas where AI research has resulted in commercially successful systems and where further developments are being unveiled every year.

Certainly the greatest commercial success of AI to date is the expert system. Starting from early medical and geological systems, expert system technology has been applied to a huge range of application areas, from insurance to travel advice, from vehicle maintenance to selecting a pet. It is no longer necessary for the developer of an expert system to be an AI expert: expert system shells that embody the reasoning and knowledge structures of an expert system require only the domain-specific information to be added.

Other areas that are having increasing commercial success are handwriting and speech recognition. Commercial pen-based computing systems are now available that allow users to interact without the use of a keyboard, entering information by hand. Such systems currently require training in order to perform accurately, and even then can usually only understand one user's writing reliably. But even this is impressive given the ambiguity in handwriting and the number of topics that may be being discussed. Similarly, there are commercially available speech recognition systems that perform accurately for single users.

Game playing was one of the areas that attracted the attention of early AI researchers, since it appeared that skilled performance of games such as chess required well-developed problem-solving skills and the application of strategy. Although it was realised that much of the skill required in such games could be distilled into the rapid searching of a set of possible moves, the resulting systems do demonstrate how well such methods work. The chess programs of today are sophisticated enough to beat a human grand master on occasion.

Much of the research in AI has been of interest to the military, and none less than that concerned with computer vision and robotics. Research has developed self-navigating cars and vehicles and systems to identify types of aircraft. Pattern recognition and classification technology is particularly promising in these areas, although care should be exercised in the light of problems like the one cited above. This technology is also finding civil applications, including identification of speeding motorists through recognition of number plates.

Robotics in the factory is already well developed, and attention is being given to producing effective robotic applications for the home. The notion of "smart buildings" that adapt to their environment (for example, by adjusting window shading) is also being extended to take us towards the "smart house".

It is clear then that although the goals and emphases of AI may have changed over time, the subject is far from dead or historical. Developments using AI techniques are being produced all the time. Indeed, some very familiar aspects of the computer tools we use regularly, such as spelling and grammar checkers, originate in AI research. It may not be long before AI is an integral part of all our lives.

In the chapters that follow we will take a relatively pragmatic approach to AI, considering first the techniques that form the building blocks for AI systems, and then showing how these can be applied in a number of important application areas, including expert systems, language understanding, computer vision and robotics.

Chapter One

Knowledge in AI

1.1 Overview

Knowledge is vital to all intelligence. In this chapter we examine four key knowledge representation schemes looking at examples of each and their strengths and weaknesses. We consider how to assess a knowledge representation scheme in order to choose one that is appropriate to our particular problem. We discuss the problems of representing general knowledge and changing knowledge.

1.2 Introduction

Knowledge is central to intelligence. We need it to use or understand language; to make decisions; to recognize objects; to interpret situations; to plan strategies. We store in our memories millions of pieces of knowledge that we use daily to make sense of the world and our interactions with it.

Some of the knowledge we possess is factual. We know what things are and what they do. This type of knowledge is known as *declarative* knowledge. We also know how to do things: *procedural* knowledge. For example, if we consider what we know about the English language we may have some declarative knowledge that the word *tree* is a noun and that *tall* is an adjective. These are among the thousands of facts we know about the English language.

However, we also have procedural knowledge about English. For example, we may know that in order to provide more information about something we place an adjective before the noun.

Similarly, imagine you are giving directions to your home. You may have declarative knowledge about the location of your house and its transport links (for example, "my house is in Golcar", "the number 301 bus runs through Golcar", "Golcar is off the Manchester Road"). In addition you may have procedural knowledge about how to get to your house ("Get on the 301 bus").

Another distinction that can be drawn is between the specific knowledge we have on a particular subject (*domain-specific knowledge*) and the general or "common-sense" knowledge that applies throughout our experience (*domain-*

independent knowledge). The fact "the number 301 bus goes to Golcar" is an example of the former: it is knowledge that is relevant only in a restricted domain – in this case Huddersfield's transport system. New knowledge would be required to deal with transport in any other city. However, the knowledge that a bus is a motorized means of transport is a piece of general knowledge which is applicable to buses throughout our experience.

General or common-sense knowledge also enables us to interpret situations accurately. For example, imagine someone asks you "Can you tell me the way to the station?". Your common-sense knowledge tells you that the person expects a set of directions; only a deliberately obtuse person would answer literally "yes"! Similarly there are thousands if not millions of "facts" that are obvious to us from our experience of the world, many acquired in early childhood. They are so obvious to us that we wouldn't normally dream of expressing them explicitly. Facts about age: a person's age increments by one each year, children are always younger than their parents, people don't live much longer than 100 years; facts about the way that substances such as water behave; facts about the physical properties of everyday objects and indeed ourselves – this is the general or "common" knowledge that humans share through shared experience and that we rely on every day.

Just as we need knowledge to function effectively, it is also vital in artificial intelligence. As we saw earlier, one of the problems with ELIZA was lack of knowledge: the program had no knowledge of the meanings or contexts of the words it was using and so failed to convince for long. So the first thing we need to provide for our intelligent machine is knowledge. As we shall see, this will include procedural and declarative knowledge and domain-specific and general knowledge. The specific knowledge required will depend upon the application. For language understanding we need to provide knowledge of syntax rules, words and their meanings, and context; for expert decision making, we need knowledge of the domain of interest as well as decision-making strategies. For visual recognition, knowledge of possible objects and how they occur in the world is needed. Even simple game playing requires knowledge of possible moves and winning strategies.

1.3   Representing knowledge

We have seen the types of knowledge that we use in everyday life and that we would like to provide to our intelligent machine. We have also seen something of the enormity of the task of providing that knowledge. However, the knowledge that we have been considering is largely experiential or internal to the human holder. In order to make use of it in AI we need to get it from the source (usually human but can be other information sources) and represent it in a form usable by the machine. Human knowledge is usually expressed through language, which, of course, cannot be accurately understood by the machine. The representation we choose must therefore be both appropriate for the computer to use and allow easy and accurate encoding from the source.

We need to be able to represent facts about the world. However, this is not all. Facts do not exist in isolation; they are related to each other in a number of ways. First, a fact may be a specific instance of another, more general fact. For example, "Spotty Dog barks" is a specific instance of the fact "all dogs bark" (not strictly true but a common belief). In a case like this, we may wish to allow *property inheritance*, in which properties or attributes of the main class are inherited by instances of that class. So we might represent the knowledge that dogs bark and that Spotty Dog is a dog, allowing us then to deduce by inheritance the fact that Spotty Dog barks. Secondly, facts may be related by virtue of the object or concept to which they refer. For example, we may know the time, place, subject and speaker for a lecture and these pieces of information make sense only in the context of the occasion by which they are related. And of course we need to represent procedural knowledge as well as declarative knowledge.

It should be noted that the representation chosen can be an important factor in determining the ease with which a problem can be solved. For example, imagine you have a 3×3 chess board with a knight in each corner (as in Fig. 1.1). How many moves (that is, chess knight moves) will it take to move each knight round to the next corner?

Figure 1.1 Four knights: how many moves?

Looking at the diagrammatic representation in Figure 1.1, the solution is not obvious, but if we label each square and represent valid moves as adjacent points

11

on a circle (see Fig. 1.2), the solution becomes more obvious: each knight takes two moves to reach its new position so the minimum number of moves is eight.

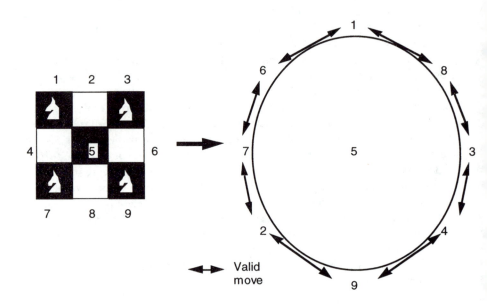

Figure 1.2 A different representation makes the solution clearer.

In addition, the granularity of the representation can affect its usefulness. In other words, we have to determine how detailed the knowledge we represent needs to be. This will depend largely on the application and the use to which the knowledge will be put. For example, if we are building a knowledge base about family relationships we may include a representation of the definition of the relation "cousin" (given here in English but easily translatable into logic, for example):

your cousin is a child of a sibling of your parent.

However, this may not be enough information; we may also wish to know the gender of the cousin. If this is the case a more detailed representation is required. For a female cousin:

your cousin is a daughter of a sibling of your parent

or a male cousin

your cousin is a son of a sibling of your parent.

Similarly, if you wanted to know to which side of the family your cousin belongs you would need different information: from your father's side your cousin is a child of a sibling of your father

or your mother's

your cousin is a child of a sibling of your mother.

A full description of all the possible variations is given in Figure 1.3. Such detail may not always be required and therefore may in some circumstances be unnecessarily complex.

> your cousin is a daughter of a sister of your mother
> your cousin is a daughter of a sister of your father
> your cousin i   daughter of a brother of your mother
> your cousin is a daughter of a brother of your father
> your cousin is a son of a sister of your mother
> your cousin is a son of a sister of your father
> your cousin is a son of a brother of your mother
> your cousin is a son of a brother of your father

Figure 1.3 Full definition of the relationship "cousin".

There are a number of knowledge representation methods that can be used. Later in this chapter we will examine some of them briefly, and identify the areas for which each is best suited. In later chapters of the book we will see how these methods can be used in specific application areas. But what makes a good knowledge representation scheme, and how can different schemes be evaluated against one another? Before going on to consider specific approaches to knowledge representation, we will look in more detail at what features a knowledge representation scheme should possess.

1.4   Metrics for assessing knowledge representation schemes

We have already looked at some of the factors we are looking for in a knowledge representation scheme. However, we can expand upon these and generate some metrics by which to measure the representations available to us. The main requirements of a knowledge representation scheme can be summarized under four headings: *expressiveness, effectiveness, efficiency* and *explanation*.

- *expressiveness.* We have already considered some of the types of knowledge that we might wish to represent. An expressive representation scheme will be able to handle different types and levels of granularity of knowledge. It will be able to represent complex knowledge and knowledge structures and the relationships between them. It will have means of representing specific facts and generic information (for example, by using variables). Expressiveness also relates to the *clarity* of the representation scheme. Ideally, the scheme should use a notation that is natural and usable both by the knowledge engineer and the domain expert. Schemes that are too complex for the latter to understand can result in incorrect knowledge being held, since the expert may not be able to critique the knowledge adequately. In summary, our representation scheme should be characterized by *completeness* and *clarity* of expression.

- *effectiveness.* The second measure of a good representation scheme is its effectiveness. In order to be effective, the scheme must provide a means of inferring new knowledge from old. It should also be amenable to computation, allowing adequate tool support.

- *efficiency.* Thirdly, the scheme should be efficient. The knowledge representation scheme must not only support inference of new knowledge from old but must do so efficiently in order for the new knowledge to be of use. In addition, the scheme should facilitate efficient knowledge gathering and representation.

- *explicitness.* Finally, a good knowledge representation scheme must be able to provide an explanation of its inferences and allow justifications of its reasoning. The chain of reasoning should be explicit.

In the rest of this chapter we will use these four metrics to compare the effectiveness of the techniques we will consider.

1.5 Logic representations

Logic representations use expressions in formal logic to represent the knowledge required. Inference rules and proof procedures can apply this knowledge to specific problems. *First-order predicate calculus* is the most common form of logic representation, with PROLOG being the most common language used to implement it.

Logic is appealing as a means of knowledge representation, as it is a powerful formalism with known inference procedures. We can derive a new piece of knowledge by proving that it is a consequence of knowledge that is already known. The significant features of the domain can be represented as logical assertions, and general attributes can be expressed using variables in logical statements. It has the advantage of being computable, albeit in a restricted form.

So how can we use logic to represent knowledge? Facts can be expressed as simple propositions. A proposition is a statement that can have one of two values:

true or false. These are known as *truth values*. So the statements *It is raining* and *I am hungry* are propositions whose values depend on the situation at the time. If I have just eaten dinner in a thunderstorm then the first is likely to be true and the second false. Propositions can be combined using operators such as *and* (∧) and *or* (∨). Returning to our dining example, we could combine the two statements: *It is raining and I am hungry* (which for convenience we will express as P ∧ Q). The truth value of the combined propositions will depend upon the truth values of the individual propositions and the operator connecting them. If the situation is still as it was then this combined propositional statement will be false, since one of the propositions (Q) is false.

Figure 1.4 shows a truth table that defines the truth values of *and* and *or*.

P	Q	P ∧ Q	P ∨ Q
T	T	T	T
T	F	F	T
F	T	F	T
F	F	F	F

Figure 1.4 Truth values for simple logic operators.

Propositional logic is limited in that it does not allow us to generalize sufficiently. Common elements within propositions cannot be used to make inferences. We need to be able to extract such common elements as parameters to the propositions, in order to allow inferences with them. Parametrized propositions give us *predicate logic*. For example, if we wish to represent our knowledge of the members of Thunderbirds' *International rescue* organization we might include such facts as

$father(Jeff, Virgil)$
$father(Jeff, Alan)$

to mean *Jeff is the father of Virgil* and *Jeff is the father of Alan* respectively. *Father* is the predicate here and *Jeff, Virgil* and *Alan* are parameters. In predicate logic, parameters can also include variables. For example,

$father(Jeff, x)$

where x is a variable that can be instantiated later with a value – the name of someone of whom Jeff is the father.

Quantifiers (universal and existential) allow the scope of the variable to be determined unambiguously. For example, in the statement above, we do not know for certain that there is value for x; that is, that Jeff is indeed someone's father (ignoring the two earlier facts for a moment). In the following statement we use the existential quantifier, ∃, to express the fact that Jeff is the father of at least one person:

$$\exists x : father(Jeff, x)$$

Similarly we can express rules that apply universally using the universal quantifier, ∀:

$$\forall x \, \forall y : father(x, y) \lor mother(x, y) \rightarrow parent(x, y)$$
$$\forall x \, \forall y \, \forall z : parent(x, y) \land parent(x, z) \rightarrow sibling(y, z)$$

The first of these states that for all values of x and y if x is the father of y or (∨) the mother of y then x is the parent of y. The second uses this knowledge to say something about siblings: for all values of x, y and z, if x is the parent of y (that is, the father or the mother), and (∧) x is the parent of z, then y and z are siblings.

Inference methods allow us to derive new facts from existing facts. There are a number of inference procedures for logic but we can illustrate the principle using the simple rule that we can substitute a universally quantified variable with any value in its domain. So, given the rule about parenthood and the facts we already know about the family from *International rescue*, we can derive new facts as shown below.

Given

$$\forall x \, \forall y : father(x, y) \lor mother(x, y) \rightarrow parent(x, y)$$
$$father(Jeff, Virgil)$$
$$father(Jeff, Alan)$$

we can derive the facts (by substitution)

$$parent(Jeff, Virgil)$$
$$parent(Jeff, Alan)$$

Similarly, given

$$\forall x \, \forall y \, \forall z : parent(x, y) \land parent(x, z) \rightarrow sibling(y, z)$$
$$parent(Jeff, Virgil)$$
$$parent(Jeff, Alan)$$

we can derive the fact

$$sibling(Virgil, Alan)$$

Facts and rules such as these can be represented easily in PROLOG. However, predicate logic and PROLOG have a limitation, which is that they operate under what is known as the *closed world assumption*. This means that we assume that all knowledge in the world is represented: the knowledge base is complete. Therefore any fact that is missing is assumed to be false. PROLOG uses a problem-solving strategy called *negation as failure*, which means that it returns a result of *false* if it is unable to prove a goal to be true. This relies on the closed world assumption (Reiter 1978). Such an assumption is useful when all relevant facts are represented but can cause problems when the knowledge base is incomplete.

In summary, logic is

- *expressive*: it allows representation of facts, relationships between facts and assertions about facts. It is relatively understandable. PROLOG is less expressive since it is not possible to represent logical negation explicitly. This in turn leads to less clarity.

- *effective*: new facts can be inferred from old. It is also amenable to computation through PROLOG.

- *efficient*: the use of predicates and variables makes the representation scheme relatively efficient, although computational efficiency depends to a degree on the interpreter being used and the programmer.

- *explicit*: explanations and justifications can be provided by backtracking.

We will return to logic and PROLOG later in the book since it is a useful method of illustrating and implementing some of the techniques we will be considering.

1.6 Procedural representation

Logic representations, such as we have been looking at, are declarative: we specify what we know about a problem or domain. We do not specify how to solve the problem or what to do with the knowledge. Procedural approaches, on the other hand, represent knowledge as a set of instructions for solving a problem. If a given condition is met then an associated action or series of actions is performed. The production system is an example of this (Newell & Simon 1972).

A production system has three components:

- a database of facts (often called *working memory*)

- a set of production rules that alter the facts in the database. These rules or *productions* are of the form

  IF <condition> THEN <action>

- an interpreter that decides which rule to apply and handles any conflicts.

1.6.1 The database

The database or working memory represents all the knowledge of the system at any given moment. It can be thought of as a simple database of facts that are true of the domain at that time. The number of items in the database is small: the analogy is to human working memory, which can hold only a small number of items at a time. The contents of the database change as facts are added or removed according to the application of the rules.

1.6.2 The production rules

Production rules are operators that are applied to the knowledge in the database and change the state of the production system in some way, usually by changing the content of the database. Production rules are sometimes called *condition–action* rules and this describes their behaviour well. If the condition of a rule is true (according to the database at that moment), the action associated with the rule is performed. This may be, for example, to alter the contents of the database by removing a fact, or to interact with the outside world in some way.

Production rules are usually unordered, in the sense that the sequence in which the rules will be applied depends on the current state of the database: the rule whose condition matches the state of the database will be selected. If more than one rule matches then conflict resolution strategies are applied. However, some production systems are programmed to apply rules in order, so avoiding conflict (this is itself a conflict resolution strategy).

1.6.3 The interpreter

The interpreter is responsible for finding the rules whose conditions are matched by the current state of the database. It must then decide which rule to apply. If there is more than one rule whose condition matches then one of the contenders must be selected using strategies such as those proposed below. If no rule matches, the system cannot proceed. Once a single rule has been selected the interpreter must perform the actions in the body of the rule. This process continues until there are no matching rules or until a rule is triggered which includes the instruction to stop.

The interpreter must have strategies to select a single rule where several match the state of the database. There are a number of possible ways to handle this situation. The most simple strategy is to choose the first rule that matches. This effectively places an ordering on the production rules, which must be carefully considered when writing the rules. An alternative strategy is to favour the most specific rule. This may involve choosing a rule that matches all the conditions of its contenders but that also contains further conditions that match, or it may mean choosing the rule that instantiates variables or qualifies a fact.

For example,

> IF <salary is high> and < age > 40>

is more specific than

> IF <salary is high>.

Similarly

> IF <salary > £40,000>

is more specific than

> IF <salary > £20,000>

since fewer instances will match it.

1.6.4   An example production system: making a loan

This production system gives advice on whether to make a loan to a client (its rules are obviously very simplistic but it is useful to illustrate the technique). Initially the database contains the following default facts:

> <client working? is unknown>
> <client student? is unknown>
> <salary is unknown>

and a single fact relating to our client:

> <AMOUNT REQUESTED is £2000>

which represents the amount of money our client wishes to borrow (we will assume that this has been added using other rules). We can use the production system to find out more information about the client and decide whether to give this loan.

Rules:

1.   IF <client working? is unknown>
     THEN   ask "Are you working?"
            read WORKING
            remove <client working? is unknown>
            add <client working? is WORKING>
2.   IF <client working? is YES> and <salary is unknown>
     THEN   ask "What is your salary?"
            read SALARY
            remove <salary is unknown>
            add <salary is SALARY>

3. IF <client working? is YES> and <salary is SALARY>
        and SALARY > (5 * AMOUNT REQUESTED)
    THEN   grant loan of AMOUNT REQUESTED
            clear database
            finish

4. IF <client working? is YES> and <salary is SALARY>
        and SALARY < (5 * AMOUNT REQUESTED)
    THEN   grant loan of (SALARY/5)
            clear database
            finish

5. IF <client working? is NO> and <client student? is unknown>
    THEN   ask "Are you a student?"
            read STUDENT
            remove <client student? is unknown>
            add <client student? is STUDENT>

6. IF <client working? is NO> and <client student? is YES>
    THEN   discuss student loan
            clear database
            finish

7. IF <client working? is NO> and <client student? is NO>
    THEN   refuse loan
            clear database
            finish

Imagine our client is working and earns £7500. Given the contents of the database, the following sequence occurs:

1. Rule 1 fires since the condition matches a fact in the database. The user answers YES to the question, instantiating the variable WORKING to YES. This adds the fact <client working? is YES> to the database, replacing the fact <client working? is unknown>

    – Database contents after rule 1 fires: <client working? is YES> <client student? is unknown> <salary is unknown> <AMOUNT REQUESTED is £2000>

2. Rule 2 fires instantiating the variable SALARY to the value given by the user. This adds this fact to the database, as above.

    – Database contents after rule 2 fires: <client working? is YES> <client student? is unknown> <salary is £7500> <AMOUNT REQUESTED is £2000>

3. Rule 4 fires since the value of SALARY is less than five times the value of AMOUNT REQUESTED. This results in an instruction to grant a loan of SALARY/5, that is £1500. The system then clears the database to the default values and finishes.

This particular system is very simple and no conflicts can occur. It is assumed that the interpreter examines the rule base from the beginning each time.

To summarize, we can consider production systems against our metrics:

- *expressiveness*: production systems are particularly good at representing procedural knowledge. They are ideal in situations where knowledge changes over time and where the final and initial states differ from user to user (or subject to subject). The approach relies on an understanding of the concept of a working memory, which sometimes causes confusion. The modularity of the representation aids clarity in use: each rule is an independent chunk of knowledge, and modification of one rule does not interfere with others.

- *effectiveness*: new information is generated using operators to change the contents of working memory. The approach is very amenable to computation.

- *efficiency*: the scheme is relatively efficient for procedural problems, and their flexibility makes it transferable between domains. The use of features from human problem solving (such as short-term memory) means that the scheme may not be the most efficient. However, to counter this, these features make it a candidate for modelling human problem solving.

- *explicitness*: production systems can be programmed to provide explanations for their decisions by tracing back through the rules that are applied to reach the solution.

1.7 Network representations

Network representations capture knowledge as a graph, in which nodes represent objects or concepts and arcs represent relationships or associations. Relationships can be domain specific or generic (see below for examples).

Networks support *property inheritance*. An object or concept may be a member of a class, and is assumed to have the same attribute values as the parent class (unless alternative values override). Classes can also have subclasses that inherit properties in a similar way. For example, the parent class may be *Dog*, which has attributes such as *has tail, barks* and *has four legs*. A subclass of that parent class may be a particular breed, say *Great Dane*, which consequently inherits all the attributes above, as well as having its own attributes (such as *tall*). A particular member (or instance) of this subclass, that is a particular Great Dane, may have additional attributes such as colour. Property inheritance is overridden where a class member or subclass has an explicit alternative value for an attribute. For example, *Rottweiler* may be a subclass of the parent class *Dog*, but may have the attribute *has no tail*.

Alternatives may also be given at the instance level: *Rottweiler* as a class may inherit the property *has tail* but a particular dog, whose tail has been docked, may have the value *has no tail* overriding the inherited property.

Semantic networks are an example of a network representation. A semantic network illustrating property inheritance is given below. It includes two generic relationships that support property inheritance: *is-a* indicating class inclusion (subclass) and *instance* indicating class membership.

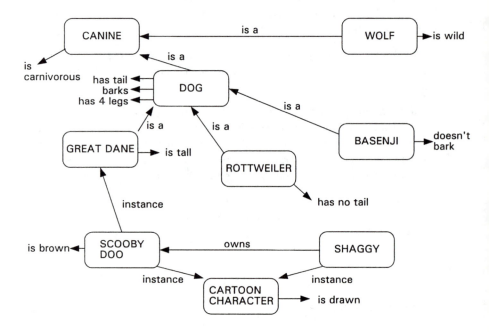

Figure 1.5 A fragment of a semantic network.

Property inheritance supports inference, in that we can derive facts about an object by considering the parent classes. For example, in the *Dog* network in Figure 1.5, we can derive the facts that a Great Dane has a tail and is carnivorous from the facts that a dog has a tail and a canine is carnivorous respectively. Note, however, that we cannot derive the fact that a Basenji can bark since we have an alternative value associated with Basenji. Note also how the network links together information from different domains (dogs and cartoons) by association.

Network representations are useful where an object or concept is associated with many attributes and where relationships between objects are important. Considering them against our metrics for knowledge representation schemes:

– *expressiveness*: they allow representation of facts and relationships between facts. The levels of the hierarchy provide a mechanism for representing general and specific knowledge. The representation is a model of human memory, and it is therefore relatively understandable.

– *effectiveness*: they support inference through property inheritance. They can also be easily represented using PROLOG and other AI languages making them amenable to computation.

– *efficiency*: they reduce the size of the knowledge base, since knowledge is stored only at its highest level of abstraction rather than for every instance or example of a class. They help maintain consistency in the knowledge base, because high-level properties are inherited by subclasses and not added for each subclass.

– *explicitness*: reasoning equates to following paths through the network, so the relationships and inference are explicit in the network links.

1.8 Structured representations

In structured representations information is organized into more complex knowledge structures. *Slots* in the structure represent attributes into which values can be placed. These values are either specific to a particular instance or default values, which represent stereotypical information. Structured representations can capture complex situations or objects, for example eating a meal in a restaurant or the content of a hotel room. Such structures can be linked together as networks, giving property inheritance. *Frames* and *scripts* are the most common types of structured representation.

1.8.1 Frames

Frames are knowledge structures that represent expected or stereotypical information about an object (Minsky 1975). For example, imagine a supermarket. If you have visited one or two you will have certain expectations as to what you will find there. These may include aisles of shelves, freezer banks and check-out tills. Some information will vary from supermarket to supermarket, for example the number of tills. This type of information can be stored in a network of frames where each frame comprises a number of slots with appropriate values. A section of a frame network on supermarkets is shown in Figure 1.6.

In summary, frames extend semantic networks to include structured, hierarchical knowledge. Since they can be used with semantic networks, they share the benefits of these, as well as

SUPERMARKET	►CHECK-OUT TILL LINE	►CHECK-OUT STATION
Instance of: SHOP	Location: Supermarket exit	Type: EPOS
Location: out of town	Number: 50	Use: billing & payment
Comprises:	Comprises:	Comprises:
check-out till	check-out stations	till
line	trolley parks	chair
shelving aisles		conveyor belt
freezer banks		

Figure 1.6 Frame representation of supermarket.

- *expressiveness*: they allow representation of structured knowledge and procedural knowledge. The additional structure increases clarity.

- *effectiveness*: actions or operations can be associated with a slot and performed, for example, whenever the value for that slot is changed. Such procedures are called *demons*.

- *efficiency*: they allow more complex knowledge to be captured efficiently.

- *explicitness*: the additional structure makes the relative importance of particular objects and concepts explicit.

1.8.2 Scripts

A script, like a frame, is a structure used to represent a stereotypical situation (Schank & Abelson 1977). It also contains slots that can be filled with appropriate values. However, where a frame typically represents knowledge of objects and concepts, scripts represent knowledge of events. They were originally proposed as a means of providing contextual information to support natural language understanding (see Ch. 7).

Consider the following description:

> Alison and Brian went to the supermarket. When they had got everything on their list they went home.

Although it is not explicitly stated in this description, we are likely to infer that Alison and Brian paid for their selections before leaving. We might also be able to fill in more details about their shopping trip: that they had a trolley and walked around the supermarket, that they selected their own purchases, that their list contained the items that they wished to buy. All of this can be inferred from our general knowledge concerning supermarkets, our expectations as to what is likely to happen at one. Our assumptions about Alison and Brian's experience of shopping would be very different if the word *supermarket* was replaced by *corner shop*.

It is this type of stereotypical knowledge that scripts attempt to capture, with the aim of allowing a computer to make similar inferences about incomplete stories to those we were able to make above. Schank and colleagues developed a number of programs during the 1970s and 1980s that used scripts to answer questions about stories (Schank & Abelson 1977). The script would describe likely action sequences and provide the contextual information to understand the stories.

A script comprises a number of elements:

- *entry conditions*: these are the conditions that must be true for the script to be activated.

- *results*: these are the facts that are true when the script ends.

- *props*: these are the objects that are involved in the events described in the script.

- *roles*: these are the expected actions of the major participants in the events described in the script.

- *scenes*: these are the sequences of events that take place.

- *tracks*: these represent variations on the general theme or pattern of the script.

For example, a script for going to a supermarket might store the following information:

Entry conditions:	supermarket open, shopper needs goods, shopper has money
Result:	shopper has goods, supermarket has less stock, supermarket has more money
Props:	trolleys, goods, check-out tills
Roles:	shopper collects food, assistant checks out food and takes money, store manager orders new stock
Scenes:	selecting goods, checking out goods, paying for goods, packing goods
Tracks:	customer packs bag, assistant packs bag

Scripts have been useful in natural language understanding in restricted domains. Problems arise when the knowledge required to interpret a story is not domain specific but general, "common-sense" knowledge. Charniak (Charniak 1972) used children's stories to illustrate just how much knowledge is required to interpret even simple descriptions. For example, consider the following excerpt about exchanging unwanted gifts:

> Alison and Brian received two toasters at their engagement party, so they took one back to the shop.

To interpret this we need to know about toasters and why, under normal circumstances, one wouldn't want two; we also need to know about shops and their normal exchange policies. In addition, we need to know about engagements and the tradition of giving gifts on such occasions. But the situation is more complicated than it appears. If instead of toasters Alison and Brian had received two gift vouchers, two books or two £20 notes they would not have needed to exchange them. So the rule that one doesn't want two of something only applies to certain items. Such information is not specific to engagements: the same would be true of birthday presents, wedding presents or Christmas presents. So in which script do we store such information?

This is indicative of a basic problem of AI, which is how to provide the computer with the general, interpretative knowledge that we glean from our experience, as well as the specific factual knowledge about a particular domain. We will consider this problem in the next section.

Scripts are designed for representing knowledge in a particular context. Within this context the method is expressive and effective, except as we have seen in representing general knowledge, but it is limited in wider application. Similarly, it provides an efficient and explicit mechanism for capturing complex structured information within its limited domain.

1.9   General knowledge

Most knowledge-based systems are effective in a restricted domain only because they do not have access to the deep, common knowledge that we use daily to interpret our world. Few AI projects have attempted to provide such general knowledge, the CYC project begun at MCC, Texas, by Doug Lenat (Lenat & Guha 1990), being a notable exception.

The CYC project aims to build a knowledge base containing the millions of pieces of common knowledge that humans possess. It is a ten-year project involving many people, meticulously encoding the type of facts that are "obvious" to us, facts at the level of "all men are people" and "children are always younger than their parents". To us, expressing such facts seems ludicrous; for the computer they need to be represented explicitly.

The project investigates whether it is possible to represent such common-sense knowledge effectively in a knowledge base, and also considers the problems of building and maintaining large-scale knowledge bases. Its critics claim that it is a waste of time and money, since such knowledge can only be gained by experience, for example the experiences children have through play. However, CYC can derive new knowledge from the facts provided, effectively learning and generalizing from its, albeit artificial, experience.

1.10 The frame problem

Throughout this chapter we have been looking at knowledge representation schemes that allow us to represent a problem at a particular point in time: a particular *state*. However, as we will see in subsequent chapters, representation schemes have to be able to represent sequences of problem states for use in search and planning. Imagine the problem of moving an automatic fork lift truck around a factory floor. In order to do this we need to represent knowledge about the layout of the factory and the position of the truck, together with information dictating how the truck can move (perhaps it can only move if its forks are raised above the ground). However, as soon as the truck makes one movement, the knowledge has changed and a new state has to be represented. Of course, not all the knowledge has changed; some facts, such as the position of the factory walls, are likely to remain the same. The problem of representing the facts that alter from state to state as well as those that remain the same is the essence of the *frame problem* (McCarthy & Hayes 1969).

In some situations, where keeping track of the sequence of states is important, it is infeasible to simply store the whole state each time – doing so will soon use up memory. So it is necessary to store information about what does and does not change from state to state. In some situations even deciding what changes is not an easy problem. In our factory we may describe bricks as being on a pallet which in turn is by the door:

$on(pallet, bricks)$

$by(door, pallet)$

If we move the pallet then we infer that the bricks also move but that the door does not. So in this case at least the relationship *on* implies no change but *by* does imply a change (the pallet is no longer by the door).

A number of solutions have been proposed to the frame problem. One approach is to include specific *frame axioms* which describe the parts that do not change when an operator is applied to move from state to state. So, for example, the system above would include the axiom

$on(x, y, s_1) \land move(x, s_1, s_2) \rightarrow on(x, y, s_2)$

to specify that when an object, y, is on object x in state s_1, then if the operation move is applied to move x to state s_2 then object y is still on object x in the new state. Frame axioms are a useful way of making change explicit, but become extremely unwieldy in complex domains.

An alternative solution is to describe the initial state and then change the state description as rules are applied. This means that the representation is always up-to-date. Such a solution is fine until the system needs to backtrack in order to explore another solution. Then there is nothing to indicate what should be done to undo the changes. Instead we could maintain the initial description but store changes each time an operator is applied. This makes backtracking easy since information as to what has been changed is immediately available, but it is again a complex solution. A compromise solution is to change the initial state description but also store information as to how to undo the change.

There is no ideal solution to the frame problem, but these issues should be considered both in selecting a knowledge representation scheme and in choosing appropriate search strategies. We will look at search in more detail in Chapter 3.

1.11 Knowledge elicitation

All knowledge representation depends upon *knowledge elicitation* to get the appropriate information from the source (often human) to the knowledge base. Knowledge elicitation is the bottleneck of knowledge-based technology. It is difficult, time consuming and imprecise. This is because it depends upon the expert providing the right information, without missing anything out. This in turn often depends upon the person trying to elicit the knowledge (the *knowledge engineer*) asking the expert the right questions in an area that he or she may know little about.

To illustrate the magnitude of the knowledge elicitation problem, think of a subject that you know something about (perhaps a hobby, a sport, a form of art or literature, a skill). Try to write down everything you know about the subject. Even more enlightening, get a friend who is not expert in the subject to question you about it, and provide answers to the questions. You will soon find that it is difficult to be precise and exhaustive in this type of activity.

A number of techniques have been proposed to help alleviate the problem of knowledge elicitation. These include structured interview techniques, knowledge elicitation tools and the use of machine-learning techniques that learn concepts from examples. The latter can be used to identify key features in examples which characterize a concept. We will look in more detail at knowledge elicitation when we consider expert systems in Chapter 6.

1.12 Summary

In this chapter we have seen the importance of an appropriate knowledge representation scheme and how we can assess potential schemes according to their expressiveness, effectiveness, efficiency and explicitness. We have considered four key representation schemes – logic, production rules, network representations and structured representations – looking at examples of each and their strengths and weaknesses. We have looked at the problems of representing general knowledge and changing knowledge. Finally, we have touched on the problem of knowledge elicitation, which we will return to in Chapter 6.

1.13 Exercises

1. UK law forbids marriage between certain relatives (for example, parents and children, brothers and sisters) but allows it between others (for example, first cousins). Use a logic formalism to represent your knowledge about UK (or your own country's) marriage laws.

2. A pet shop would like to implement an expert system to advise customers on suitable pets for their circumstances. Write a production system to incorporate the following information (your system should elicit the information it needs from the customer).

   A budgie is suitable for small homes (including city flats) where all the members of the family are out during the day. It is not appropriate for those with a fear of birds or who have a cat.

   A guinea pig is suitable for homes with a small garden where the occupants are out all day. It is particularly appropriate for children. However, it will require regular cleaning of the cage.

   A cat is suitable for most homes except high-rise flats, although the house should not be on a main road. It does not require exercise. Some people are allergic to cats.

   A dog is suitable for homes with a garden or a park nearby. It is not suitable if all occupants are out all day. It will require regular exercise and grooming.

3. Construct a script for a train journey. (You can use a natural language representation but you should clearly indicate the script elements.)

4. Working in pairs, one of you should take the role of expert, the other of knowledge engineer. The expert should suggest a topic in which he or she is expert and the knowledge engineer should ask questions of the expert to elicit information on this topic. The expert should answer as precisely as possible. The knowledge engineer should record all the answers given. When enough information has been gathered, choose an appropriate representation scheme and formalize this knowledge.

1.14   Recommended further reading

Ringland, G. A. & D. A. Duce 1988. *Approaches to knowledge representation: an introduction.* Chichester: John Wiley.

Explains the issues of knowledge representation in more detail than is possible here: a good next step.

Brachman, R. J., H. J. Levesque, R. Retier (eds) 1992. *Knowledge representation.* Cambridge, MA: MIT Press.

A collection of papers that makes a good follow-on from the above and covers more recent research into representation for symbolic reasoning.

Bobrow D. G. & A. Collins (eds) 1975. *Representation and understanding: studies in cognitive science.* New York: Academic Press.

A collection of important papers on knowledge representation.

Chapter Two

Reasoning

2.1 Overview

Reasoning is the ability to use knowledge to draw new conclusions about the world. Without it we are simply recalling stored information. There are a number of different types of reasoning, including induction, abduction and deduction. In this chapter we consider methods for reasoning when our knowledge is unreliable or incomplete. We also look at how we can use previous experience to reason about current problems.

2.2 What is reasoning?

Mention of reasoning probably brings to mind logic puzzles or "whodunit" thrillers, but it is something that we do every day of our lives. Reasoning is the process by which we use the knowledge we have to draw conclusions or infer something new about a domain of interest. It is a necessary part of what we call "intelligence": without the ability to reason we are doing little more than a lookup when we use information. In fact this is the difference between a standard database system and a knowledge-based or expert system. Both have information that can be accessed in various ways but the database, unlike the expert system, has no reasoning facilities and can therefore answer only limited, specific questions.

Think for a moment about the types of reasoning you use. How do you know what to expect when you go on a train journey? What do you think when your friend is annoyed with you? How do you know what will happen if your car has a flat battery? Whether you are aware of it or not, you will use a number of different methods of reasoning depending on the problem you are considering and the information that you have before you.

The three everyday situations mentioned above illustrate three key types of reasoning that we use. In the first case you know what to expect on a train journey because of your experience of numerous other train journeys: you infer that the new journey will share common features with the examples you are aware of.

This is *induction*, which can be summarized as *generalization from cases seen to infer information about cases unseen*. We use it frequently in learning about the world around us. For example, every crow we see is black; therefore we infer that all crows are black. If you think about it, such reasoning is unreliable: we can never prove our inferences to be true, we can only prove them to be false. Take the crows again. To prove that all crows are black we would have to confirm that all crows that exist, have existed or will exist are black. This is obviously not possible. However, to disprove the statement, all we need is to produce a single crow that is white or pink. So at best we can amass evidence to support our belief that all crows are black. In spite of its unreliability, inductive reasoning is very useful and is the basis of much of our learning. It is used particularly in machine learning, which we will meet in Chapter 4.

The second example we suggested was working out why a friend is annoyed with you, in other words trying to find an explanation for your friend's behaviour. It may be that this particular friend is a stickler for punctuality and you are a few minutes late to your rendezvous. You may therefore infer that your friend's anger is caused by your lateness. This uses *abduction*, the process of reasoning back from something to the state or event that caused it. Of course this too is unreliable; it may be that your friend is angry for another reason (perhaps you had promised to telephone but had forgotten). Abduction can be used in cases where the knowledge is incomplete, for example where it is not possible to use deductive reasoning (see below). Abduction can provide a "best guess" given the evidence available.

The third problem is usually solved by *deduction*: you have knowledge about cars such as "if the battery is flat the headlights won't work"; you know the battery is flat so you can infer that the lights won't work. This is the reasoning of standard logic. Indeed, we could express our car problem in terms of logic: given that

a = *the battery is flat* and b = *the lights won't work*

and the axioms

$$\forall x : a(x) \rightarrow b(x)$$

$$a(my\ car)$$

we can deduce $b(my\ car)$. Note, however, that we cannot deduce the inverse: that is, if we know $b(my\ car)$ we cannot deduce $a(my\ car)$ This is not permitted in standard logic, but is of course another example of abduction. If our lights don't work we may use abduction to derive this explanation. However, it could be wrong; there may be another explanation for the light failure (for example, a bulb may have blown).

Deduction is probably the most familiar form of explicit reasoning. Most of us at some point have been tried with syllogisms about Aristotle's mortality and the like. It can be defined as the process of deriving the *logically* necessary conclusion for the initial premises. So, for example,

Elephants are bigger than dogs

Dogs are bigger than mice

Therefore

Elephants are bigger than mice.

However, it should be noted that deduction is concerned with logical validity, not actual truth. Consider the following example; given the facts, can we reach the conclusion by deduction?

Some dogs are greyhounds

Some greyhounds run fast

Therefore

Some dogs run fast.

The answer is no. We cannot make this deduction because we do not know that all greyhounds are dogs. The fast greyhounds may therefore be the greyhounds that are not dogs. This of course is nonsensical in terms of what we know (or more accurately have induced) about the real world, but it is perfectly valid based on the premises given. You should therefore be aware that deduction does not always correspond to natural human reasoning.

2.3   Forward and backward reasoning

As well as coming in different "flavours", reasoning can progress in one of two directions: forwards to the goal or backwards from the goal. Both are used in AI in different circumstances. *Forward reasoning* (also referred to as *forward chaining, data-driven reasoning, bottom-up* or *antecedent-driven*) begins with known facts and attempts to move towards the desired goal. *Backward reasoning* (*backward chaining, goal-driven reasoning, top-down, consequent-driven* or *hypothesis-driven*) begins with the goal and sets up subgoals which must be solved in order to solve the main goal.

Imagine you hear that a man bearing your family name died intestate a hundred years ago and that solicitors are looking for descendants. There are two ways in which you could determine if you are related to the dead man. First, follow through your family tree from yourself to see if he appears. Secondly, trace his family tree to see if it includes you. The first is an example of forward reasoning, the second backward reasoning. In order to decide which method to use, we need to consider the number of start and goal states (move from the smaller to the larger – the more states there are the easier it is to find one) and the number of possibilities that need to be considered at each stage (the fewer the better). In the above example there is one start state and one goal state (unless you are related to the dead man more than once), so this does not help us. However, if you use forward reasoning there will be two possibilities to consider from each node (each person will have two parents), whereas with backward reasoning there may be many more (even today the average number of children is 2.4; at the beginning of the century it was far more).

In general, backward reasoning is most applicable in situations where a goal or hypothesis can be easily generated (for example, in mathematics or medicine), and where problem data must be acquired by the solver (for example, a doctor asking for vital signs information in order to prove or disprove a hypothesis). Forward reasoning, on the other hand, is useful where most of the data is given in the problem statement but where the goal is unknown or where there are a large number of possible goals. For example, a system which analyzes geological data in order to determine which minerals are present falls into this category.

2.4   Reasoning with uncertainty

In Chapter 1 we looked at knowledge and considered how different knowledge representation schemes allow us to reason. Recall, for example, that standard logics allow us to infer new information from the facts and rules that we have.

Such reasoning is useful in that it allows us to store and utilize information efficiently (we do not have to store everything). However, such reasoning assumes that the knowledge available is complete (or can be inferred) and correct, and that it is consistent. Knowledge added to such systems never makes previous knowledge invalid. Each new piece of information simply adds to the knowledge. This is called *monotonic* reasoning. Monotonic reasoning can be useful in complex knowledge bases since it is not necessary to check consistency when adding knowledge or to store information relating to the truth of knowledge. It therefore saves time and storage.

However, if knowledge is incomplete or changing an alternative reasoning system is required. There are a number of ways of dealing with uncertainty. We will consider four of them briefly:

- non-monotonic reasoning

- probabilistic reasoning

- reasoning with certainty factors

- fuzzy reasoning

2.4.1   Non-monotonic reasoning

In a non-monotonic reasoning system new information can be added that will cause the deletion or alteration of existing knowledge. For example, imagine you have invited someone round for dinner. In the absence of any other information you may make an assumption that your guest eats meat and will like chicken. Later you discover that the guest is in fact a vegetarian and the inference that your guest likes chicken becomes invalid.

We have already met two non-monotonic reasoning systems: abduction and property inheritance (see Ch. 1). Recall that abduction involves inferring some information on the basis of current evidence. This may be changed if new evidence comes to light, which is a characteristic of non-monotonic reasoning. So, for example, we might infer that a child who has spots has measles. However, if evidence comes to light to refute this assumption (for example, that the spots are yellow and not red), then we replace the inference with another.

Property inheritance is also non-monotonic. An instance or subclass will inherit the characteristics of the parent class, unless it has alternative or conflicting values for that characteristic. So, as we saw in Chapter 1, we know that dogs bark and that Rottweilers and Basenjis are dogs. However, we also know that Basenjis don't bark. We can therefore infer that Rottweilers bark (since they are dogs and we have no evidence to think otherwise) but we cannot infer that Basenjis do, since the evidence refutes it.

A third non-monotonic reasoning system is the truth maintenance system or TMS (Doyle 1979). In a TMS the truth or falsity of all facts is maintained. Each piece of knowledge is given a support list (SL) of other items that support (or refute) belief in it. Each piece of knowledge is labelled for reference, and an item can be supported either by another item being true (+) or being false (-). Take, for example, a simple system to determine the weather conditions:

(1) It is winter (SL ()())
(2) It is cold (SL (1+)(3-))
(3) It is warm

Statement (1) does not depend on anything else: it is a fact. Statement (2) depends on statement (1) being true and statement (3) being false. It is not known at this point what statement (3) depends on. It has no support list. Therefore we could assume that "it is cold" since we know that "it is winter" is true (it is a fact) and we have no information to suggest that it is warm (we can therefore assume that this is false). However, if "it is warm" becomes true, then "it is cold" will become false. In this way the TMS maintains the validity and currency of the information held.

2.4.2 Probabilistic reasoning

Probabilistic reasoning is required to deal with incomplete data. In many situations we need to make decisions based on the likelihood of particular events, given the knowledge we have. We can use probability to determine the most likely cause.

Simple probability deals with independent events. If we know the probability of event A occurring (call it $p(A)$) and the probability of event B occurring ($p(B)$), the probability that both will occur ($p(AB)$) is calculated as $p(A) * p(B)$. For example, consider an ordinary pack of 52 playing cards, shuffled well. If I select a card at random, what is the likelihood of it being the king of diamonds? If we take event A to be the card being a diamond and event B to be the card being a king, we can calculate the probability as follows:

$p(A) = \frac{13}{52} = 0.25$ (there are 13 diamonds)

$p(B) = \frac{4}{52} = 0.077$ (there are four kings)

$p(AB) = \frac{52}{2704} = \frac{1}{52} = 0.0192$ (there is one king of diamonds)

However, if two events are interdependent and the outcome of one affects the outcome of the other, then we need to consider conditional probability. Given the probability of event A ($p(A)$) and that of a second event B which depends on it, $p(B|A)$ (B given A), the probability of both occurring is $p(A) * p(B|A)$. So, returning to our pack of cards, imagine I take two cards. What is the probability that they are both diamonds? Again, event A is the first card being a diamond, but this time event B is the second card also being a diamond:

$p(A) = \frac{13}{52} = 0.25$ (there are 13 diamonds)

$p(B|A) = \frac{12}{51} = 0.235$ (there are 12 diamonds left and 51 cards)

$p(AB) = \frac{156}{2652} = 0.058$

This is the basis of *Bayes theorem* and several probabilistic reasoning systems. Bayes theorem calculates the probabilities of particular "causes" given observed "effects".

The theorem is as follows:

$$p(h_i|e) = p(e|h_i)p(h_i)/\sum_{j=1}^{n} p(e|h_j)p(h_j)$$

where

$p(h_i|e)$ is the probability that the hypothesis h_i is true given the evidence e

$p(h_i)$ is the probability that h_i in the absence of specific evidence

$p(e|h_i)$ is the probability that evidence e will be observed if hypothesis h_i is true

n is the number of hypotheses being considered.

For example, a doctor wants to determine the likelihood of particular causes, based on the evidence that a patient has a headache. The doctor has two hypotheses, a common cold (h_1) and meningitis (h_2), and one piece of evidence, the headache (e), and wants to know the probability of the patient having a cold.

Suppose the probability of the doctor seeing a patient with a cold, $p(h_1)$, is 0.2 and the probability of seeing someone with meningitis, $p(h_2)$, is 0.000 001. Suppose also that the probability of a patient having a headache with a cold, $p(e|h_2)$, is 0.8 and the probability of a patient having a headache with meningitis, $p(e|h_2)$, is 0.9.

Using Bayes theorem we can see that the probability that the patient has a cold is very high:

$$p(h_1) = \frac{0.8 \times 0.2}{(0.8 \times 0.2) + (0.9 \times 0.000\,001)} = \frac{0.16}{0.16 + 0.000\,000\,9} = 0.99$$

In reality, of course, the cost of misdiagnosis of meningitis is also very high, and therefore many more factors would have to be taken into account.

Bayes theorem was used in the expert system, PROSPECTOR (Duda et al. 1979), to find mineral deposits. The aim was to determine the likelihood of finding a specific mineral by observing the geological features of an area. PROSPECTOR has been used to find several commercially significant mineral deposits.

In spite of such successful uses, Bayes theorem makes certain assumptions that make it intractable in many domains. First, it assumes that statistical data on the relationships between evidence and hypotheses are known, which is often not the case. Secondly, it assumes that the relationships between evidence and hypotheses are all independent. In spite of these limitations Bayes theorem has been used as the base for a number of probabilistic reasoning systems, including certainty factors, which we will consider next.

2.4.3 Certainty factors

As we have seen, Bayesian reasoning assumes information is available regarding the statistical probabilities of certain events occurring. This makes it difficult to operate in many domains. Certainty factors are a compromise on pure Bayesian reasoning. The approach has been used successfully, most notably in the MYCIN expert system (Shortliffe 1976). MYCIN is a medical diagnosis system that diagnoses bacterial infections of the blood and prescribes drugs for treatment. Its knowledge is represented in rule form and each rule has an associated certainty factor.

For example, a MYCIN rule looks something like this:

If (a) the gram stain of the organism is gram negative and

(b) the morphology of the organism is rod and

(c) the aerobicity of the organism is anaerobic

> then there is suggestive evidence (0.5) that identity of the organism
> is Bacteroides

In this system, each hypothesis is given a certainty factor (CF) by the expert providing the rules, based on his or her assessment of the evidence. A CF takes a value between 1 and -1, where values approaching -1 indicate that the evidence against the hypothesis is strong, and those approaching 1 show that the evidence for the hypothesis is strong. A value of 0 indicates that no evidence for or against the hypothesis is available.

A CF is calculated as the amount of belief in a hypothesis given the evidence ($MB(h|e)$) minus the amount of disbelief ($MD(h|e)$). The measures are assigned to each rule by the experts providing the knowledge for the system as an indication of the reliability of the rule. Measures of belief and disbelief take values between 0 and 1. Certainty factors can be combined in various ways if there are several pieces of evidence. For example, evidence from two sources can be combined to produce a CF as follows:

$$CF(h|e_1, e_2) = MB(h|e_1, e_2) - MD(h|e_1, e_2)$$

where

$$MB(h|e_1, e_2) = MB(h|e_1) + \{MB(h|e_2)[1 - MB(h|e_1)]\}$$
(or 0 if $MD(h|e_1, e_2) = 1$)

and

$$MD(h|e_1, e_2) = MD(h|e_1) + \{MD(h|e_2)[1 - MD(h|e_1)]\}$$
(or 0 if $MB(h|e_1, e_2) = 1$)

The easiest way to understand how this works is to consider a simple example. Imagine that we observe the fact that the air feels moist (e_1). There may be a number of reasons for this (rain, snow, fog). We may hypothesize that it is foggy, with a measure of belief ($MB(h|e_1)$) in this being the correct hypothesis of 0.4. Our disbelief in the hypothesis given the evidence ($MD(h|e_1)$) will be low, say 0.1 (it may be dry and foggy but it is unlikely). The certainty factor for this hypothesis is then calculated as

$$CF(h|e_1) = MB(h|e_1) - MD(h|e_1) = 0.5 - 0.1 = 0.4$$

We then make a second observation, e_2, that visibility is poor, which confirms our hypothesis that it is foggy, with $MB(h|e_2)$ of 0.7. Our disbelief in the hypothesis given this new evidence is 0.0 (poor visibility is a characteristic of fog). The certainty factor for it being foggy given this evidence is

$$CF(h|e_2) = MB(h|e_2) - MD(h|e_2) = 0.7 - 0.0 = 0.7$$

However, if we combine these two pieces of evidence we get an increase in the overall certainty factor:

$MB(h|e_1, e_2) = 0.5 + (0.7 * 0.5) = 0.85$

$MD(h|e_1, e_2) = 0.1 + (0.0 * 0.9) = 0.1$

$CF(h|e_1, e_2) = 0.85 - 0.1 = 0.75$

Certainty factors provide a mechanism for reasoning with uncertainty that does not require probabilities. Measures of belief and disbelief reflect the expert's assessment of the evidence rather than statistical values. This makes the certainty factors method more tractable as a method of reasoning. Its use in MYCIN shows that it can be successful, at least within a clearly defined domain.

2.4.4 Fuzzy reasoning

Probabilistic reasoning and reasoning with certainty factors deal with uncertainty using principles from probability to extend the scope of standard logics. An alternative approach is to change the properties of logic itself. *Fuzzy sets* and *fuzzy logic* do just that.

In classical set theory an item, say a, is either a member of set A or it is not. So a meal at a restaurant is either expensive or not expensive and a value must be provided to delimit set membership. Clearly, however, this is not the way we think in real life. While some sets are clearly defined (a piece of fruit is either an orange or not an orange), many sets are not. Qualities such as size, speed and price are relative. We talk of things being very expensive or quite small.

Fuzzy set theory extends classical set theory to include the notion of *degree* of set membership. Each item is associated with a value between 0 and 1, where 0 indicates that it is not a member of the set and 1 that it is definitely a member. Values in between indicate a certain degree of set membership.

For example, although you may agree with the inclusion of Porsche and BMW in the set $FastCar$, you may wish to indicate that one is faster than the other. This is possible in fuzzy set theory:

$$FastCar = \left\{ \begin{array}{l} (Porsche\ 944, 0.9), \\ (BMW\ 316, 0.5), \\ (Vauxhall\ Nova\ 1.2, 0.1) \end{array} \right\}$$

Here the second value in each pair is the degree of set membership.

Fuzzy logic is similar in that it attaches a measure of truth to facts. A predicate, P, is given a value between 0 and 1 (as in fuzzy sets). So, taking an element from our fuzzy set, we may have a predicate

$fastcar(Porsche\ 944) = 0.9$

Standard logic operators, such as *and*, *or* and *not*, can be applied in fuzzy logic and are interpreted as follows:

$P \wedge Q = min(P, Q)$

$$P \vee Q = max(P, Q)$$
$$notP = 1 - P$$

So, for example, we can combine predicates and get new measures:

$fastcar(Porsche\,944) = 0.9$

$pretentiouscar(Porsche\,944) = 0.6$

$fastcar(Porsche\,944) \wedge pretentiouscar(Porsche\,944) = 0.6$

2.4.5 Reasoning by analogy

Analogy is a common tool in human reasoning (Hall 1989). Given a novel problem, we might compare it with a familiar problem and note the similarities. We might then apply our knowledge of the old problem to solving the new. This approach is effective if the problems are comparable and the solutions transferable.

Analogy has been applied in AI in two ways: *transformational analogy* and *derivational analogy*. Transformational analogy involves using the solution to an old problem to find a solution to a new. Reasoning can be viewed as a state space search where the old solution is the start state and operators are used (employing means–ends analysis, for example) to transform this solution into a new solution.

An alternative to this is derivational analogy, where not only the old solution but the process of reaching it is considered in solving the new problem. A history of the problem-solving process is used. Where a step in the procedure is valid for the new problem, it is retained; otherwise it is discarded. The solution is therefore not a copy of the previous solution but a variation of it.

2.4.6 Case-based reasoning

A method of reasoning which exploits the principle of analogy is case-based reasoning (CBR). All the examples (called cases in CBR) are remembered in a case base. When a new situation is encountered, it is compared with all the known cases and the best match is found. If the match is exact, then the system can perform exactly the response suggested by the example. If the match is not exact, the differences between the actual situation and the case are used to derive a suitable response (see Fig. 2.1).

Where there is an exact match, the CBR is acting as a rote learning system, but where there is no exact match, the combination of case selection and comparison is a form of generalization. The simplest form of CBR system may just classify the new situation, a form of concept learning. In this case, the performance of the system is determined solely by the case selection algorithm. In a more

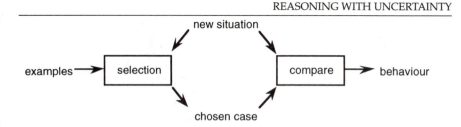

Figure 2.1 Case-based reasoning.

complicated system, the response may be some form of desired action depending on the encountered situation. The case base consists of examples of stimulus–action pairs, and the comparison stage then has to decide how to modify the action stored with the selected case. This step may involve various forms of reasoning.

Imagine we have the following situation:

situation: buy(fishmonger,cod), owner(fishmonger,Fred),
cost(cod,£3)

The case base selects the following best match case:

stimulus: buy(postoffice,stamp), owner(postoffice,Dilys),
cost(stamp,25p)
action: pay(Dilys,25p)

The comparison yields the following differences:

fishmonger → postoffice, cod → stamp, Fred → Dilys, £3 → 25p

The action is then modified correspondingly to give "pay(Fred,£3)".

In this example, the comparison and associated modification is based on simple substitution of corresponding values. However, the appropriate action may not be so simple. For example, consider a blocks-world CBR (Fig. 2.2). The situation is:

situation: blue(A), pyramid(A), on(A,table),
green(B), cube(B), on(B,table),
blue(C), ball(C), on(C,B),

The CBR has retrieved the following case:

stimulus: blue(X), pyramid(X), on(X,table),
green(Y), cube(Y), on(Y,table),
blue(Z), cube(Z), on(Z,table),
action: move(X,Y)

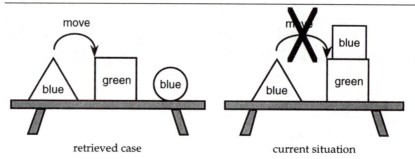

move

green

blue

blue

blue

retrieved case

move

blue

green

blue

current situation

Figure 2.2 Modifying cases.

A simple pattern match would see that the action only involves the first two objects, X and Y, and the situation concerning these two objects is virtually identical. So, the obvious response is "move(A,B)". However, a more detailed analysis would show that moving the blue pyramid onto the green cube is not possible because, in the current situation, the blue ball is on it. A more sophisticated difference procedure could infer that a more appropriate response would be: move(C,table), move(A,B).

Note how the comparison must be able to distinguish irrelevant differences such as ball(C) vs. cube(Z) from significant ones such as on(C,B) vs. on(Z,table). This is also a problem for the selection algorithm. In practice there may be many attributes describing a situation, only a few of which are really important. If selection is based on a simple measure such as "least number of different attributes", then the system may choose "best match" cases where all the irrelevant attributes match, but none of the relevant ones! At the very least some sort of weighting is needed. For example, if one were developing a fault diagnosis system for a photocopier, the attributes would include the error code displayed, the number of copies required, the paper type, whether the automatic feeder was being used, and so on. However, one would probably give the error code a higher weighting than the rest of the attributes. Where the comparison yields differences which invalidate the response given in the case and no repair is possible, the CBR can try another close match case. So, a good selection mechanism is important, but some poor matches can be corrected.

Case-based reasoning has some important advantages. The most important is that it has an obvious and clear explanation for the user: "the current situation is similar to this given case and so I did a similar response". Indeed, one option is to do no comparison at all, simply to present the user with similar cases and allow the user to do the comparison between the current situation and the selected cases. Arguably, because the human does the "intelligent" part, this is not really CBR but simply a case memory, a sort of database.

Another advantage of CBR is that it is not difficult to incorporate partial descriptions, in both the cases and the presented situations. This is because it is fairly easy to generalize measures of similarity to cases where some of the attributes are missing or unknown. For example, we could score +1 for each matching attribute, −1 for each non-match and 0 for any attributes that are missing from either the case or situation (weighted of course!). This is an important feature of CBR, as it is often the case that records are incomplete. For example, if we start to build a CBR based on past medical records, we will find that many symptoms are unrecorded – the doctor would not have taken the heart rate of someone with a skin complaint. Other reasoning methods can deal with such problems, but not so simply as CBR.

2.5 Summary

In this chapter we have considered a number of different types of reasoning, including induction, abduction and deduction. We have seen that the knowledge that we are reasoning about is often incomplete and therefore demands reasoning methods that can deal with uncertainty. We have considered four approaches to reasoning with uncertainty: non-monotonic reasoning, probabilistic reasoning, reasoning with certainty factors and fuzzy reasoning. We have considered analogical reasoning and case-based reasoning.

2.6 Exercises

1. Distinguish between *deductive, inductive* and *abductive* reasoning, giving an example of the appropriate use of each.

2. Alison is trying to determine the cause of overheating in Brian's car. She has two theories: a leak in the radiator or a broken thermostat. She knows that leaky radiators are more common than broken thermostats: she estimates that 10% of cars have a leaky radiator while 2% have a faulty thermostat. However, 90% of cars with a broken thermostat overheat whereas only 30% overheat with a leaky radiator. Use Bayes theorem to advise Alison of the most likely cause of the problem.

3. Alison then checks the water level in Brian's car and notices it is normal. She knows that a car with a leaky radiator is very unlikely not to lose water (perhaps 1% chance), whereas water loss is not seen in 95% of cases of faulty thermostats. How would this new evidence affect your advice to Alison? (Use Bayes theorem again and assume for simplicity that all evidence is independent.)

2.7 Recommended further reading

Shafer, G. & J. Pearl (eds) 1990. *Readings in uncertain reasoning.* Los Altos: Morgan Kaufmann.

A collection of articles which provide a useful introduction to reasoning with uncertainty.

Riesbeck, C. K. & R. Schank 1989. *Inside case based reasoning.* Hillsdale, NJ: Lawrence Erlbaum.

A useful introduction to case-based reasoning.

Chapter Three

Search

3.1 Introduction

When we want to solve a problem, we consider various alternatives, some of which fail to solve the problem. Of those that succeed, we may want to find the best solution, or the easiest to perform. The act of enumerating possibilities and deciding between them is *search*. AI systems must search through sets of possible actions or solutions, and this chapter discusses some of the algorithms that are used. Before we go on to consider specific algorithms, we need to look at the sorts of problems that we are likely to face, as the appropriate algorithm depends on the form of the problem. The set of possible solutions is not just an amorphous bag, but typically has some structure. This structure also influences the choice of search algorithm.

3.1.1 Types of problem

State and path

In some problems we are only interested in the state representing the solution, whereas in other cases we also want to know how we got to the solution – the path. A crossword puzzle is an example of the former: the important thing is that the crossword is eventually completed; the order in which the clues were solved is only of interest to the real crossword fanatic. The *eight queens problem* and solving *magic squares* are similar problems (see Fig. 3.1). Typically with pure state-finding problems the *goal state* is described by some properties. In the case of the magic square, the states are the set of all 3×3 squares filled in with numbers between 1 and 9, and the property is that each row, column and diagonal adds up to 15.

Mathematical theorem proving has always been a driving force in AI. If we consider this, we see that it is not only important that we solve the required theorem, but that the steps we take are recorded – that is, the proof. Other path problems include various finding route problems, puzzles such as the *Towers of Hanoi* (Fig. 3.2) and algorithms for planning actions such as *means–ends analysis* (Ch. 9). In all these problems we know precisely what the goal state is to be; it is

A magic square is a square of numbers where each row, column and diagonal adds up to the same number. Usually the numbers have to be consecutive. So, for example, the 3 × 3 square would contain the numbers 1, 2, 3, 4, 5, 6, 7, 8 and 9. Here are some examples, one 3 × 3 square and one 4 × 4 square:

7	13	12	2
10	4	5	15
1	11	14	8
16	6	3	9

8	1	6
3	5	7
4	9	2

The 3 × 3 square is the simplest. (There are no 2 × 2 squares and the 1 × 1 square 1 is rather boring!) So, when we talk about the "magic squares" problem in this chapter, we will always mean finding 3 × 3 squares.

The eight queens problem is another classic placing problem. In this case we must position eight queens on a chess board so that no queen is attacking another. That is, so that no queen is on the same row, column or diagonal as any other. There are similar problems with smaller numbers of queens on smaller chess boards: for example, a solution of the four queens problem is:

Figure 3.1 Magic squares and the eight queens problem.

only the means of getting there that is required. The solution to such problems must include not just a single goal state, but instead a sequence of states visited and the moves made between them. In some problems the moves are implicit from the sequence of states visited and can hence be omitted.

In fact, some route problems do not specify their goal state in advance. For example, we may want to find the fastest route from Zuata, Venezuela, to any international airport with direct flights to Sydney, Australia. In this case we want to find a route (sequence of places) where the goal state is a city that satisfies the property

$P(s) = $ "s has an international airport with direct flights to Sydney"

In a monastery in deepest Tibet there are three crystal columns and 64 golden rings. The rings are different sizes and rest over the columns. At the beginning of time all the rings rested on the leftmost column, and since then the monks have toiled ceaselessly moving the rings one by one between the columns. It is said that when all the rings lie on the centre column the world will end in a clap of thunder and the monks can at last rest.

The monks must obey two rules:

1. They may move only one ring at a time between columns.
2. No ring may rest on top of a smaller ring.

With 64 rings to move, the world will not end for some time yet. However, we can do the same puzzle with fewer rings. So, with three rings the following would be a legal move:

But this would not be:

In the examples in this chapter, we will consider the even simpler case of two rings!

Figure 3.2 Towers of Hanoi.

In fact, the *travelling salesman problem* is more complex again. Imagine a salesman has to visit a number of towns. He must plan a route that visits each town exactly once and that begins and ends at his home town. He wants the route to be as short as possible. Although the final state is given (the same as the start state), the important property is one of the whole path, namely that each place is visited exactly once. It would be no good to find a route which reached the goal state by going nowhere at all! The last chapter was all about the importance of the choice of representation. In this example, it may well be best to regard the travelling salesman problem as a state problem where the state is a path!

Any solution or best solution

When finding a proof to a theorem (path problem), or solving the magic square or eight queens problem (state problems), all we are interested in is finding some solution – any one will do so long as it satisfies the required conditions (although some proofs may be more elegant than others).

However, if we consider the travelling salesman problem, we now want to find the *shortest* route. Similarly, we may want to choose a colouring for a map that uses the fewest colours (to reduce the costs of printing), or simply be looking for the shortest path between two places. In each of these examples, we are not only interested in finding a solution that satisfies some property, we are after the *best* solution – that is, search is an *optimization* problem. The definition of best depends on the problem. It may mean making some measure as big as possible (for example, profit), or making something as small as possible (for example, costs). As profits can be seen as negative costs (or vice versa), we can choose whichever direction is easiest or whichever is normal for a particular problem type.

For a state problem such as map colouring, the costs are associated with the solution obtained, whereas in a path problem it is a combination of the "goodness" of the final solution and the cost of the path:

$$\text{total cost} = cost(\text{route}) - benefit(\text{goal state})$$

However, one finds that for many path problems there is no second term; that is, all goal states are considered equally good.

In general, the specification of a problem includes both a property (or constraints), which must be satisfied by the goal state (and path), and some cost measure. A state (and path) that satisfies the constraints is said to be em feasible and a feasible state that has the least cost is *optimal*. That is, real problems are a mixture of finding any solution (feasibility) and finding the best (optimality). However, for simplicity, the examples within this chapter fall into one camp or the other. Where constraints exist in optimization problems, they are often satisfied "by construction". For example, a constraint on map-colouring problems is that adjacent countries have different colours. Rather than constructing a colouring and then checking this condition, one can simply ensure as one adds each colour that the constraint is met.

Deterministic vs. adversarial

All the problems considered so far have been *deterministic*, that is totally under the control of the problem solver. However, some of the driving problems of AI have been to do with game playing: chess, backgammon and even simple noughts and crosses (tic-tac-toe). The presence of an adversary radically changes the search problem: as the solver tries to get to the best solution (that is, win), the adversary is trying to stop it! Most games are state based: although it is interesting to look back over the history of a game, it is the state of the chess board *now* that matters. However, there are some path-oriented games as well, for example bridge or poker, where the player needs to remember all past moves, both of other players and their own, in order to choose the next move.

Interaction with the physical environment can be seen as a form of game playing also. As the solver attempts to perform actions in the real world, new knowledge is found and circumstances may occur to help or hinder. If one takes a pessimistic viewpoint, one can think of the world as an adversary which, in the worst case, plays to one's downfall. (Readers of Thomas Hardy will be familiar with this world view!)

A further feature in both game playing and real-world interaction is chance. Whereas chess depends solely on the abilities of the two players, a game like backgammon also depends on the chance outcome of the throwing of dice. Similarly, we may know that certain real-world phenomena are very unlikely and should not be given too great a prominence in our decision making.

This chapter will only deal with deterministic search. Chapter 5 will deal with game playing and adversarial search.

Perfect vs. good enough

Finally, we must consider whether our problem demands the absolutely best solution or whether we can make do with a "good enough" solution. If we are looking for the best route from Cape Town to Addis Ababa, we are unlikely to quibble about the odd few miles. This behaviour is typical of human problem solving and is called *satisficing*. Satisficing can significantly reduce the resources needed to solve a problem, and when the problem size grows may be the only way of getting a solution at all.

There is a parallel to satisficing when we are simply seeking any solution. In such cases, we may be satisfied with a system that replies

YES   – here is your solution
NO   – there is no solution
SORRY – I'm not sure

In practice theorem provers are like this. In most domains, not only is it very expensive to find proofs for all theorems, it may be fundamentally impossible. (Basically, Godel showed that in sufficiently powerful systems (like the numbers) there are always things that are true yet which can never be proved to be true (Kilmister 1967).)

3.1.2 Structuring the search space

Generate and test – combinatorial explosion

The simplest form of search is *generate and test*. You list each possible candidate solution in turn and check to see if it satisfies the constraints. You can either stop when you reach an acceptable goal state or, if you are after the best solution, keep track of the best so far until you get to the end.

Figure 3.3 shows this algorithm applied to the 3×3 magic square. However,

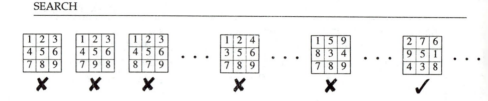

Figure 3.3 Generate and test – finding solutions to the magic square.

this is an extremely inefficient way to look for a solution. If one examines the solutions in the *lexicographic* order (as in the figure), the first solution is found only after rejecting 75 231 candidates. In fact, the whole search space consists of 9! = 362 880 possible squares of which only eight satisfy the goal conditions – and that is after we have been careful not to generate squares with repeated digits! This problem is called *combinatorial explosion* and occurs whenever there are a large number of nearly independent parameters.

In practice, only the most ill-structured problems require this sledge-hammer treatment. One can structure most problems to make the search space far more tractable.

Trees

The first square in Figure 3.3 fails because $1 + 2 + 3 \neq 15$. So does the second square, the third ... in fact the first 720 squares all fail for exactly the same reason. Then the next 720 fail because $1 + 2 + 4 \neq 15$, etc. In each case, you do not need to look at the full square: the *partial state* is sufficient to fail it.

The space of potential magic squares can be organized into a *tree*, where the leaf nodes are completed squares (all 362 880 of them), and the internal nodes are partial solutions starting off at the top left-hand corner. Figure 3.4 shows part of this search tree. The advantage of such a representation is that one can instantly ignore all nodes under the one starting 123, as all of these will fail. There are 504 possible first lines, of which only 52 add up to 15 (the first being $\boxed{1}\,\boxed{5}\,\boxed{9}$). That is, of 504 partial solutions we only need to consider 52 of them further – an instant reduction by a factor of 10. Of course, each of the subtrees under those 52 will be able to be similarly *pruned* – the gains compound.

There are many ways to organize the tree. Instead of doing it in reading order, we could have filled out the first column first, or the bottom right, and so on. However, some organizations are better than others. Imagine we had built the tree so that the third level of partial solution got us to partial solutions like the following:

?	2	?
1	?	?
?	?	3

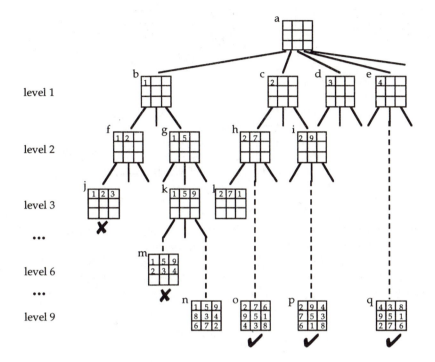

Figure 3.4 Magic square – search tree of potential solutions.

Clearly, we would not be able to prune the tree so rapidly. Choosing the best organization for a particular problem is somewhat of an art, but there are general guidelines. In particular, you want to be able to test constraints as soon as possible.

Branching factor and depth

We can roughly characterize a tree by the number of children each node has – the *branching factor* – and the distance from the root of the tree to the leaves (bottom nodes) – the *depth*. The tree for magic squares has a branching factor of 9 at the root (corresponding to the nine possible entries at the top left), and a depth of 9 (the number of entries in the square). However, the branching factor reduces as one goes down the tree: at the second level it is 8, at the third level 7, and so on. For a game of chess, the branching factor is 20 for the first move (two possibilities for each pawn and four knight moves). For Go, played on a 19 × 19 board, the branching factor is 361! For a uniform tree, if the branching factor is b there are b^n nodes at level n. That is, over 10 billion possibilities for the first four moves in Go – you can see why Go-playing computers aren't very good!

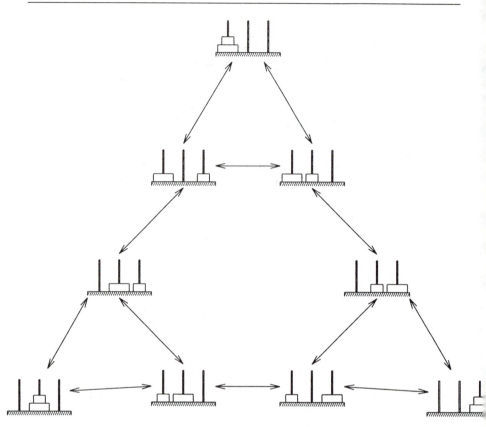

Figure 3.5 Towers of Hanoi: graph of possible states and moves.

Graphs

When one considers a problem consisting of states with moves between them, it is often the case that several move sequences get one from a particular start state to the same final state. That is, the collection of moves and states can be best thought of as a *directed graph*, where the nodes of the graph are the states and the arcs between nodes are the moves. Figure 3.5 shows the complete graph of states of the Towers of Hanoi (with only two rings!). Notice how even such a simple puzzle has a reasonably complex graph.

With the Towers of Hanoi, each arc is bidirectional, because each move between two states can be undone by a move in the reverse direction. This is not always so, for example when a piece is taken in chess; if the nodes represented states while making a cake, there would be no move backwards once the cake was cooked. When the arcs are directional, we can distinguish between the *forward branching*

52

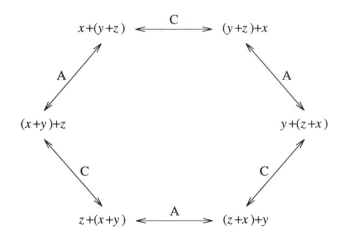

Figure 3.6 Addition proof graph.

factor – the number of arcs coming from a node – and the *backward branching factor* – the number of arcs going to a node. If the backward factor is smaller than the forward factor, it suggests that searching backwards from the goal state towards the start state may be more efficient than searching forwards.

Some algorithms search this graph directly. However, they will usually keep track of the path travelled through the graph as this will be part of the solution. For example, in the Towers of Hanoi puzzle, the path represents the moves to solve the puzzle. Similarly, Figure 3.6 shows a graph of states in a proof system. The states are addition formulae involving three variables, and the arcs are rewrites of the formulae using the associative and commutative laws of addition:

A: $L + (M + N)$ = $(L + M) + N$ associative law
C: $M + N$ = $N + M$ commutative law

(Note that the commutative law is only applied to the outermost (unbracketed) addition in order to simplify the graph.)

If we wanted to prove, for instance, that

$$x + (y + z) = y + (z + x)$$

we could trace a path through the graph going clockwise. We begin at the start state $x + (y + z)$, apply first the commutative law getting us to state $(y + z) + x$, and then the associative law getting us to the goal state $y + (z + x)$. The two steps (commutative law followed by associative law) constitute the proof of the equality.

Notice that there are several paths to the same goal state – we could have followed the graph anti-clockwise (ACAC). If we want to distinguish the paths

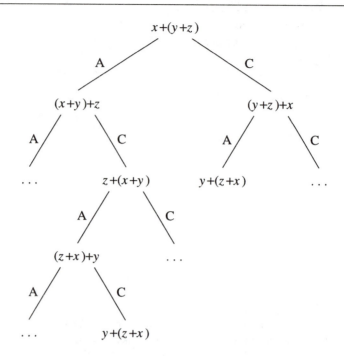

Figure 3.7 Addition proof tree.

more clearly, we can represent the graph by a tree. Figure 3.7 shows a portion of the proof tree for the same expression. The root is the start state and the children are those expressions that can be reached by applying one or other of the laws. The ellipses in the tree represent nodes where the tree "stutters": that is, the child node is the same as its parent. The figure stops expanding the tree when the goal state is reached, but in a sense the full tree reaches out below, as one could continue to apply arithmetic laws.

Note that in the tree representation, the goal state appears twice – once for each path to it. In fact, if one continued to expand the "stuttering" nodes one would uncover more goal states corresponding to "wasteful" proofs such as CCCA.

Adding information

We have already seen that the way we organized the magic square search affected our ability to rule out nodes. This ability to detect that searching down certain paths of the tree is fruitless is a particularly simple (but very useful) form of *heuristic*. (Although arguably it is not a heuristic as the information it provides is exact.) Heuristics are information that tells us something about the future of our search, before we have investigated a path fully. Heuristics may tell us about the likelihood of finding a solution down a path, about how far we may have to search or how good the solution is likely to be. Heuristics are usually approximations – they give some indication but are not guaranteed to be right. Obviously the more accurate the heuristic and the more we *know* about its accuracy, the better it can inform our search. Section 3.3 is all about searching using heuristic information.

There are two major types of heuristic: those that tell us about a node – whether it is worth investigating further – and those which, when we are considering a node, suggest an order in which to search its children. Obviously information of the former category can be used to order the children, but only when the heuristic information for each child has been calculated. As this is sometimes expensive to do in its own right, or there may be an infinite number of children, a separate way of ordering the children may be required. The majority of the search algorithms in this chapter concentrate on the first type of heuristic. Furthermore these algorithms will simply use a *heuristic evaluation function*, a single number calculated for each node, which says how good or bad it is likely to be. Such heuristics are rather simple, but can be surprisingly powerful. In Section 3.4 we will discuss more complex heuristics.

Virtual trees and real trees

It is important to note that the trees and graphs that we have been discussing are not necessarily real. That is, they will not in general be constructed in the computer's memory. Indeed, given the size of the spaces (often infinite) they would be impossible to construct. Instead, they represent the space of possible solutions of which a system may only investigate a part. For example, we can imagine the graph of all chess games linked by possible moves. However, if we play chess we do not by any means "construct" this graph in our heads and play using it. Neither will the algorithms we consider here!

3.2 Exhaustive search and simple pruning

In this section we consider simple search algorithms that do not use heuristic information.

3.2.1 Depth and breadth first search

Consider the following simple logic problem:

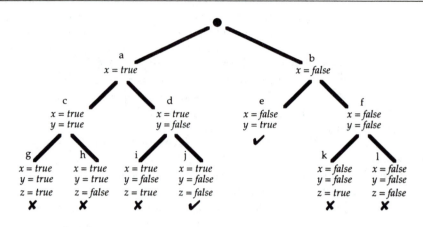

Figure 3.8 Tree of potential solutions for logic problem.

find x, y, z such that $(\neg x \wedge y) \vee (x \wedge \neg y \wedge \neg z)$ is true
that is: (not x and y) or (x and not y and not z)

Figure 3.8 shows a complete search tree for the problem based on choosing the variables in order. The tree is slightly ragged as the formula is true when x is *false* and y is *true* irrespective of the value of z. Note also that there are two solutions, marked with ticks.

We now consider two algorithms for searching this space of potential solutions: *depth first* and *breadth first*. Depth first search starts off at the root of the tree (the empty solution) and then works down the left-hand branch considering the partial solutions until it gets to a leaf. If this is not a goal state it backs up and tries the next path down. That is, the algorithm tries to get as deep as possible as fast as possible, hence its name. Figure 3.9 shows the order in which this algorithm visits the nodes of the graph. In terms of the logic variables, one is considering them in the following order:

a:	$x = true$			– ?
c:	$x = true$	$y = true$		– ?
g:	$x = true$	$y = true$	$z = true$	– NO
h:	$x = true$	$y = true$	$z = false$	– NO
d:	$x = true$	$y = false$		– ?
i:	$x = true$	$y = false$	$z = true$	– NO
j:	$x = true$	$y = false$	$z = false$	– YES

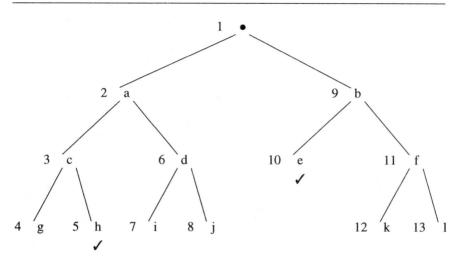

Figure 3.9 Depth first search – order of visiting nodes.

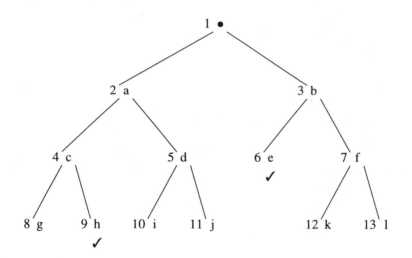

Figure 3.10 Breadth first search – order of visiting nodes.

In contrast, breadth first search moves back and forth through the search tree, only looking at the children of a node when all other nodes at a level have been examined. Figure 3.10 shows the order in which this algorithm visits the nodes, and the search progresses as follows:

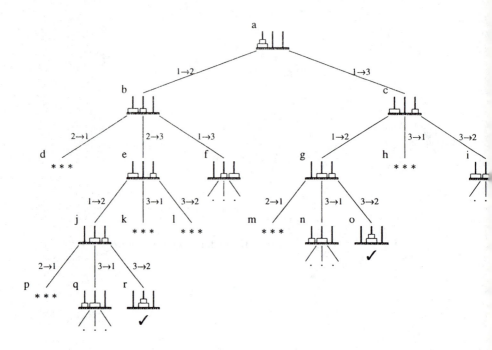

Figure 3.11 Towers of Hanoi – search tree.

a:	$x = true$		– ?
b:	$x = false$		– ?
c:	$x = true$	$y = true$	– ?
d:	$x = true$	$y = false$	– ?
e:	$x = false$	$y = true$	– YES

3.2.2 Comparing depth and breadth first searches

Note that the two searches encounter a different goal state first. Often, one stops at the first goal state found – in this case, depth first and breadth first searches would return different solutions to the problem. Depth first always finds the first solution, reading the tree left to right, whereas breadth first finds the shallowest solution.

If we consider human problem solving it is usually a mixture of depth first (looking at individual detailed options) and breadth first (considering the complete range of options at an abstract level). If anything, the tendency is towards depth first examination of a small part of the possible space, but this is combined with an almost uncanny ability to spot the right portion of the state space to explore. To some extent this ability is guided by *heuristics*, which enable us to make suitable choices. Algorithms that mimic this will be dealt with in Section 3.3.

To some extent depth first is the computationally easier method. However, breadth first searching has several advantages. First of all, it finds the shallowest solution. Often the depth in the tree is related to the complexity of the solution and hence shallowest is, in a sense, best. This is true, for example, of mathematical proofs, where a short proof is usually considered superior to a long one.

Even ignoring the issue of which solution is best, there are disadvantages to using depth first search. Consider the proof tree in Figure 3.7: the nodes represented by ellipses were those that stuttered; that is, the move reversed the effect of the previous move. If this were not detected, it would lead to an infinite search, for example continuously applying the commutativity axiom, and so moving back and forth for ever between the expressions $(x + y) + z$ and $x + (y + z)$. Figure 3.11 shows a similar tree for the Towers of Hanoi problem. In this case there are nodes that stutter (marked with asterisks ***) but, in addition, paths that go on for ever without repeating. For example, if we performed the moves 1–2, 1–3, 2–3, we would get to the state where all the rings are on the third column; another sequence of moves would return us to the initial state. One can avoid this terminal problem by keeping track of the states visited along the current path and *backtracking* whenever the current state is found on the path. In more complex domain, infinite paths may exist that never repeat and, even where there are no infinite paths, the leftmost branch of the search tree could be immoderately large, making depth first search impractical.

3.2.3 Programming and space costs

From the previous discussion it would seem that breadth first search was a hands-down winner, except in the case where we were definitely seeking the leftmost solution in the search space. However, when we consider ease of programming and space costs, the situation is reversed.

To see this we will look at a simple implementation of the depth and breadth first algorithms. Both search algorithms must keep track of which nodes need to be examined next. This collection of nodes is known as the *open list*. The open list starts off containing only the root node. To search the tree the algorithm selects a node from the open list. The node is checked to see if it is a goal state: if it is, we have succeeded; if not, we add the children of the node to the open list and start again. The algorithm stops when the open list is exhausted. At that point the entire tree has been searched and therefore the algorithm reports failure.

The pseudo-code for the algorithm is in Figure 3.12. (Note that this version of

```
Initialize Open=[Root]
while Open is not empty
   take first node N from Open
   if N is a goal state
            return N and SUCCESS!
   otherwise generate C: the set of children of N
                                (if it has any)
** add C to Open
if Open becomes empty with no success return FAILURE
```

Figure 3.12 Depth/breadth first search – generic algorithm.

the algorithm does not check for repeated states.) The difference between depth and breadth first search is in the line marked **. If we add the children to the front of the open list (a stack), we get depth first search; if we add them to the end (a queue), we get breadth first search. It is truly amazing that such a small difference to the algorithm makes such a big difference to the order of the search.

Consider now a tree of depth d and branching factor b, and the largest open lists that can accumulate in the two algorithms. For depth first, the worst case is when it reaches the leftmost leaf node. At this point the open list contains the $b - 1$ siblings at each of the d levels. That is, the open list can contain up to $(b - 1) \times d$ nodes. The worst case for breadth first is when the algorithm is about to start looking at the leaf nodes. At this point all b^d leaf nodes will be in the open list – the space is exponential in the depth of the tree. So, space usage would discourage one from using breadth first search.

We turn now to ease of programming. In depth first search, the open list is a stack. By using recursion, either in procedural languages or in PROLOG, we can effectively use the language's own run-time stack to give us depth first search almost for free. Indeed, PROLOG's execution can be seen as a search process that is itself depth first (with consequent problems of infinite regress!).

3.2.4 Iterative deepening and broadening

We have seen that breadth first search may give an answer far faster if the search tree has some solutions closer to the root. However, breadth first search uses far more space, so much that searching large spaces will become prohibitive. One way to avoid this is an algorithm called *iterative deepening*. This is basically depth first search except with a maximum depth cut-off. The search is repeated with the depth increasing at each pass until a solution is found. If the depth is increased by one on each pass, the solution found will be precisely the same as that found by breadth first search. Like breadth first search it is immune to infinitely deep branches and hence is guaranteed to find a solution if one exists.

It seems as if iterative deepening would do a great deal of work, as it keeps searching the tree again and again. However, because of the exponential growth in the number of nodes at each level in the search tree, most of the work is done at the deepest level. Repeating work at higher levels has very little effect on the cost.

The worst case is when the tree is of constant depth. In this case, for a tree with branching factor b the extra work is only $1/(b-1)$ of the normal breadth first time. For example, if $b = 6$, iterative deepening only takes 20 per cent longer. In contrast, if the tree has any infinite or very deep branches, the saving can be enormous.

Iterative deepening avoids the problems associated with very deep, or infinitely deep, branches. However, sometimes there is an infinite *branching factor*. For example, we may want to find a positive integer solution to the equation $x^2 + y^2 = z^2$. As with the logic example at the start of this section, we could look at all the possibilities for x: 1, 2, 3, . . . – it might take some time! A second variation, *iterative broadening*, can deal with this problem by putting a bound on the number of children that are examined on each pass. Iterative broadening can be used on its own in conjunction with depth first or breadth first search, or combined with iterative deepening. In the latter case, one has to decide at each pass how much to increase both depth and branching cut-offs.

3.2.5 Finding the best solution – branch and bound

So far, we have only been concerned with finding the first solution. Now consider the case when we have cost associated with solutions. We cannot stop when we have found the first solution; instead we must keep track of the solution and its cost and then continue the search in case there is a better solution further on. We have to continue until the whole space is exhausted, all the time keeping track of the best solution encountered so far. This process could be combined with any of the search strategies we have encountered. However, every node must eventually be examined, so there is no advantage to using it with anything but depth first search.

If the cost function is associated solely with the final state, we can make no improvement to the algorithm without further heuristic guidance. However, if the path also has a cost, we can do somewhat better. We assume that the cost always increases with path length, as we shall do with all path costs. Examples of such costs include the distance travelled along a route, the time taken to perform actions between states, or a simple count of the moves taken. In fact all these costs are also additive, and are the sum of the costs of each move; however, this

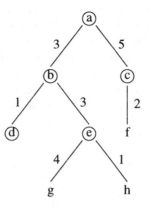

Figure 3.13 Search tree with path costs.

is not necessary for the algorithm to work.

Imagine we have found a solution g with cost $c(g)$. We go on to look for a further solution, and are about to examine a node at the end of a path p from the root of the tree. Now n and any state below n will have cost at least $c(p)$, so if $c(p) > c(g)$, it is not worth pursuing this path further – all nodes below it will exceed the current best cost. The algorithm resulting from this insight is called *branch and bound*. Figure 3.13 shows a search tree with costs associated with each path. Node d is optimal with path cost $3 + 1 = 4$. Assuming it is visited first, nodes below e and c need not be examined, as their partial path costs are $3 + 3 = 6$ and 5 respectively. Thus only the circled nodes are examined.

There are again variants of branch and bound associated with depth first, breadth first and iterative deepening. For the latter, the cut-offs can be based on the cost of the path rather than the depth. So long as the costs of the path increase suitably with path length, this will still be safe from infinitely deep branches.

3.2.6 Graph search

Several of the example trees we have been searching have been trees of graph nodes, for example the arithmetic proof tree. Indeed, the problem of repeated states arose directly because of their graph-related nature. A tree generated from partial solutions, such as the magic square tree in Figure 3.4 or the logic problem in Figure 3.8, cannot have repeated states down a branch.

Notice also that, when a graph is considered as a tree, nodes can be repeated along different branches. This is seen in the Towers of Hanoi tree in Figure 3.11. It is not as serious a problem as repeats down a single branch, since it does not lead to infinite work. However, if the same node is repeated on different branches, time is wasted examining nodes that have already been searched.

To avoid infinite branches we checked that the new node was not already in the current path. A similar technique can be used with graph searching. In addition to the open list, we also keep a *closed list*, keeping track of all those nodes that have already been examined. If a node is in this list it will not be examined again.

One can use branch and bound on graphs as well, simply by adding the cost check. However, a second visit to a node might be via a cheaper path. One therefore has to compare the new cost with the old one and, if cheaper, remove the node from the closed list and add it again to the open.

Depending on where we add the children, we can search the graph in a depth or breadth first fashion. However, we cannot now avoid space costs as the closed list will expand until it includes the whole space. In addition to the space cost, this means that the lookup to see whether a state has been visited previously gets progressively more expensive. One option is to limit the size of the closed list, discarding some entries when it gets full. This will certainly reduce the space and time costs, but leaves the possibility of repeated work and infinite loops.

3.3 Heuristic search

Recall from Section 3.1.2 that *heuristics* give us some information from a node part-way through a search about the nodes that lie beyond. Strictly, a heuristic could be any information, but is most usually a simple number representing how good or bad that path is likely to be. In a state problem, the evaluation will usually only depend on the node itself $ev(n)$, but in a path problem it must also depend on the path to the node $ev(n, p)$.

Figure 3.14 shows the search tree for finding the way through a maze. This is a state problem, as we are not interested in the shortest way through, just any way. The start is marked with a bullet and the exit (goal state) is marked g. The rest of the letters mark the choice points in the maze. The figures in square brackets show the heuristic evaluation for each node. The evaluation function chosen is the distance from the node to the goal measured using the *Manhattan block distance*. (That is, the sum of the distances in the x and y directions.)

Notice the following about the maze search tree:

- *misleading directions*: at node a, it at first appears that b is the most promising direction. Unfortunately, it leads to a dead end.

- *local minima*: from node b nowhere looks any better; whatever path you take you appear (in terms of the heuristic) to get further from the goal. Hence b is called a *local minimum*. A simple search might stop at b and never reach g, which is the *global minimum*.

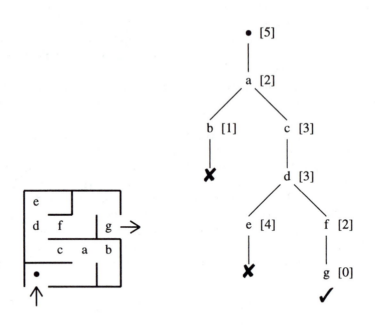

Figure 3.14 Maze search tree.

- *plateaux*: the heuristic evaluation does not change between c and d; there is no sense of progress. In more complex problems there may be whole areas of the search space with no change of heuristic. When this happens, the heuristic ceases to give any guidance about possible direction.

- *getting worse to get better*: in order to progress towards the goal one has to get temporarily further away from it.

To be fair, a maze is designed to be hard to get through, and hence it is no wonder that a simple distance measure (or indeed any measure) is unhelpful. However, all these problems do occur in real scenarios and must be faced by any efficient search algorithm.

3.3.1 Hill climbing and best first – goal-directed search

We can use heuristic evaluation functions to improve basic depth first and breadth first searches. Both algorithms search the children of nodes in a left-to-right fashion. If instead we search the child with the largest heuristic value first, we get *hill climbing with backtracking* and *best first search*. The difference between the two is that once hill climbing has chosen to follow a node it continues to do so in a depth first fashion, even if the heuristic value of the node's children are higher than the value for previously visited nodes. In contrast, best first will consider all previously visited nodes at each stage, choosing the best so far.

Hill climbing is named after those situations where the biggest number is best (benefit rather than cost), and so the algorithm is constantly following the direction that gives the fastest rate of increase – a rather keen climber who always chooses the steepest path! (Perhaps in situations where lowest is best, we ought to use a downhill skier analogy?) However, the algorithm is prepared to back up and try a different path if the steepest ascent leads to a dead end, hence the addition "with backtracking". Because best first search considers the whole open list at each stage, it doesn't need to backtrack, but consequently has to remember more nodes and to consider more possibilities at each step.

In the case of the maze tree, both algorithms would search the space in the same order, but this will not always be the case. Consider the tree in Figure 3.15. Like the maze tree, it represents some sort of goal-seeking search, where the heuristic is an estimated distance to a goal. The non-goal leaves are given an evaluation of 99 to represent the fact that they are no good at all! The heuristic evaluation function is rather better this time, especially as one gets closer to the goal nodes. This is typical of real-world examples. However, just as in the real world, it is not perfect – indeed, node f has quite a good evaluation, but no goal state is found beneath it.

Notice that the two algorithms reach different goal states. In fact, both algorithms are guaranteed to reach a goal state if one is there, as in the end they will both search the entire space. However, one hopes that the heuristic will so guide the search that a goal state is found when only a small portion of the space has been examined.

3.3.2 Finding the best solution – the A* algorithm

Given good enough heuristics, hill climbing and best first searches can find a solution faster than exhaustive searches. However, when a solution is found, they cannot tell whether it is the best one. Consider the tree in Figure 3.15. The heuristic on the goal nodes represents how good they are. We see that the hill climbing algorithm gets to a suboptimal solution, l. In this case, best first does manage to find the optimal solution h, but this will not always be the case. If the heuristic had been a little less helpful and node d had had value 4, then best first would have found node e – again suboptimal.

The problem is that given a goal state and an open list, we cannot determine whether there are as yet unseen nodes with lower cost. The heuristic guides us to the good nodes, but does not give enough information to guarantee we have found the optimum. Recall from Section 3.2.5 that branch and bound search did far better. It was able to prune whole areas of the search tree as unfruitful. This is because the cost of the path to a node serves as a *lower bound* on the cost of the

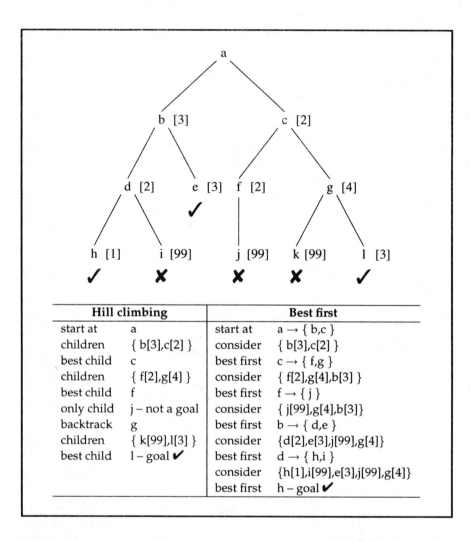

Figure 3.15 Trace of hill climbing and best first searches.

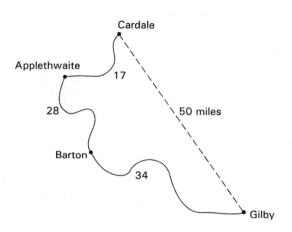

Figure 3.16 Using the A* algorithm.

nodes below it. If we have a heuristic function $ev(n, p)$ that has this property, we can have algorithms that guarantee an optimal solution.

A method of search that does this is the A* algorithm, which is effectively a modified form of best first. It is used especially on path problems where the cost of a path is the sum of the costs of the moves. However, it is not limited to such situations.

Rather than looking at the algorithm in detail, we shall simply consider the way it works in the case of real route finding on roads or around obstacles. We know that the shortest distance between two places must be at least as long as the straight-line distance. It may be longer if there is an obstacle in the way or if the roads are not straight, but, excluding cosmic worm-holes, it cannot be shorter.

Imagine we are looking for routes between Applethwaite and Gilby (see Fig. 3.16). We have already found a route via Barton that is 62 miles long. We then go on to look for further routes. We find the shortest path from Applethwaite to Cardale is 17 miles, but we see that the straight-line distance from Cardale to Gilby is 50 miles. So, any route from Applethwaite to Gilby via Cardale must be at least 67 miles. As this is longer than the route we have already found, we can stop looking for routes via Cardale. That is, we have *pruned* the search tree at Cardale.

Using this sort of reasoning the A* algorithm can prune many fruitless paths, but still guarantee to find the best solution.

Unfortunately, being a variant of breadth first, the A* algorithm inherits its storage problems for the open list. However, there are depth first and iterative deepening versions of the algorithm that can be used to overcome the problem.

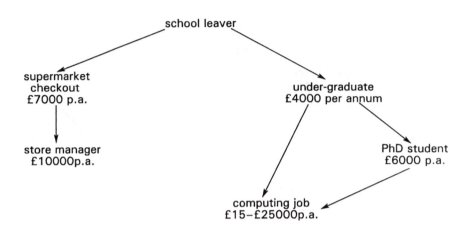

Figure 3.17 Graph of possible career moves.

3.3.3 Inexact search

Hill climbing revisited

As we noted in Section 3.1.1, we are often content with a good enough solution rather than the best. We saw that this would be the case if we used the first solution from best first or hill climbing. Furthermore, if all leaf nodes are *feasible* (although some are better than others), hill climbing will not need to do any backtracking. Thus we can use *forgetful hill climbing*; that is, we need only keep track of the current node and forget where we have been – no open list, no stack.

As the search space becomes very large, exhaustive search, even when guided by a heuristic, becomes impractical, and so this sort of inexact method is acceptable. Recall, however, the problems of hill climbing, plateaux and local minima (or maxima depending on the definition of best), making it hard to determine which direction to follow. Indeed, at a local minimum, one cannot even know if it is the best solution or not. Consider the career graph in Figure 3.17; the hill climbing school leaver would not get far!

In order to make progress in such domains (including running mazes), one needs to be prepared to accept some downhill movement. One way to proceed is periodically to make random moves, or to start at several random positions and compare the outcome of hill climbing from each start position.

An advantage of hill climbing over the exact techniques discussed earlier is that it can be used in continuous as well as discrete domains. An example of this would be driving a car. The parameters to control include both discrete values (gear selected, choke on) and continuous ones (depression of accelerator, steering wheel position). Choosing continuous parameters is beyond the scope of tree-searching techniques. On the other hand, traditional mathematical optimization techniques deal *only* with continuous variables. However, hill climbing can be used with these rather difficult *hybrid problems*.

To apply hill climbing to the continuous part of the problem, one must choose some small step and look at the change in cost, or alternatively use the derivative of the cost function in that parameter. When one considers continuous parameters a new phenomenon is encountered: the *ridge*. This is, like a real rocky ridge, a direction where the system is slowly moving uphill, but where it drops sharply downhill on either side. The problem is that if you are slightly off the ridge, the uphill direction is not to move along the ridge, but to ascend nearly directly up it. Unfortunately, the need to take discrete steps means that one frequently overshoots, leading to a wasteful zig-zag up the ridge, potentially missing it entirely. The equivalent problem where it occurs in discrete systems leads to a sequence of local minima occurring along the line of the ridge.

Simulated annealing

A slightly more systematic approach is *simulated annealing*. At each step one considers a random move. If the move is uphill, one always follows that direction. However, even if the move is downhill, it is sometimes followed, with a probability that diminishes as the distance downhill increases. Slight downhill movements are likely, large ones less likely. As the process proceeds, the system is "cooled" – that is, it is made gradually less likely that a downhill step is taken. Basically when the system is hot the behaviour is almost a *random walk*; when it is cold, it is simple hill climbing. Note that although the discussion here compares it with hill climbing, the algorithm is usually described with the best state having the lowest value, or "energy".

Simulated annealing is not guaranteed to find the global minimum, but usually gets somewhere close. It can be made somewhat more systematic by keeping track of a fixed number of good past states. If the search seems to get stuck in the "lowlands" it can be restarted from one of these positions.

Simulated annealing has proved to be a very robust and flexible technique for solving problems that seem particularly intractable (for example, timetabling), yet is very simple to program. However, one may feel uncomfortable using such a "random" algorithm for any critical application, such as medical diagnosis. In these cases it would need to be surrounded by *firewalls* to prevent mistakes.

Like hill climbing, simulated annealing is particularly powerful in *hybrid problems* where continuous and discrete parameters are mixed. The change in a continuous parameter can be chosen randomly, and the size of change can be arranged to reduce as the system is cooled, leading to smaller jumps and fine adjustment.

Genetic algorithms

As the name suggests, *genetic algorithms* are based on an analogy with biotic genetics and natural selection. The problem state is coded into separate parameters (the *genes*). A random set of states (individuals) is then allocated. The system then goes through a series of *generations*. In each generation, some of the individuals die, some breed and occasionally some mutate:

- *death*: some of the individuals are randomly killed (removed from the set). In order to simulate natural selection, those individuals that are considered good, as measured by the relevant cost function on the state, have a greater probability of survival.

- *breeding*: pairs of individuals are chosen and a new individual formed by mixing the genes of its parents. The exact nature of this mixing will depend on the particular parametrization chosen for the problem.

- *mutation*: as the original "gene pool" is not necessarily complete (or genes may be lost through deaths), occasionally parts of an individual's state may randomly change.

The idea is that the individuals that survive will gradually become better, as measured by the same costs that drive the natural selection. This algorithm has again proved fruitful in many domains where traditional techniques have found great difficulty. However, its success depends crucially on the choice of representation. To work the mixing of the genes from two good parents should lead (at least some of the time) to a good child. This is true where a problem consists of several almost independent parts. A good example of this is a crossword puzzle. Given a complete (but not necessarily correct) puzzle, we can measure goodness by the number of words that are in the English language. If one puzzle has good words in its top left and another good words in its bottom right, then combining the two is likely to lead to a reasonably promising solution. The parts of the puzzle are almost independent, but not entirely so (as some words will cross between the two).

The particular advantage of genetic algorithms is that work spent on making one part right is not thrown away because another part is wrong. In a simple tree-based search, only the decisions near the root are re-used. Those near the leaves are constantly being discarded, even where different parts of the space have similar structure.

The language of genetics is helpful in discussing the general problem of search. The *genotype* is the internal description – in the case of search, the parameters in the state description. The *phenotype* is the external attribute – the goodness measure or cost of the state. Systematic progress can only be made in a search if the phenotype and genotype have a reasonably simple mapping. For example, simulated annealing and hill climbing rely on the fact that small changes in the *genotype* (state) will normally result in small changes in the *phenotype* (goodness measure). In addition, genetic algorithms rely on that mapping having reasonably good structural properties.

3.4 Knowledge-rich search

The different algorithms that have been presented so far have depended upon the general type of problem (optimization, game playing, etc.), but have been *domain independent*. They could be applied to solving crossword puzzles or controlling a chemical factory. Of course, the algorithms would not work equally well in all cases, but they are not intrinsically designed for a particular situation.

However, for many problems more domain knowledge is required, and the general algorithms must be tuned to the specific problem. There are obviously as many fine tunings as there are problems, so this section will briefly discuss two of the more general classes of problem: constraint satisfaction and means–ends analysis.

We have already explicitly assumed the use of domain knowledge in the *heuristic evaluation function*. Although this does in a sense embody knowledge about the domain, it is quite crude – a single number. Furthermore, it may be difficult to code knowledge about the goodness of a state into a number. We may be able to look at two states and say that one is better or more interesting than the other, but not be able to put a number to it. Note too that the word *heuristic* means more than just this evaluation function, but indeed any knowledge used to guide search.

In addition to the evaluation function, there have been several places where we have implicitly assumed that domain knowledge would or could be used:

- *ordering children*: in depth or breadth first search, we assumed that there was some ordering of the children of a node. A good choice of this ordering makes an enormous difference to the search efficiency. In minimax, examining the best child first can double the depth to which it is possible to search in a given time. Even where an evaluation is being used, we may need extra guidance where there are many plateaux.

- *ordering the tree*: that is, choosing which decisions to make first in producing the tree. This is applicable to trees where the states represent partial solutions, and we have already seen in Section 3.1.2 how the order in which we expand the magic square search tree makes a big difference to our ability to prune impossible solutions.

In addition, in Chapter 5, we will consider the *minimax algorithm* for searching game tree searches. An important parameter in the minimax algorithm is the *search horizon*, which determines how deep the search looks down the game tree. The choice of search horizon will vary for different parts of the tree and embodies a great deal of the knowledge of the particular game.

In this section, we will look at constraint satisfaction and see how a good order of search can be determined dynamically. In Chapter 9, we will see examples of knowledge-rich search algorithms for planning and route finding.

3.4.1 Constraint satisfaction

Consider again the magic square tree shown in Figure 3.4. In fact, the magic square is an example of a *constraint satisfaction* problem. The goal is to have a state described by parameters $m_{11} \ldots m_{33}$, corresponding to the positions in the square:

m_{11}	m_{12}	m_{13}
m_{21}	m_{22}	m_{23}
m_{31}	m_{32}	m_{33}

These parameters are to be different integers in the range 1 to 9 and must satisfy the following *constraints*:

1.	$m_{11} + m_{12} + m_{13} = 15$		5.	$m_{12} + m_{22} + m_{32} = 15$
2.	$m_{21} + m_{22} + m_{23} = 15$		6.	$m_{13} + m_{23} + m_{33} = 15$
3.	$m_{31} + m_{32} + m_{33} = 15$		7.	$m_{11} + m_{22} + m_{33} = 15$
4.	$m_{11} + m_{21} + m_{31} = 15$		8.	$m_{13} + m_{22} + m_{31} = 15$

Constraints 1–3 say that the rows add up to 15; 4–6 say the same for the columns and 7 and 8 for the diagonals.

These constraints are arithmetic equalities, but constraints can also be inequalities or logical formulae. The logic problem in Section 3.2.1 is an example of the latter.

We can use the constraints to:

- *check* the correctness of a partial solution and hence prune fruitless branches.

- *calculate* some parameters from others. For example, once we know m_{11} and m_{12} we can calculate that

$$m_{13} = 15 - m_{11} + m_{12}$$

- *choose* which parameter to fix next.

In keeping with the idiom, the fixing of a parameter value can be thought of as adding a new (albeit simple) constraint. However, we must remember to distinguish those constraints that are given as part of the problem and those that are guesses and may thus be changed later (*backtracking*).

The first of these, checking, reduces the effective breadth of the tree, as it means some branches need not be examined. The second, calculation, reduces the effective depth as some choices are made "for free". These two can be accomplished using a general software method called *constraint propagation*. However, it is the third choice that is ultimately most powerful.

Recall how the particular order in which the magic square was searched led to rapid pruning of unfruitful paths, whereas an expansion that led to partial solutions of the form

?	2	?
1	?	?
?	?	3

was clearly unsuitable. The reason for this is that the chosen order filled in the parameters of constraints that could then be checked (in fact the third choice could have been made by calculation).

A general heuristic is to choose to fix parameters that will complete constraints. So, for example, once we have chosen to fix $m_{11} = 1$, there are only two more parameters required on constraints 1, 4 and 7. This suggests that we next choose to fix one of the other parameters in these constraints, say m_{12} (as in the tree) or m_{22}. A general heuristic is thus to choose a parameter that is in the constraint with the fewest free slots. Where this heuristic yields several possible parameters, we can choose one that reduces most other constraints. For example, this would suggest that for the first parameter we ought to choose m_{22}, as this is in four constraints as opposed to only three for m_{11}.

As one focuses in on more specific problems, these general heuristics are also honed. In particular, we find that the choice of order can no longer be made *statically*. All the arguments we have used for the magic tree could be made without looking at a single node. We can look at the constraints and choose a search order (not square!) such as the following

2	6	4
8	1	9
5	7	3

In other problems it may not be clear what order to choose until one has explicit information. This is particularly true where the constraints are complex logical formulae such as

$$(a \wedge b \wedge c \wedge d \wedge e \wedge f) \vee (g \wedge h)$$

Initially this has a lot of parameters in it, and would be far down our list of interesting constraints. However, as soon as we begin to examine the branch with $a = false$, the whole left-hand side of the constraint becomes false and it reduces to $(g \wedge h)$, suggesting that we next fix g or h.

3.5 Summary

Search problems can be classified in a number of ways:

- state or path based

- any or best solution

- deterministic or adversarial

- perfect solution or just good enough

Search spaces can be structured as trees or graphs. In some problems the interior nodes of a search tree may represent partial solutions. Trees can be characterized by their branching factor and their depth, either of which may be infinite.

Search can be guided by heuristic evaluation functions or by domain knowledge, or can be virtually unguided.

Blind search algorithms include depth first search, breadth first search, iterative broadening, iterative deepening and branch and bound. Depth first search is simple to program and uses relatively little space compared with breadth first search, but has problems with very deep branches. Iterative deepening and iterative broadening algorithms deal with problems of very (or infinitely) deep and very broad trees respectively. Where costs are associated with moves, branch and bound can reduce the number of nodes searched by pruning nodes of the search tree. But it is still guaranteed to find the best solution.

Heuristic evaluation functions can guide search. Hill climbing with backtracking and best first search use the heuristic value to choose the order to investigate nodes. But both must search the entire tree to be sure of finding the best solution. If the heuristic evaluation function gives a lower bound on the final cost, the A* algorithm can prune nodes and so avoid searching all the tree, but still will get the best solution.

Exact methods are often impractical. Forgetful hill climbing can often find good solutions, but suffers from problems caused by local mimima and plateaux in the search space. Genetic algorithms and simulated annealing use randomness in different ways to search complex spaces including problems with some discrete and some continuous parameters. They often find near optimal solutions.

However, more knowledge is needed to tune algorithms for specific problem domains. Algorithms that include such knowledge include constraint satisfaction, as well as specialist algorithms discussed in later chapters.

3.6 Exercises

1. In Section 3.1.1, it was said that for many path problems the cost was a function of the route only and not the goal state reached. Think of an example of a problem where both the goodness of the goal state and the cost of the path are important.

2. In Section 3.3.3 it was suggested that a genetic algorithm was a possible way to solve crossword puzzles. Find an online dictionary and extract all words of four letters. You are trying to produce 4×4 acrostics. That is, four lines of four characters so that each row and each column forms a word. The states will be lists of 16 characters, and goodness can be measured by the number of four-letter words (8 is perfect). For example, take the (incorrect) acrostic

```
P I N S
A M E O
I Q A N
L O T S
```

It has five correct words (pins, lots, pail, neat and sons) and three incorrect (ameo, iqan and imqo). Its goodness is therefore 5. Choose a method to combine two acrostics and use a genetic algorithm on it.

3.7 Recommended further reading

Pearl, J. 1984. *Heuristics: intelligent search strategies for computer problem solving.* Reading, MA: Addison Wesley.
 A detailed, mathematically precise expositon of the main search strategies and their application in AI.

Chapter Four

Machine learning

4.1 Overview

In this chapter, we will see that machine learning is an important and necessary part of artificial intelligence. We will also discuss the general pattern of machine learning and some of the issues that arise. Several specific machine learning methods will be described: deductive learning, inductive learning, and explanation-based learning. Most of the chapter will concentrate on two specific inductive learning algorithms: the version-space method and ID3. We will conclude with a description of an experimental system that uses machine learning in an intelligent database interface.

4.2 Why do we want machine learning?

One response to the idea of artificial intelligence is to say that computers can never think because they only do what their programmers tell them to do. Of course, it is not always easy to tell what a particular program will do (!), but at least given the same inputs and conditions it will do the same things – dependable if not predictable. If the program gets something right once it will always get it right. If it makes a mistake once it always makes the same mistake. In contrast, people tend to learn from their mistakes; attempt to work out why things went wrong; try alternatives. Also, we are able to notice similarities between things, and so generate new ideas about the world we live in. An intelligence, however artificial or alien, that did not learn would not be much of an intelligence. So, machine learning is a prerequisite for any mature programme of artificial intelligence.

Of course, many practical applications of AI do not make use of machine learning. The relevant knowledge is built in at the start. Although perhaps fundamentally limited, such systems are useful and do their job. However, even where we do not require a system to learn "on the job", machine learning has a part to play. One of the most difficult problems in the building of expert systems is capturing the knowledge from the experts. There are many knowledge elicitation techniques to aid this process (see Ch. 6), but the fundamental problem remains:

things that are normally implicit, inside the expert's head, must be externalized and made explicit (Fig. 4.2).

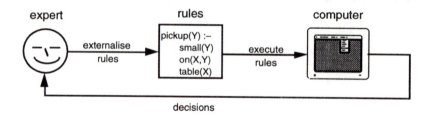

Figure 4.1 The knowledge elicitation bottleneck.

Using machine learning this problem can be eased. Experts may find it hard to say what rules they use to assess a situation, but they can usually tell you what factors they take into account. A machine learning program can take descriptions of situations couched in terms of these factors and then infer rules that match the expert's behaviour. The expert can then critique these rules and verify that they seem reasonable (it is easier to recognize correct rules than to generate them). If the rules are wrong, the expert may be able to suggest counter-examples that can guide further learning (Fig. 4.2).

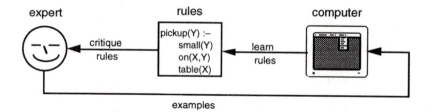

Figure 4.2 Machine learning avoids the bottleneck.

4.3 How machines learn

In previous chapters we have discussed reasoning, knowledge representation and search. All are important for machine learning. In addition, there are various other factors that influence the choice and efficacy of a learning system, for example the amount of domain knowledge used by the system.

In this section we will look at several of these issues, which will be important when we look at particular learning algorithms later in this chapter. It will give a context to these algorithms and we shall mention them where appropriate. We suggest that you revisit this section after reading the rest of the chapter. We'll start by looking at the phases in a typical machine learning system (Fig. 4.3). The different issues will then be discussed in relation to the data and processes involved.

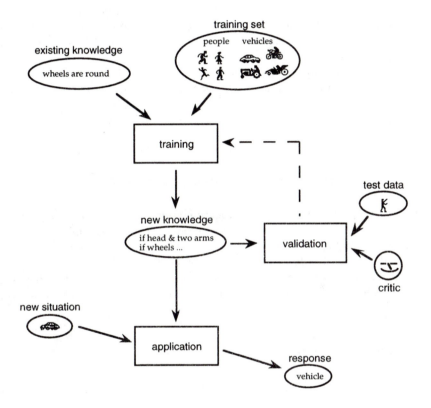

Figure 4.3 Phases of machine learning.

4.3.1 Phases of machine learning

Machine learning typically follows three phases:

- *training*: a training set of examples of correct behaviour is analyzed and some representation of the newly learnt knowledge is stored. This is often some form of rules.

– *validation*: the rules are checked and, if necessary, additional training is given. Sometimes additional test data are used, but instead a human expert may validate the rules (as in Fig. 4.2), or some other automatic knowledge-based component may be used. The role of the tester is often called the critic.

– *application*: the rules are used in responding to some new situation.

These phases may not be distinct. Often there is no explicit validation phase; instead the learning algorithm guarantees some form of correctness. Also, in some circumstances, systems learn "on the job" – that is, the training and application phases overlap.

Obviously the training stage is the most important and we will look in turn at the inputs to training (the training set and existing background knowledge), the outputs (the new knowledge learnt), and then the process of training itself. First, however, we'll look at how rote learning fits into this picture.

4.3.2 Rote learning and the importance of generalization

The simplest kind of learning is rote learning. In this case examples of correct behaviour are stored and when a new situation is encountered it is matched with the learnt examples. If one of the examples matches, the relevant response is given. In this kind of learning there is no prior knowledge. Training consists simply of memorization, and the output of training is just the stored training set. For example, the system may be given the following set of stimulus–response pairs:

24°C	–	75°F
−3°C	–	26°F
176°F	–	80°C
17°C	–	62°F
41°F	–	5°C
89°F	–	32°C
0°C	–	32°F

From these it might be able to respond to a stimulus "41°F" and give the response "5°C". However, it would not be able to respond to an unseen stimulus such as "15°C". Rote learning is clearly a very limited form of learning and is arguably not "real" learning at all.

Real learning involves some form of generalization. We would like a system to infer that when a stimulus of the form "<a number>°C" is received, it should multiply the number by 9/5 and add 32. Note how this is not a simple arithmetic rule. The system would have to learn that different formulae should be used depending on whether the stimulus included "°C" or "°F". In fact, in most of the learning algorithms we will discuss, the rules learnt will be symbolic rather than numeric.

However, one should not underestimate the importance of rote learning. After all, the ability to remember vast amounts of information is one of the advantages of using a computer, and it is especially powerful when combined with other techniques. For example, heuristic evaluation functions are often expensive to compute; during a search the same node in the search tree may be visited several times and the heuristic evaluation wastefully recomputed. Where sufficient memory is available a rote learning technique called *memorizing* can help. The first time a node is visited the computed value can be remembered. When the node is revisited this value is used instead of recomputing the function. Thus the search proceeds faster and more complex (and costly) evaluation functions can be used.

4.3.3   Inputs to training

In Figure 4.3, we identified two inputs to the training process: the training set and existing knowledge. Most of the learning algorithms we will describe are heavily example based; however, pure deductive learning (Section 4.4) uses no examples and only makes use of existing knowledge. There is a continuum (Fig. 4.4) between knowledge-rich methods that use extensive domain knowledge and those that use only simple domain-independent knowledge. The latter is often implicit in the algorithms; for example, inductive learning is based on the knowledge that if something happens a lot it is likely to be generally true.

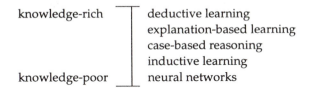

knowledge-rich · · · · · · · · · deductive learning
explanation-based learning
case-based reasoning
inductive learning
knowledge-poor · · · · · · · · · neural networks

Figure 4.4 Knowledge continuum.

Where examples are being used it is important to know what the source is. The examples may be simply measurements from the world, for example transcripts of grand master chess tournaments. If so, do they represent "typical" sets of behaviour or have they been filtered to be "representative"? If the former is true then we can infer information about the relative probability from the frequency in the training set. However, unfiltered data may also be noisy, have errors, etc., and examples from the world may not be complete, since infrequent situations may simply not be in the training set.

Alternatively, the examples may have been generated by a teacher. In this case we can assume that they are a helpful set, covering all the important cases and including near miss examples. Also, one can assume that the teacher will not be deliberately ambiguous or misleading. For example, a helpful teacher trying to teach a relationship between numbers would not give the example (2, 2, 4), as this might be multiplication or addition.

Finally, the system itself may be able to generate examples by performing experiments on the world (for robots), asking an expert, or using an internal model of the world.

We also have to decide on a representation for the examples. This may be partly determined by the context, but often we will have some choice. Often the choice of representation embodies quite a lot of the domain knowledge.

A common representation is as a set of attribute values. For example, in Section 4.5.1, we will describe children's play tiles using four attributes: shape, colour, size and material. A particular example could be: triangle, blue, large, wood. In vision applications (see Ch. 8), the representation is often even cruder – simply a bitmap. On the other hand, more knowledge-rich learning often uses more expressive descriptions of the structure of the examples, using predicate logic or semantic nets.

4.3.4   Outputs of training

To a large extent the outputs of learning are determined by the application. What is it we want to do with our new knowledge? Many machine learning systems are classifiers. The examples they are given are from two or more classes, and the purpose of learning is to determine the common features in each class. When a new unseen example is presented, the system then uses the common features to determine in which class the new example belongs. The new knowledge is thus effectively in the form of rules such as

> **if**   example satisfies condition
> **then**   assign it to class X

In machine learning, this job of classification is often called concept learning (see Section 4.5.1). The simplest case is when there are only two classes, of which one is seen as the desired "concept" to be learnt and the other is everything else. In this case we talk about positive and negative examples of the concept. The "then" part of the rules is then always the same and so the learnt rule is simply a predicate describing the concept.

The form of this predicate, or of the condition part of a more complex rule, varies between machine learning algorithms. In some it is an arbitrary logical predicate, but more commonly its form is much simpler. In Section 4.5.1 we will consider predicates that are of the form

> attribute1 = value1 **and** attribute2 = value2 **and** ...

That is, conjunctions of simple tests on attributes. In Section 4.5.2 more complex predicates in the form of decision trees will be considered. We will see that there is a trade-off between the allowable set of rules and the complexity of the learning process. The desire for simple rules is determined partly by computational tractability, but also by the application of Occam's razor – always prefer simpler explanations: they are more likely to be right and more likely to generalize.

Not all learning is simple classification. In applications such as robotics one wants to learn appropriate actions. In this case, the knowledge may be in terms of production rules or some similar representation. More complex rules also arise in theorem provers and planning systems.

An important consideration for both the content and representation of learnt knowledge is the extent to which explanation may be required for future actions. In some cases the application is a black box. For example, in speech recognition, one would not ask for an explanation of why the system recognizes a particular word or not, one just wants it to work! However, as we shall see in Chapter 6, many applications require that the system can give a justification for decisions. Imagine you asked an expert system "is my aircraft design safe" and it said "yes". Would you be happy? Probably not. Even worse, imagine you asked it to generate a design – it might do a very good job, but unless it could justify its decisions would you be happy? Because of this, the learnt rules must often be restricted to a form that is comprehensible to humans. This is another reason for having a bias towards simple rules.

4.3.5 The training process

As we noted, real learning involves some generalization from past experience and usually some coding of memories into a more compact form. Achieving this generalization requires some form of reasoning. In Chapter 2, we discussed the difference between deductive reasoning and inductive reasoning. This is often used as the primary distinction between machine learning algorithms. Deductive learning works on existing facts and knowledge and deduces new knowledge from the old. In contrast, inductive learning uses examples and generates hypotheses based on similarities between them. In addition, abductive reasoning may be used and also reasoning by analogy (see Ch. 2).

Imagine we are analyzing road accidents. One report states that conditions were foggy, another that visibility was poor. With no deductive reasoning it would be impossible to see the similarity between these cases. However, a bit of deduction based on weather knowledge would enable us to reason that in both cases visibility was poor. Indeed, abductive reasoning would suggest that visibility being poor probably means that it was foggy anyway, so the two descriptions are in fact identical. However, using this sort of reasoning is expensive both during learning and because it is dependent on having coded much of the background knowledge. If learning is being used to reduce the costs of knowledge elicitation, this is not acceptable. For this reason many machine learning systems depend largely on inductive reasoning based on simple attribute–value examples.

One way of looking at the learning process is as search. One has a set of examples and a set of possible rules. The job of the learning algorithm is to find suitable rules that are correct with respect to the examples and existing knowledge. If the set of possible rules is finite, one could in principle exhaustively search to find the best rule. We will see later in this chapter that the sizes of the search spaces make this infeasible. We could use some of the generic search methods from Chapter 3. For example, genetic algorithms have been used for rule learning. In practice, the structure of rules suggests particular forms of the algorithms. For example, the version-space method (Section 4.5.1) can be seen as a special case of a branch and bound search. This exhaustive search works because the rules used by version spaces are very limited. Where the rule set is larger exhaustive search is not possible and the search must be extensively heuristic driven with little backtracking. For example, the inductive learning algorithm ID3 discussed in Section 4.5.2 will use an entropy-based heuristic.

4.4 Deductive learning

Deductive learning works on existing facts and knowledge and deduces new knowledge from the old. For example, assume you know that Alison is taller than Clarise and that Brian is taller than Alison. If asked whether Brian is taller than Clarise, you can use your knowledge to reason that he is. Now, if you remember this new fact and are asked again, you will not have to reason it out a second time, you will know it – you have learnt.

Arguably, deductive learning does not generate "new" knowledge at all, it simply memorizes the logical consequences of what you know already. However, by this argument virtually all of mathematical research would not be classed as learning "new" things. Note that, whether or not you regard this as new knowledge, it certainly can make a reasoning system more efficient. If there are many rules and facts, the search process to find out whether a given consequence is true or not can be very extensive. Memorizing previous results can save this time.

Of course, simple memorization of past results would be a very crude form of learning, and real learning also includes generalization. A proof system has been asked to prove that $3 + 3 = 2 \times 3$. It reasons as follows:

$$
\begin{aligned}
3 + 3 &= 1 \times 3 + 1 \times 3 && \text{(because for any number } n, 1 \times n = n) \\
&= (1 + 1) \times 3 && \text{(distributivity of } \times) \\
&= 2 \times 3
\end{aligned}
$$

Although this looks trivial, a real proof system might find it quite difficult. The step that uses the fact that 3 can be replaced by 1×3 is hardly an obvious one to use! Rather than simply remembering this result, the proof system can review the proof and try to generalize. One way to do this is simply to attempt to replace constants in the proof by variables. Replacing all the occurrences of "3" by a variable a gives the following proof:

$$
\begin{aligned}
a + a &= 1 \times a + 1 \times a \quad &\text{(because for any number } a, 1 \times a = a\text{)} \\
&= (1 + 1) \times a \quad &\text{(distributivity of } \times\text{)} \\
&= 2 \times a
\end{aligned}
$$

The proof did not depend on the particular value of 3; hence the system has learnt that in general $a + a = 2 \times a$. The system might try other variables. For example, it might try replacing 2 with a variable to get $3 + 3 = b \times 3$, but would discover that for this generalization the proof fails. Hence, by studying the way it has used particular parts of a situation, the system can learn general rules. We will see further examples of deductive learning in Chapter 9, when we consider planning, and in Chapter 11, in the SOAR architecture. In this chapter, we will not look further at pure deductive learning, although explanation-based learning (Section 4.6) and case-based reasoning (Ch. 2) both involve elements of deductive learning.

4.5   Inductive learning

Rather than starting with existing knowledge, inductive learning takes examples and generalizes. For example, having seen many cats, all of which have tails, one might conclude that all cats have tails. This is of course a potentially unsound step of reasoning, and indeed Manx cats have no tails. However, it would be impossible to function without using induction to some extent. Indeed, in many areas it is an explicit assumption. Geologists talk about the "principle of uniformity" (things in the past work the same as they do now) and cosmologists assume that the same laws of physics apply throughout the universe. Without such assumptions it is never possible to move beyond one's initial knowledge – deductive learning can go a long way (as in mathematics) but is fundamentally limited. So, despite its potential for error, inductive reasoning is a useful technique and has been used as the basis of several successful systems.

One major subclass of inductive learning is concept learning. This takes examples of a concept, say examples of fish, and tries to build a general description of the concept. Often the examples are described using simple attribute–value pairs. For example, consider the fish and non-fish in Table 4.1.

There are various ways we can generalize from these examples of fish and non-fish. The simplest description (from the examples) is that a fish is something that does not have lungs. No other single attribute would serve to differentiate the fish. However, it is dangerous to opt for too simple a classification. From the first

	swims	has fins	flies	has lungs	is a fish
herring	yes	yes	no	no	✔
cat	no	no	no	yes	✘
pigeon	no	no	yes	yes	✘
flying fish	yes	yes	yes	no	✔
otter	yes	no	no	yes	✘
cod	yes	yes	no	no	✔
whale	yes	yes	no	yes	✘

Table 4.1 Fish and non-fish.

four examples we might have been tempted to say that a fish was something that swims, but the otter shows that this is too general a description. Alternatively, we might use a more specific description. A fish is something that swims, has fins and has no lungs. However, being too specific also has its dangers. If we had not seen the example of the flying fish, we might have been tempted to say that a fish also did not fly. This trade-off between learning an overgeneral or overspecific concept is inherent in the problem.

Notice also the importance of the choice of attributes. If the "has lungs" attribute were missing it would be impossible to tell that a whale was not a fish.

The two inductive learning algorithms described in detail in this section – version spaces and ID3 – are examples of concept learning. However, inductive learning can also be used to learn plans and heuristics. The final part of this section will look at some of the problems of rule induction.

4.5.1 Version spaces

When considering the fish, we used our common sense to find the rule from the examples. In an AI setting we need an algorithm. This should take a set of examples such as those above and generate a rule to classify new unseen examples. We will look first at concept learning using version spaces, which uses examples to home in on a particular rule (Mitchell 1978).

Consider again Table 4.1. Imagine we have only seen the first four examples so far. There are many different rules that could be used to classify the fish. A simple class of rules are those that consist of conjunctions of tests of attributes:

if   *attribute1 = value1* **and** *attribute2 = value2* . . .
then   is a fish

Even if we restrict ourselves to these, there are seven different rules that correctly classify the fish in the first four examples:

R1.	**if**	swims = yes
	then	is a fish
R2.	**if**	has fins = yes
	then	is a fish
R3.	**if**	has lungs = no
	then	is a fish
R4.	**if**	swims = yes **and** has fins = yes
	then	is a fish
R5.	**if**	swims = yes **and** has lungs = no
	then	is a fish
R6.	**if**	has fins = yes **and** has lungs = no
	then	is a fish
R7.	**if**	swims = yes **and** has fins = yes **and** has lungs = no
	then	is a fish

If we only had the first four examples, what rule should we use? Notice how rules R1 and R2 are more general than rule R4, which is in turn more general than R7. (By more general, one means that the rule is true more often.) One option is to choose the most specific rule that covers all the positive examples, in this case R7. Alternatively, we could look for the most general rule. Unfortunately, there is no single most general rule. The three rules R1, R2 and R3 are all "most" general in that there is no correct rule more general than them, but they are all "most" general in different ways. Figure 4.5 shows these rules as a lattice with the most general rules at the top and the most specific at the bottom.

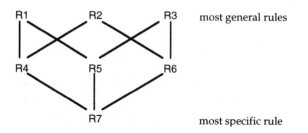

Figure 4.5 Rule lattice.

Further examples may restrict this set of possible rules further. If one takes the next example, the otter, it swims, but is not a fish. Therefore rule R1 can be removed from the set of candidate rules. This gives rise to an algorithm:

1. start off with the set of all rules
2. for each positive example p
   2.1. remove any rules which p doesn't satisfy
3. for each negative example n
   3.1. remove any rules which n does satisfy

4. if there are no rules left FAIL

5. when there is one rule left it is the result

The only problem with this algorithm is that you have to keep track of all rules. If there are n attributes with m values each, then there are $(m + 1)^n$ rules! Clearly this is infeasible for any realistic problem.

Version spaces reduce this number by only keeping track of the most specific and most general rules: all the other possible rules lie somewhere between these. Positive examples change the set of most specific rules, forcing them to become more general in order to include the new examples. Negative examples change the set of the most general rules, forcing them to become more specific in order to exclude the new examples.

In addition, because we are looking for a single final rule we can further prune the two sets. After a positive example we examine the set of most general rules (G) and remove any that are not above (more general than) any of those in the set of most specific examples (S). Similarly, after a negative example we can prune S to remove any which are not below some rule in G.

An example

Let's see how this would work when given the examples of tiles in Table 4.2. As a shorthand, rules will be represented by a tuple of the attributes they select. For example, the rule "**if** colour = blue **and** material = wood" is represented by the tuple (?,blue,?,wood). The question marks denote attributes which the rule doesn't test. The most general rule is (?,?,?,?), which doesn't care about any of the attributes.

	shape	colour	size	material	
ex1	triangle	blue	large	wood	✔
ex2	square	blue	small	wood	✘
ex3	triangle	blue	small	plastic	✔
ex4	triangle	green	large	plastic	✘

Table 4.2 Example tiles.

After seeing the first example, the most specific rule is (triangle,blue,large,wood), which only matches ex1. The most general rule is (?,?,?,?), which matches anything. This is because we have not seen any negative examples yet and so cannot rule out anything. The state of the algorithm can thus be summarized:

set of most specific rules (S) = { (triangle,blue,large,wood) }

set of most general rules (G) = { (?,?,?,?) }

The second example is negative and so the set of most general rules must be modified to exclude it. However, the new most general rules should not contradict the previous examples, and so only those that are more general than all those in S are allowed. This gives rise to a new state:

set of most specific rules (S) = { (triangle,blue,large,wood) }
set of most general rules (G) = { (triangle,?,?,?), (?,?,large,?),
(?,?,?,wood) }

The third example is positive. It does not satisfy (triangle,blue,large,wood), so S is generalized (again consistent with G):

set of most specific rules (S) = { (triangle,blue,?,?) }

However, at this stage we can also use the pruning rules to remove the second two rules from (G), as neither is more general than (triangle,blue,?,?):

set of most general rules (G) = { (triangle,?,?,?) }

Finally, we look at the fourth example, which is negative. It satisfies (triangle,?,?,?), so we must make G more specific. The only rule that is more specific than (triangle,?,?,?), but that is also more general than those in S, is (triangle,blue,?,?). Thus this becomes the new G. The set S is not changed by this new example.

set of most specific rules (S) = { (triangle,blue,?,?) }
set of most general rules (G) = { (triangle,blue,?,?) }

At this point $S = G$ and so we can finish successfully – which is just as well as we have reached the end of our examples!

Different kinds of rules – bias

The version-space algorithm depends on being able to generate rules that are just a little more or less specific than a given rule. In fact, any class of rules which have a method of making them slightly more or less specific can be used, not just the simple conjunctions that we have dealt with so far. So, if an attribute has values that themselves have some form of generalization hierarchy, then this can be used in the algorithm. For example, assume the shape attribute has a hierarchy as in Figure 4.6. We can then generalize from two rules (circle,?,small,?) (ellipse,?,small,?) to get (rounded?,small,?).

The rules can get even more complicated. With full boolean predicates generalization can be achieved by adding disjunctions or turning constants into variables; specialization by adding conjunctions or turning variables into constants. This sounds like a very general learning mechanism – but wait. If we allow more complicated rules, then the number of examples needed to learn those rules increases. If we are not careful, we end up with rules like

if *new example = ex1* **or** *new example = ex2* **or** ...

These are not only difficult to learn, but fairly useless – rote learning again.

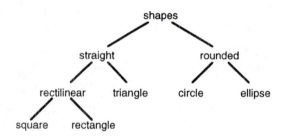

Figure 4.6 Shape taxonomy.

A learning algorithm must have some bias – a tendency to choose certain types of rules rather than others. This reduces the set of possible rules, and in so doing makes the learning task both tractable and useful. Restricting the rules in the version-space method to conjunctions introduced just such a bias and so enabled the algorithm to learn. However, the downside of a bias is that it means that some sorts of rule cannot be learnt. In this case, we would not be able to learn rules of the form

    if shape = triangle **or** colour = blue

Noise and other problems

The version-space method has several problems. It is very sensitive to noise – if any wrong examples are given the algorithm will fail completely. It also demands a complete set of examples, in the sense that there must be exactly one rule that classifies them all. Finally, it is not well suited to multi-way classification (for example, sorting animals into fish/bird/mammal). One must effectively treat these as several yes/no distinctions.

4.5.2 ID3 and decision trees

Decision trees are another way of representing rules. For example, Figure 4.7 shows a decision tree for selecting all blue triangles. Imagine a tile coming in at the top of the tree. If it satisfies the condition at the top node it passes down the yes (Y) branch; if it doesn't it passes down the no (N) branch. It is passed down node by node until it comes to one of the leaves, which then classifies the tile.

Several algorithms, of which the most well known is ID3 (Quinlan 1979), learn by building decision trees in a top-down fashion.

Consider again the tiles in Table 4.2. We start off with the four examples and choose some condition to be the root of the tree, say "shape = triangle". Three of

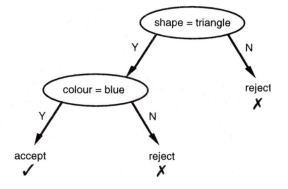

Figure 4.7 Decision tree.

the tiles (ex1, ex3 and ex4) satisfy this, and one doesn't (ex2). The N branch has all negative examples, and so no further action is taken on that branch. The Y branch has a mixture of positive and negative examples, and so the same procedure is taken recursively (Fig. 4.8).

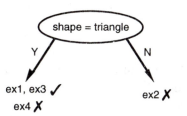

Figure 4.8 Starting to build a decision tree.

We now choose another condition for this branch, say "colour = blue". The three examples are sorted by this condition and now both branches have examples of one type. At this point we stop and label the leaves in the obvious manner (Fig. 4.9).

A different choice of condition at the root would lead to a different tree. For example, if we had instead chosen "material = wood", we would get to the stage in Figure 4.10. This time both branches have mixed examples and we must build subtrees at each.

If we chose the same condition "size = large" for each branch, we would end up with the decision tree in Figure 4.11.

Note that this not only is a different tree from Figure 4.9, but also represents a completely different rule:

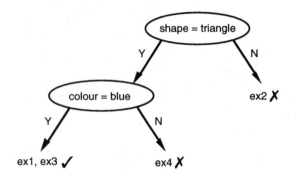

Figure 4.9 Completed tree.

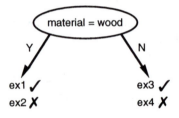

Figure 4.10 Starting a different tree.

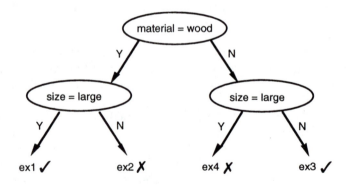

Figure 4.11 A different decision tree.

if   material = wood **and** size = large

    or material ≠ wood **and** size ≠ large

as opposed to the original rule

if   shape = triangle **and** colour = blue

How do we choose between these?

Well, one way would be to find the smallest tree (or at least one of the smallest). Unfortunately, the number of trees is huge and so an exhaustive search would be impractical. Instead, the algorithms are careful about the choice of condition at each node and use a condition that looks as though it will lead to a good tree (but might not). This decision is usually based on the numbers of positive and negative examples that are sent to the Y and N branches.

In Figure 4.12 these are tabulated for the two top-level conditions "shape = triangle" and "material = wood". In the first table, we see that the Y branch has two positive examples and one negative example giving three in total. The N branch has no positive examples and one negative example. In comparison the "material = wood" condition is very even handed with one positive and one negative example down each branch.

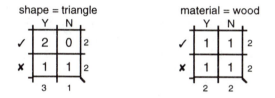

Figure 4.12 Contingency tables for different choices.

Of the two, the first is a more promising candidate as it makes the branches more uneven. Unevenness is important because we want the final tree to be very uneven – leaves must be either totally positive or totally negative. Indeed, one would expect a totally irrelevant attribute to give rise to an even split, as in the second table. Algorithms use different measures of this unevenness and use this to choose which condition to use at the node.

ID3 uses an entropy-based measure. The entropy of a collection of probabilities p_i is given by

$$\text{entropy} = -\sum p_i \log_2(p_i)$$

We calculate the entropy of each branch and then the average entropy (weighted by the number of examples sent down each branch). For example, take the "shape = triangle" table. The Y branch has entropy

$$-[2/3 \times \log 2(2/3) + 1/3 \times \log 2(1/3)] = 0.918$$

The N branch has entropy

$$-[0 \times \log 2(0) + 1 \times \log 2(1)] = 0$$

The average entropy is thus

$$3/4 \times 0.918 + 1/4 \times 0 = 0.689$$

(NB When calculating entropy one assumes that $0 \times \log_2(0) = 0$. This usually has to be treated as a special case to avoid an overflow error when calculating $\log_2(0)$.)

In contrast, the entropy of the "material = wood" decision is:

$$2/4 \times -[0.5 \times \log_2(0.5) + 0.5 \times \log_2(0.5)]$$
$$+2/4 \times -[0.5 \times \log_2(0.5) + 0.5 \times \log_2(0.5)] = -\log_2(0.5) = 1$$

Small values of entropy correspond to greatest disorder; hence the first decision would be chosen.

The original ID3 algorithm did not use simple yes/no conditions at nodes; instead it chose an attribute and generated a branch for each possible value of the attribute. However, it was discovered that the entropy measure has a bias towards attributes with large numbers of values. Because of this, some subsequent systems used binary conditions at the nodes (as in the above examples). However, it is also possible to modify the entropy measure to reduce the bias. Other systems use completely different measures of unevenness similar to the χ^2 statistical test. In fact, the performance of decision tree inductive learning has been found to be remarkably independent of the actual choice of measure.

As with the version-space method, decision tree building is susceptible to noise. If wrongly classified examples are given in training then the tree will have spurious branches and leaves to classify these. Two methods have been proposed to deal with this. The first is to stop the tree growing when no condition yields a suitable level of unevenness. The alternative is to grow a large tree that completely classifies the training set, and then to prune the tree, removing nodes that appear to be spurious. The second option has several advantages, as it allows one to use properties of the whole tree to assess a suitable cut-off point, and is the preferred option in most modern tree-building systems.

The original ID3 algorithm only allowed splits based on attribute values. Subsequent algorithms have used a variety of conditions at the nodes, including tests of numerical attributes and set membership tests for attribute values. However, as the number of possible conditions increases, one again begins to hit computational problems in choosing even a single node condition. Set membership tests are particularly bad, as an attribute with m values gives rise to 2^{m-1} different possible set tests!

The above description of decision tree learning used only a binary classification. However, it is easy to allow multi-way classification, and this is present in the original ID3 algorithm. The leaves of multi-way decision trees simply record a particular classification rather than just accept/reject. During training, the measure of unevenness must be able to account for multiple classifications, but the entropy measure easily allows this.

4.5.3 Rule induction

In both the version-space method and decision tree induction, the rules that are learnt are of the form "if condition then classify". The training can see whether a rule works simply by seeing whether the response it gives matches the desired response – that is, it classifies correctly. However, in more complicated domains it is not so easy to see whether a particular rule is correct. A classic example is pole balancing (Fig. 4.13). The task is to move the railway carriage so that the upright pole does not fall over and so that the carriage stays between the buffers. At each moment, the system must choose whether to move the carriage to the right or left depending on its position and the position and velocity of the pole. However, if the pole falls over, which rule is held "responsible" – the last rule applied? In fact, in such tasks the mistake often happened much earlier, and subsequent rules might be good ones.

Figure 4.13 Pole balancing.

This problem is called the credit assignment problem. It arises in many domains. For example, in computer chess – if the computer won, which moves were the good ones? If it lost, which should be blamed? A human expert might be needed at this stage to analyze the game in order to tell the computer what went wrong.

There is no simple solution to this problem. The human expert will be useful in some circumstances, but often the nature of the problem makes this undesirable or impractical – for example, a human expert would find it hard to assign credit in the pole-balancing problem. If the problem domain is internal to the computer it may be able to backtrack to each decision point and try alternatives. However, this approach will often be computationally infeasible. Sometimes there are special solutions dependent on the domain. For example, LEX, a theorem-proving program, searches for minimal proofs of mathematical propositions. All the heuristics that give rise to a minimal proof are deemed "good" – LEX assigns credit uniformly.

4.6 Explanation-based learning

Algorithms for inductive learning usually require a very large number of examples in order to ensure that the rules learnt are reliable. Explanation-based learning addresses this problem by taking a single example and attempting to use detailed domain knowledge in order to explain the example. Those attributes which are required in the explanation are thus taken as defining the concept.

Imagine you are shown a hammer for the first time. You notice that it has a long wooden handle with a heavy metal bit at the end. The metal end has one flat surface and one round one. You are told that the purpose of a hammer is to knock in nails. You explain the example as follows. The handle is there so that it can be held in the hand. It is long so that the head can be swung at speed to hit the nail. One surface of the hammer must be flat to hit the nail with. So, the essential features extracted are: a long handle of a substance that is easy to hold, and a head with at least one flat surface, made of a substance hard enough to hit nails without damage. A couple of years ago, one of the authors bought a tool in Finland. It was made of steel with rubber covering the handle. The head had one flat surface and one flat sharp edge (for cutting wood, a form of adze). Despite the strange shape and not having a wooden handle it is recognizably a hammer.

Notice how explanation-based learning makes up for the small number (one!) of examples by using extensive domain knowledge: how people hold things; the hardness of nails; the way long handles can allow one to swing the end at speed. If the explanation is complete, then one can guarantee that the description is correct (or at least not overinclusive). Of course, with all that domain knowledge, a machine could, in theory, generate a design for a tool to knock in nails without ever seeing an example of a hammer. However, this suffers both from the search cost problem and because the concepts deduced in isolation may not correspond to those used by people (but it might be an interesting tool!).

In addition, explanations may use reasoning steps that are not sound. Where gaps are found in the explanation an EBL system may use abduction or induction to fill them. Both forms of reasoning are made more reliable by being part of an explanation.

Consider abduction first. Imagine one knows that hitting a nail with a large object will knock it into wood. If we have not been shown the hammer in use, merely told its function, we will have to use an abductive step to reason that the heavy metal head is used to knock in the nail. However, the match between features of the example and the possible cause makes it far more likely that the abductive step is correct than if we looked at causes in general (for example, that the nail is driven into the wood by drilling a hole and then pushing it gently home).

Similarly, the inductive steps can be made with greater certainty if they are part of an explanation. Often several examples with very different attributes require the same assumption in order to explain them. One may thus make the inductive inference that this assumption is true in general.

Even if no non-deductive steps are made, explanation-based learning gives an important boost to deductive learning – it suggests useful things to learn. This is especially true if the explanation is based on a low-level, perhaps physical, model. The process of looking at examples of phenomena and then explaining them can turn this physical knowledge into higher-level heuristics. For example, given the example of someone slipping on ice, an explanation based on physical knowledge could deduce that the pressure of the person melted the ice and that the presence of the resulting thin layer of water allowed the foot to move relative to the ice. An analysis of this explanation would reveal, amongst other things, that thin layers of fluid allow things to move more easily – the principle of lubrication.

4.7   Example: Query-by-Browsing

As an example of the use of machine learning techniques we will look briefly at Query-by-Browsing (QbB). This is an experimental "intelligent" interface for databases that uses ID3 to generate queries for the user. This means that the user need only be able to recognize the right query, not actually produce it.

4.7.1   What the user sees

Initially Query-by-Browsing shows the user a list of all the records in the database. The user browses through the list, marking each record either with a tick if it is wanted or a cross if it is not (see Fig. 4.14). After a while the system guesses what sort of records the user wants, highlights them and generates a query (in SQL or an appropriate query method). The query is shown in a separate window so that the user can use the combination of the selected records and the textual form of the query to decide whether it is right (Fig. 4.15).

Whereas so-called Query-by-Example works by making the user design a sort of answer template, Query-by-Browsing is really "by example" – the user works from examples of the desired output.

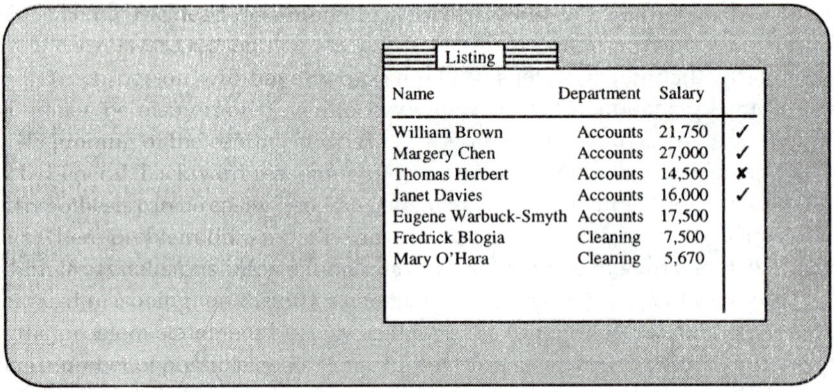

Figure 4.14 Query-by-Browsing – user ticks interesting records.

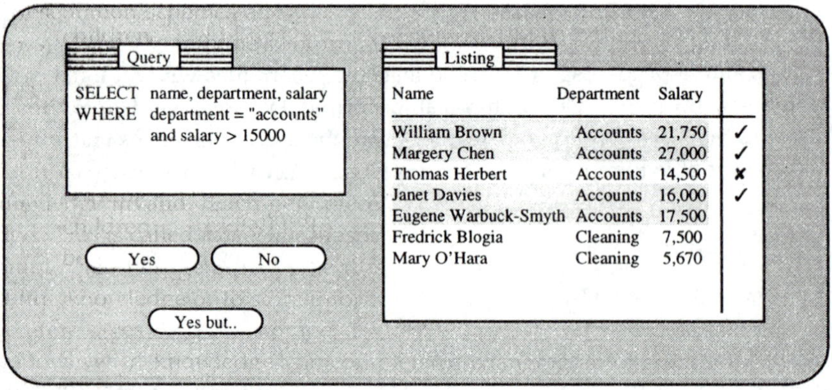

Figure 4.15 Query-by-Browsing – system highlights inferred selection.

4.7.2 How it works

The form of examples used by ID3, attribute–value tuples, is almost exactly the same as that of the records found in a relational database. It is thus an easy job to take the positive and negative examples of records selected by the user and feed them into the ID3 algorithm. The output of ID3, a decision tree, is also reasonably easy to translate into a standard database query.

In fact, QbB uses a variant of the standard ID3 algorithm in that it also allows branches based on cross-attribute tests (for example, "overdraft > overdraft-limit") as these are deemed important for effective queries. Otherwise the implementation of the basic system is really as simple as it sounds.

4.7.3 Problems

Even a very simple implementation of QbB works very well – when the system gets it right. When it doesn't things are rather more complicated. First of all the algorithm produces some decision tree which correctly classifies the records. However, there are typically many such trees. Sometimes the system produces a "sensible" answer, sometimes not. Although the answers are always "correct" they are not always the sort a reasonable human expert would produce. When QbB gets the wrong answer, the user can tell it and give more examples to help clarify the desired result. At some point the system generates a new query. However, the algorithm used starts from scratch each time and so there may be no obvious relationship between the first attempt and subsequent guesses. Although the earlier queries were wrong, the resulting behaviour can appear odd, and reduce one's confidence in the system.

The above problems can be tackled by modifying the algorithm in various ways, but the lesson they give us is that applications of machine learning must do more than work, they must work in a way that is comprehensible to those who use them. Sometimes the machine intelligence can be hidden away in a "black box", where the mechanisms are invisible and hence don't matter, but more often than not someone will have to understand what is going on. This is a point we shall return to in the next chapter.

4.8 Summary

In this chapter, we have discussed the importance of machine learning, its general pattern, and some of the issues that arise. Several specific machine learning methods have been described, including deductive learning, inductive learning, and explanation-based learning. In particular we have examined two inductive learning algorithms: the version-space method and ID3. We ended the chapter with a discussion of an experimental system that uses machine learning in an intelligent database interface.

4.9   Recommended further reading

Anzai, Y. 1992. *Pattern recognition and machine learning.* San Diego: Academic Press.
   Provides more detail of many of the algorithms discussed here including concept learning and decision trees.

Chapter Five

Game playing

5.1 Overview

Game playing has been an important part of the history of AI. The techniques for game playing can also be applied to other situations where factors are unknown but will be discovered only after action is taken. This chapter will consider algorithms for playing standard games (non-probabilistic, open, two-person, turn-taking, zero-sum games). Such games include chess, draughts, tic-tac-toe and Go. In particular, we will look at minimax search techniques and alpha–beta pruning. This builds on the search techniques studied in Chapter 3. The chapter will also consider other types of game where co-operation is important, where players can take simultaneous moves and where random events happen (such as the throw of a die). We will see in Chapter 9 that acting in the presence of uncertainty is essential for robotics and other practical planning tasks, and this chapter will show how game-playing algorithms can be used to tackle such non-gaming problems.

5.2 Introduction

Game playing has always been an important part of AI. Indeed, the earliest attempts at game-playing computer programs predate the field. Even Babbage considered programming his analytic engine to play chess.

Games have been seen as a good testing ground for two reasons. First, because the mixture of reasoning and creative flair seems to epitomize the best of human intelligence. Secondly, because the constrained environment of play with clearly formulated rules is far more conducive to computation than the confused and open problems of everyday life. However, more recently this latter advantage has often been seen as a weakness of game playing as a measure of intelligence. Instead human intelligence is regarded as being more thoroughly expressed in the complexity of open problems and the subtlety of social relationships. Many now look at the current state of the art in chess programs and say that the brute force approaches that are being applied are no longer mainstream AI.

This critique of game playing should not detract from its own successes and its enormous importance in the development of the field of AI. When chess programs were still struggling at club level they were regarded as a challenge to AI; now they compete at grand master level. Game-playing programs have also led to the development of general purpose AI algorithms; for example, iterative deepening (discussed in Ch. 3) was first used in CHESS 4.5 (Slate & Atkin 1977). Game playing has also been a fertile ground for experiments in machine learning.

> The single problem that has received most attention from the artificial intelligence community is the playing of chess, a game whose whole attraction is that it runs to precise rules within which billions of games are possible. As Stephen Rose, the British brain biologist, says, getting a computer to do this is not too great a wonder. Get one to play a decent game of poker, he says, and he might be more impressed.
>
> Martin Ince, THES(1994)

Most interesting games defy pure brute force approaches because of the sheer size of their branching factor. In chess there are typically around 30 legal moves at any time (although only a few "sensible" ones), and it is estimated around 10^{75} legal chess games. We say "legal" games, as few would be sensible games. In order to deal with this enormous search space the computer player must be able to recognize which of the legal moves are sensible, and which of the reachable board positions are desirable. Search must be heuristic driven, and the formulation of these heuristics means that the programs must to some extent capture the strategy of a game.

These factors are exemplified by the game of Go. Its branching factor is nearly 400, with as many moves. Furthermore, the tactics of the game involve both local and global assessment of the board position, making heuristics very difficult to formulate. However, effective heuristics are essential to the game. The moves made in the early part of the game are critical for the final stages; effectively one needs to plan for the end game, hundreds of moves later. But the huge branching factor clearly makes it impossible to plan for the precise end game; instead one makes moves to produce the right kind of end game.

Applying machine learning and neural networks to Go also encounters problems. The tactical advantage of a move is partly determined by its absolute position on the board (easy to match), but partly also by the local configuration of pieces. We will see in Chapter 8 that position independence is a major problem for pattern matching, and so this is not a parochial problem for game playing. Perhaps advances in Go and other games will give rise to general AI methods in the same way as chess and other simpler games have done over the years.

5.3   Characteristics of game playing

Game playing has an obvious difference from the searches in Chapter 3: while you are doing your best to find the best solution, your adversary is trying to stop you! One consequence of this is that the distinction between *planning* and *acting* is stronger in game play. When working out how to fill out a magic square, one could always backtrack and choose a different solution path. However, once one has made a choice in a game there is no going back. Of course, you can look ahead, guessing what your opponent's moves will be and planning your responses, but it remains a guess until you have made your move and your opponent has responded – it is then too late to change your mind.

The above description of game playing is in fact only of a particular sort of game: a non-probabilistic, open, two-person, turn-taking, zero-sum game.

- *non-probabilistic*: no dice, cards or any other random effects.

- *open*: each player has complete knowledge of the current state of play, as opposed to games like "battleships" where different players have different knowledge.

- *two-person*: no third adversary and no team playing on your side, as opposed to say bridge or football.

- *turn-taking*: the players get alternate moves, as opposed to a game where they can take multiple moves, perhaps based on their speed of play.

- *zero-sum*: what one player wins, the other loses.

In addition, the games considered by AI are normally non-physical (a football-playing computer?). With a bit of effort one can think of games that have alternatives to all the above, but the "standard" style of game is most heavily studied, with the occasional addition of some randomness (for example, backgammon).

As with deterministic search, we can organize the possible game states into trees or graphs, with the nodes linked by moves. However, we must also label the branches with the player who can make the choice between them. In a game tree alternate layers will be controlled by different players.

Like deterministic problems, the game trees can be very big and typically have large branching factors. Indeed, if a game tree is not complex the game is likely to be boring. Even a trivial game like noughts and crosses (tic-tac-toe) has a game tree far too big to demonstrate here. Because of the game tree's size it is usually only possible to examine a portion of the total space.

Two implications can be drawn from the complexity of game trees. First, *heuristics* are important – they are often the only way to judge whether a move is good or bad, as one cannot search as far as the actual winning or losing state. Secondly, the choice of which nodes to expand is critical. A human chess player only examines a small number of the many possible moves, but is able to identify those moves that are "interesting". This process of choosing directions to search is knowledge rich and therefore expensive. More time spent examining each node means fewer nodes examined – in fact, the most successful chess programs have relatively simple heuristics, but examine vast numbers of moves. They attain grand master level and are clearly "intelligent", but the intelligence is certainly "artificial".

5.4 Standard games

5.4.1 A simple game tree

In order to demonstrate a complete game tree, we consider the (rather boring) game of "placing dominoes". Take a squared board such as a chess board. Each player in turn places a domino that covers exactly two squares. One player always places pieces right to left, the other always places them top to bottom. The player who cannot place a piece loses. The complete game tree for this when played on a 3×3 board is shown in Figure 5.1. In fact, even this tree has been simplified to fit it onto the page, and some states that are equivalent to others have not been drawn. For example, there are two states similar to b and four similar to c.

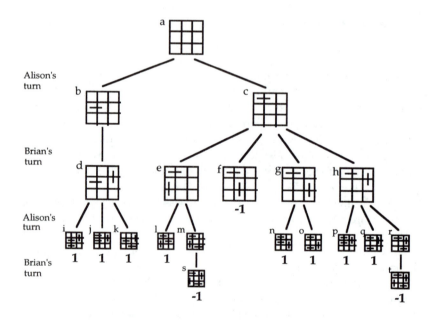

Figure 5.1 Game tree for "placing dominoes".

The adversaries are called Alison and Brian. Alison plays first and places her pieces left to right. Consider board position j. This is a win for Alison, as it is Brian's turn to play and there is no way to play a piece top to bottom. On the other hand, position s is a win for Brian, as although neither player can place a piece it is Alison's turn to play.

We can see some of the important features of game search by looking at this tree. The leaves of the tree are given scores of +1 (win for Alison) or −1 (win for Brian – Alison loses). This scoring would of course be replaced by a heuristic value where the search is incomplete. The left-hand branch is quite simple – if Alison makes this move, Brian has only one move (apart from equivalent ones) and from there anything Alison does will win. The right branch is rather more interesting. Consider node m: Brian has only one possible move, but this leads to a win for him (and a loss for Alison). Thus position m should be regarded as a win for Brian and could be labelled "−1". So, from position e Alison has two choices, either to play to l – a win – or to play to m – a loss. If Alison is sensible she will play to l. Using this sort of argument, we can move up the tree marking nodes as win or lose for Alison.

In a win–lose game either there will be a way that the first player can always win, or alternatively the second player will always be able to force a win. This game is a first-player win game; Alison is a winner! If draws are also allowed then there is the third alternative that two good players should always be able to prevent each other from winning – all games are draws. This is the case for noughts and crosses, and it is suspected that the same is true in chess. The reason that chess is more interesting to play than noughts and crosses is that no-one knows; and even if it were true that in theory the first player would always win, the limited ability to look ahead means that this does not happen in practice.

5.4.2 Heuristics and minimax search

In the dominoes game we were able to assign each leaf node as a definite win either for Alison or for Brian. By tracing back we were able to assign a similar value for each intermediate board position. As we have discussed, we will not usually have this complete information, and will have to rely instead on heuristic evaluation. As with deterministic search, the form of this will depend on the problem. Examples are

- *chess*: one can use the standard scoring system where a pawn counts as 1, a knight as 3, and so on.

- *noughts and crosses*: one can use a sum based on the value of each square where the middle counts most, the corners less and the sides least of all. You add up the squares under the crosses and subtract those under the noughts.

105

Note that these heuristics may give values outside the range 1 to −1, so one must either suitably scale them or choose large enough values to represent winning and losing positions.

Figure 5.2 shows an example game tree with heuristic values for each position. The heuristic values are the unbracketed numbers (ignore those in brackets for the moment). Alison's moves are shown as solid lines and Brian's moves are dashed. This is not the whole game tree, which would extend beyond the nodes shown. We will also ignore for now the difficult issue of how we decided to search this far in the tree and not, for example, to look at the children of node k. The portion of the tree that we have examined is called the *search horizon*.

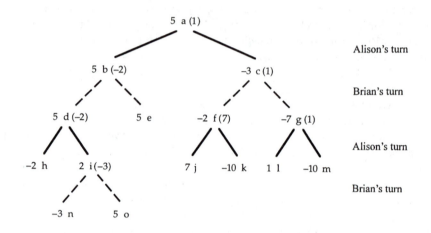

Figure 5.2 Minimax search on a game tree.

It is Alison's move. There are obviously some good positions for her (with scores 5 and 7) and some very bad ones (−10). But she cannot just decide to take the path to the best position, node j, as some of the decisions are not hers to make. If she moves to position c then Brian might choose to move to position g rather than to f. How can she predict what Brian will do and also make her own decision?

We can proceed up the tree rather as we did with the dominoes game. Consider position i. It is Brian's move, and he will obviously move to the best position for him, that is the child with the *minimum* score, n. Thus, although the heuristic value at node i was 2, by looking ahead at Brian's move we can predict that the actual score resulting from that move will be −3. This number is shown in brackets. Look next at node d. It is Alison's move. If she has predicted Brian's move (using the argument above), her two possible moves are to h with score −2, or to i with score −3. She will want the best move for her, that is the *maximum* score. Thus the move made would be to h and position d can be given the revised score of −2. This process has been repeated for the whole tree. The numbers in brackets show the revised scores for each node, and the solid lines show the chosen moves from each position.

With this process one alternately chooses the minimum (for the adversary's move) and the maximum (for one's own move). The procedure is thus called *minimax search*. Pseudocode for minimax is shown in Figure 5.3.

```
to find minimax score of n
        find minimax score of each child of n
        if it is Alison's turn
                score of n is the maximum of the children's scores
        if it is Brian's turn
                score of n is the minimum of the children's scores
```

Figure 5.3 Minimax pseudocode.

Note that the numbers on the positions are the worst score that you can get assuming you always take the indicated decisions. Of course you may do better if your adversary makes a mistake. For example, if Alison moves to c and Brian moves to f, Alison will be able to respond with a move to j, giving a score of 7 rather than the worst case score of 1. However, if you don't take the indicated moves, a good opponent will fight down your score to below the minimax figure. Minimax is thus a risk averse search.

5.4.3   Horizon problems

It is important to remember that the portion of tree examined in determining the next move is *not* the whole tree. So although minimax gives the worst case score *given the nodes that have been examined*, the actual score may be better or worse as the game proceeds, and one gets to previously unconsidered positions. For example, imagine that Alison looks ahead only two moves, to the level d–g. A minimax search at this level gives scores of 5 to b and −2 to c, so Alison will move to b, whereas by looking further ahead we know that c would be better. Looking even further ahead, our choice might change again. These rapid changes in fortune are a constant problem in detemining when to stop in examining the game tree. Figure 5.4 shows a particularly dramatic example. The white draught is crowned, so it can jump in any direction, and it is white's move. A simple heuristic would suggest that black is unassailable, but looking one move further we find that white jumps all black's draughts and wins the game!

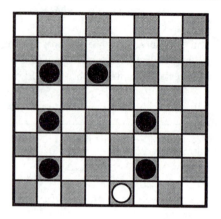

Figure 5.4 Horizon effect – simple heuristics can be wrong!

Look again at Figure 5.2. Positions a, b, d and e all have the same heuristic score. That is, they form a plateau rather like we saw in hill climbing. While we only look at the positions within a plateau, minimax can tell us nothing. In the example tree, the search horizon went beyond the plateau, and so we were able to get a better estimate of the score for each position. In fact, if you examine the suggested chess heuristic this only changes when a piece is taken. There are likely to be long play sequences with no takes, and hence plateaux in the game tree.

Plateaux cause two problems. First, as already noted, minimax cannot give us a good score. Secondly, and perhaps more critically, it gives us no clue as to which nodes to examine further. If we have no other knowledge to guide our search, the best we can do is examine the tree around a plateau in a breadth first manner. In fact, one rule for examining nodes is to look precisely at those where there is a lot of change – that is, ignore the plateaux. This is based on the observation that rapid changes in the evaluation function represent interesting parts of the game.

5.4.4 Alpha–beta pruning

The minimax search can be speeded up by using branch and bound techniques. Look again at Figure 5.2. Imagine we are considering moves from d. We find that h has score −2. We then go on to look at node i – its child n has score −3. So, *before* we look at o we know that the minimax score for i will be *no more than* −3, as Brian will be minimizing. Thus Alison would be foolish to choose i, as h is going to be better than i whatever score o has.

We can see similar savings on the dominoes game tree (Fig. 5.1). Imagine we are trying to find the move from position c. We have evaluated e and its children and f, and are about to look at the children of nodes g and h. From Brian's point of view (minimization), f is best so far. Now as soon as we look at node n we can see that the minimax score for g will be at least 1 (as Alison will play to maximize), so there is no reason to examine node o. Similarly, having seen node f, nodes p and q can be skipped. In fact, if we look a bit further up we can see that even less search is required. Position b has a minimax score of 1. As soon as we have seen that node f has score "−1" we know that Brian could choose this path and that the minimax score of c is at most −1. Thus nodes g and h can be ignored completely. This process is called alpha–beta pruning and depends on carrying around a best-so-far (α) value for Alison's choices and a worst-so-far (β) for Brian's choices.

5.4.5 The imperfect opponent

Minimax and alpha–beta search both assume that the opponent is a rational player using the same sort of reasoning as the algorithm. Imagine two computers, AYE and BEE, playing against one another. AYE is much more powerful than BEE and is to move first. There are two possible moves. If one move is taken then a draw is inevitable. If the other move is taken then, by looking ahead 20-ply, AYE can see that BEE can force a win. However, all other paths lead to a win for AYE. If AYE knows that BEE can only look ahead 10-ply, then AYE should probably play the slightly risky move in the knowledge that BEE will not know the correct moves to make and so almost certainly lose.

For a computer to play the same trick on a human player is far more risky. Even though human players can consider nowhere near as many moves as computers, they may look very far ahead down promising lines of moves (actually computers do so too). Because AYE knew that BEE's search horizon was fixed, it could effectively use probabilistic reasoning. The problem with human opponents, or less predictable computer ones, is that they might pick exactly the right path. Assuming random moves from your opponent under such circumstances is clearly foolhardy, but minimax seems somewhat unadventurous. In preventing the worst, it throws away golden opportunities.

5.5 Non-zero-sum games and simultaneous play

In this section we will relax some of the assumptions of the standard game. If we have a non-zero-sum game, there is no longer a single score for each position. Instead, we have two values representing how good the position is for each player. Depending on the rules of play, different players control different choice points, and they seek to maximize their own score. This formulation allows one to consider not only competitive but also co-operative situations, where the choices are made independently, but where the players' ideas of "good" agree with one another. This leads into the area of *distributed AI*, where one considers, for example, shop-floor robots co-operating in the building of a motor car (see Ch. 10). However, there we will consider the opposite extreme, where all parties share a common goal. In this section we will consider the in-between stage when the players' goals need not agree, but may do so. We will also examine simultaneous play, that is when both parties make a move in ignorance of each other's choice.

5.5.1 The prisoner's dilemma

A classic problem in game theory is the prisoner's dilemma. There are several versions of this. The one discussed in Section 5.5.4 is the most common, but we will deal with a more tractable version first! This comes in several guises, and the most common is as follows. Imagine two bank-robbers have been arrested by the police and are being questioned individually. The police have no evidence against them, and can only prosecute if one or the other decides to confess.

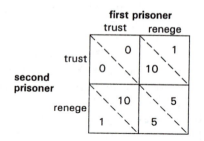

Figure 5.5 The prisoner's dilemma.

Before they were arrested, the criminals made a pact to say nothing. Each now has the choice either to remain silent – and trust their colleague will do the same – or to renege on their promise. Is there honour among thieves?

If neither confesses then the police will eventually have to let them go. If both confess then they will each get a long, five-year sentence. However, the longest sentence will be for a prisoner who doesn't confess when the other does. If the first prisoner confesses then the other prisoner will get a ten-year sentence, whereas the first prisoner will only be given a short, one-year sentence. Similarly, if the second prisoner confesses and the first does not, the first will get the ten-year sentence. The situation is summarized in Figure 5.5. In each square the first prisoner's sentence is in the upper right and the second in the lower left.

Let's consider the first prisoner's options. If he trusts his colleague, but she reneges then he will be in prison for ten years. However, if he confesses, reneging on his promise, then the worst that can happen to him is a five-year sentence. A minimax strategy would suggest reneging. The second prisoner will reason in exactly the same way – so both confess.

5.5.2 Searching the game tree

The above problem was drawn as a matrix rather than a tree, because neither prisoner knew the other's moves. If instead the two 'played' in turn then the situation would be far better. In this case we can draw the prisoner's dilemma as a game tree (see Fig. 5.6). At each terminal node we put the two values and use a minimax-like algorithm on the tree.

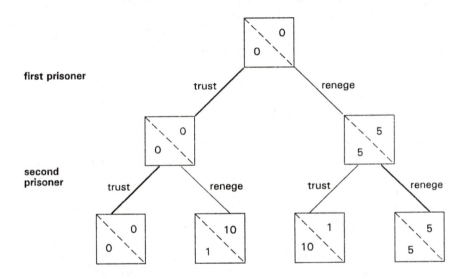

Figure 5.6 Game tree for prisoner's dilemma.

Imagine the first prisoner has decided not to confess, and the second prisoner knows this. Her options are then to remain silent also and stay out of prison, or to renege and have a one-year sentence. Her choice is clear. On the other hand, if the first prisoner has already reneged, then it is clear that she should also do so (honour aside!). Her choices are indicated by bold lines, and the middle nodes have been given pairs of scores based on her decisions.

Assuming the first prisoner can predict his partner's reasoning, he now knows the scores for each of his options. If he reneges he gets five years; if he stays silent he walks away free – no problem!

Notice that although this is like the minimax algorithm, it differs when we consider the second prisoner's moves. She does not seek to minimize the first prisoner's score, but to maximize her own. More of a maximax algorithm?

So, the game leads to a satisfactory conclusion (for the prisoners) if the moves are open, but not if they are secret (which is why the police question them separately). In real-life decision making, for example many business and diplomatic negotiations, some of the choices are secret. For example, the Cuban missile crisis can be cast in a similar form to the prisoner's dilemma. The "renege" option here would be to take pre-emptive nuclear action. Happily, the range of options and the level of communication were substantially higher.

Although there are obvious differences, running computer simulations of such games can be used to give some insight into these complex real-world decisions. In the iterated prisoner's dilemma, the same pair of players are constantly faced with the same secret decisions. Although in any one game they have no knowledge of the other's moves, they can observe their partner's previous behaviour. A successful strategy for the iterated prisoner's dilemma is tit-for-tat, where the player "pays back" the other player for reneging. So long as there is some tendency for the players occasionally to take a risk, the play is likely to end up in extended periods of mutual trust.

5.5.3   No alpha–beta pruning

Although the slightly modified version of the minimax algorithm works fine on non-zero-sum games, alpha–beta pruning cannot be used. Consider again the game tree in Figure 5.6. Imagine this time that you consider the nodes from right to left. That is, you consider each renege choice before the corresponding trust choice. The third and fourth terminal nodes are considered as before, and the node above them scored. Thus the first prisoner knows that reneging will result in five years in jail. We now move on to the second terminal node. It has a penalty of ten years for the first prisoner. If he applied alpha–beta pruning, he would see that this is worse than the reneging option, and so not bother to consider the first node at all.

Why does alpha–beta fail? The reason is that it depends on the fact that in zero-sum games the best move for one player is the worst for the other. This holds in the right-hand branch of the game tree, but not in the left-hand branch. When the first prisoner has kept silent, then the penalties for both are minimized when the second prisoner also remains silent. What's good for one is good for both.

5.5.4   Pareto-optimality

In the form of the prisoner's dilemma discussed above, the option when both remain silent was best for both. However, when there is more than one goal, it is not always possible to find a uniformly best alternative. Consider the form of the prisoner's dilemma in Figure 5.7. This might arise if the police have evidence of a lesser crime, perhaps possession of stolen goods, so that if neither prisoner confesses they will still both be imprisoned for two years. However, if only one confesses, that prisoner has been promised a lenient sentence on both charges.

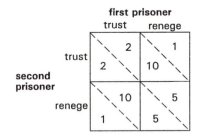

Figure 5.7 Modified prisoner's dilemma.

This time, there is no uniformly optimal solution. Neither prisoner will like the renege–renege choice, and the trust–trust one is better for both. However, it is not best overall as each prisoner would prefer the situation when only they confess. The trust–trust situation is called Pareto-optimal. This means that there is no other situation that is uniformly better. In general, there may be several different Pareto-optimal situations favouring one or other party.

Now see what happens when the prisoners make their choices. The first prisoner wonders what the second prisoner might do. If she reneges, then he certainly ought to as well. But if she stays silent it is still better for him to renege as this will reduce his sentence from two years to one. The second prisoner reasons similarly and so they end up in the renege–renege situation.

This time, having an open, turn-taking game does not help. Figure 5.8 shows the game tree for this version of the dilemma, which also leads to the renege–renege option. Even though both prisoners would prefer the Pareto-optimal trust–trust option to the renege–renege one, the latter is still chosen. Furthermore, if they both did decide to stay silent, but were later given the option of changing their decision, both would do so. The Pareto-optimal decision is, in this case, unstable.

The lesson is that, in order to get along, both computers and people have to negotiate and be able to trust one another. Some early work has begun on endowing software agents (see Ch. 10) with ideas of trust.

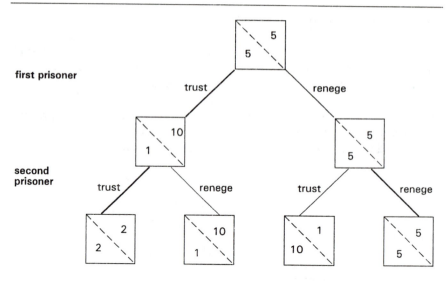

Figure 5.8 Non-Pareto-optimal solution.

5.5.5 Multi-party competition and co-operation

The above can easily be extended to the case of multiple players. Instead of two scores, one gets a tuple of scores, one for each player. The modified minimax algorithm can again be used. At each point, as we move up the tree, we assume each player will maximize their own part of the tuple. The same problems arise with secret moves and non-Pareto-optimal results.

5.6 The adversary is life!

Game playing is similar to interacting with the physical environment – as you act, new knowledge is found, or circumstances change to help or hinder you. In such circumstances the minimax algorithm can be used where the adversary is replaced by events from the environment. This effectively assumes that the worst thing will always happen.

Consider the following coin-weighing problem:

King Alabonzo of Arbicora has nine golden coins. He knows that one is a counterfeit (but not which one). He also knows that fake coins are slightly lighter than true ones. The local magician Berzicaan has a large and accurate balance, but demands payment in advance for each weighing required. How many weighings should the king ask for and how should he proceed?

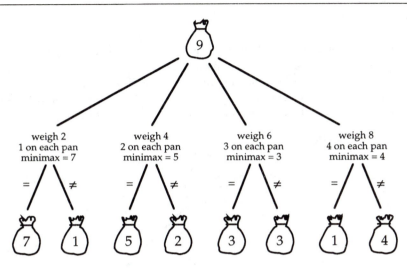

Figure 5.9 Minimax search for King Alabonzo's counterfeit coin.

Figure 5.9 shows the search space, expanded to one level. The numbers in bags represent the size of the pile that has the heavier coin in it. This starts off as size 9. The king can weigh two coins (one on each side of the balance), four, six or eight. If the balance is equal the coin must be in the remaining pile; if unequal he can confine his search to the heavier pile.

For example, imagine the king chose to weigh four coins. If the balance was unequal, he would know that the lighter side had the fake coin in it; hence the pile to test would now consist of only two coins. If, on the other hand, the balance had been equal, the king would know that the fake coin was among the five unweighed coins. Thus if we look at the figure, the choice to weigh four coins has two branches, the "=" branch leading to a five-coin bag and the "≠" branch leading to a two-coin bag.

The balance acts as the adversary and we assume it "chooses" to weigh equal or unequal to make things as bad as possible for King Alabonzo! Alabonzo wants the pile as small as possible, so he acts as minimizer, while the balance acts as maximizer. Based on this, the intermediate nodes have been marked with their minimax values. We can see that, from this level of look-ahead, the best option appears to be weighing six coins first. In fact, this is the best option and, in this case, the number of coins remaining acts as a very good heuristic to guide us quickly to the shallowest solution.

5.7 Probability

Many games contain some element of randomness, perhaps the toss of a coin or the roll of a die. Some of the choice points are replaced by branches with probabilities attached. This may be done both for simple search trees and for game trees. There are various ways to proceed. The simplest is to take the expected value at each point and then continue much as before.

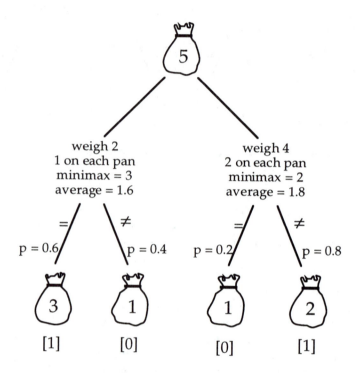

Figure 5.10 Probabilistic game tree for King Alabonzo's counterfeit coin.

In the example of Alabonzo's coins we deliberately avoided probabilities by saying he had to pay in advance for the number of weighings, so only the worst case mattered. If instead he paid per weighing when required, he might choose to minimize the expected cost. This wouldn't necessarily give the same answer as minimax. Figure 5.10 shows part of the tree starting with five coins. The lower branches have been labelled with the probability that they will occur. For example, if two coins are weighed then there is a probability of 2/5 that one of them will be the counterfeit and 3/5 that it will be one of the three remaining coins. At the bottom of the figure, the numbers in square brackets are the expected number of further weighings needed to find the coin. In the case of one coin remaining, that must be the counterfeit and so the number is zero. In the cases

116

of two or three coins, one further weighing is sufficient.

With five coins the king can choose to weigh either two or four coins. The average number of weighings for each has been calculated. For example, when weighing two coins there is that weighing, and if the scales are equal (with a probability of 0.6) then a further weighing is required, giving an average number of 1.6.

See how the average number of weighings required is 1.6 when two coins are weighed and 1.8 when four are weighed. So, it is better to weigh two. However, if the number of coins in the piles is used as a heuristic, the minimax score is better for four weighings. In general the two methods will not give the same answer, as minimax will concentrate on the worst outcome no matter how unlikely its occurrence.

One problem with calculating the average pay-off is that it leads to a rapid increase in the search tree. For example, in a two-dice game, like backgammon, one has to investigate game situations for all 21 different pairs of die faces (or 13 sums). One way to control this is by using a probability-based cut-off for the search. It is not worth spending a lot of effort on something that is very unlikely to happen.

Averages are not the only way to proceed. One might prefer a choice with a lower average pay-off (or higher cost), if it has less variability – that is, a strategy of *risk avoidance*. On the other hand, a gambler might prefer a small chance of a big win. This may not be wise against a shrewd opponent with no randomness, but may be perfectly reasonable where luck is involved.

Because of the problem with calculating probabilities, game-playing programs usually use complex heuristics rather than deep searches. So, a backgammon program will play more like a human than a chess program. However, there are some games where the calculation of probabilities can make a computer a far better player than a person. In casinos, the margin towards the house is quite narrow (otherwise people would lose their money too quickly!), so a little bit of knowledge can turn a slow loss into a steady win. In card games, the probability of particular cards occurring changes as the pack is used up. If you can remember every card that has been played, then you can take advantage of this and win. But don't try it! Counting (as this is called) is outlawed. If the management suspects, it will change the card packs, and anyone found in the casino using a pocket computer will find themselves in the local police station – if not wearing new shoes at the bottom of the river!

5.8 Summary

In this chapter we have looked at algorithms for playing standard games (non-probabilistic, open, two-person, turn-taking, zero-sum games). Such games include chess, draughts, tic-tac-toe and Go. We considered minimax search techniques and alpha–beta pruning, which relate to the search techniques studied in Chapter 3. We also discussed games where co-operation is important, where players can take simultaneous moves and where random events happen (such as the throw of a die). We will see in Chapter 9 that acting in the presence of uncertainty is essential for robotics and other practical planning tasks, and this chapter will show how game-playing algorithms can be used to tackle such non-gaming problems.

5.9 Exercises

1. Consider the alternatives to the "standard" game (the non-probabilistic, open, two-person, turn-taking, zero-sum game). Confining yourself to turn-taking games, consider all possible combinations of game types, and attempt to find a game to fit in each category. Only worry about the "zero-sum" property for two-person games, so that you should have 12 categories in all. For example, find a game that is probabilistic, open and not two person.

2. Consider the three-person game hex-lines, a variant of "placing dominoes". A piece of paper is marked with dots in a triangular pattern. Different sizes and shapes of playing area give rise to different games. Each person in turn connects two adjacent points. However, they are only allowed to use points that have not yet been used. The players each have a direction and are only allowed to draw lines parallel to their direction. We'll assume that the first player draws lines sloping up (/), the second horizontal (—) and the third sloping down (\). If players cannot draw their direction of line then they are out of the game. When no player can draw a line the lines for each player are counted, giving the final score.

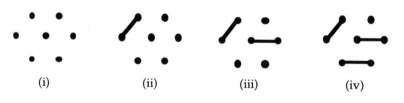

(i)   (ii)   (iii)   (iv)

Figure 5.11 Hex-lines.

Consider an example game on a small hexagonal playing area. The board positions through the game are shown in Figure 5.11. The initial configuration is (i).

(a) First player draws sloping up (ii).

(b) Second player draws horizontal (iii).

(c) Third player cannot play and is out.

(d) First player cannot play either and is out.

(e) Second player draws again giving (iv).

The final score is thus [1,2,0] (1 for the first player, 2 for the second and 0 for the third).

Taking the same initial configuration draw the complete game tree. Could the first player have done better?

5.10 Recommended further reading

Pearl, J. 1984. *Heuristics: intelligent search strategies for computer problem solving.* Reading, MA: Addison-Wesley.
   Part 3 of this book concentrates on game-playing strategies and heuristics.

Chapter Six

Expert systems

6.1 Overview

Expert systems are one of the most successful commercial applications of artificial intelligence. In this chapter we examine expert systems, looking at a basic system architecture, some classic applications, and the stages involved in building an expert system. In particular, we consider the important problem of knowledge elicitation. Finally, we discuss some of the limitations of current expert system technology and some possible solutions for the future.

6.2 What are expert systems?

Of all the applications of AI techniques, expert systems are perhaps the most familiar and are certainly, as yet, the most commercially successful. But what exactly is an expert system? What is it used for, and how is it built? This chapter will attempt to answer these questions. In our discussion we will return to several of the techniques we have already examined and see how they operate together to produce a useful artefact.

An expert system is an AI program that uses knowledge to solve problems that would normally require a human expert. The knowledge is collected from human experts and secondary knowledge sources, such as books, and is represented in some form, often using logic or production rules. The system includes a reasoning mechanism as well as heuristics for making choices and navigating around the search space of possible solutions. It also includes a mechanism for passing information to and from the user. Even from this brief overview you can probably see how the techniques that we have already considered might be used in expert system development.

In this chapter we will look at the main uses of expert systems and the components that make up an expert system, before going on to consider a number of well-known and, in a sense, classic expert systems. We will then look more closely at the process of building an expert system and the tools that are available to support this process. Finally, we will consider the problems facing expert system technology and look to the future.

6.3 Uses of expert systems

If an expert system is a program that performs the work of human experts, what type of work are we talking about? This is not an easy question to answer since the possibilities, if not endless, are extensive. Commercial expert systems have been developed to provide financial, tax-related and legal advice; to plan journeys; to check customer orders; to perform medical diagnosis and chemical analysis; to solve mathematical equations; to design everything from kitchens to computer networks and to debug and diagnose faults. And this is not a comprehensive list. Such tasks fall into two main categories: those that use the evidence to select one of a number of hypotheses (such as medical diagnosis and advisory systems) and those that work from requirements and constraints to produce a solution which meets these (such as design and planning systems).

So why are expert systems used in such areas? Why not use human experts instead? And what problems are candidates for an expert system? To take the last question first, expert systems are generally developed for domains that share certain characteristics. First, human expertise about the subject in question is not always available when it is needed. This may be because the necessary knowledge is held by a small group of experts who may not be in the right place at the right time. Alternatively it may be because the knowledge is distributed through a variety of sources and is therefore difficult to assimilate. Secondly, the domain is well defined and the problem clearly specified. At present, as we discovered in Chapter 1, AI technology cannot handle common sense or general knowledge very well, but expert systems can be very successful for well-bounded problems. Thirdly, there are suitable and willing domain experts to provide the necessary knowledge to populate the expert system. It is unfeasible to contemplate an expert system when the relevant experts are either unwilling to co-operate or are not available. Finally, the problem is of reasonable scope, covering diagnosis of a particular class of disease, for example, rather than of disease in general.

If the problem fits this profile it is likely to benefit from the use of expert system technology. In many cases the benefits are in real commercial terms such as cost reduction, which may go some way to explaining their commercial success. For example, expert systems allow the dissemination of information held by one or a small number of experts. This makes the knowledge available to a larger number of people, and less skilled (so less expensive) people, reducing the cost of accessing information. Expert systems also allow knowledge to be formalized. It can then be tested and potentially validated, reducing the costs incurred through error. They also allow integration of knowledge from different sources, again reducing the cost of searching for knowledge. Finally, expert systems can provide consistent, unbiased responses. This can be a blessing or a curse depending on which way you look at it. On the positive side, the system is not plagued by human error or prejudice (unless this is built into the knowledge and reasoning), resulting in more consistent, correct solutions. On the other hand, the system is unable to make value judgements, which makes it more inflexible

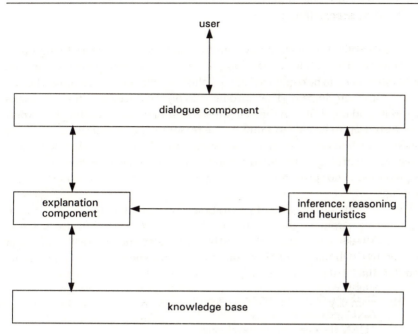

Figure 6.1 Typical expert system architecture.

than the human (for example, a human assessing a loan application can take into account mitigating circumstances when assessing previous bad debts, but an expert system is limited in what it can do).

6.4 Architecture of an expert system

An expert system comprises a number of components, several of which utilize the techniques we have considered so far (see Fig. 6.1).

Working from the bottom up, we require knowledge, a reasoning mechanism and heuristics for problem solving (for example, search or constraint satisfaction), an explanation component and a dialogue component. We have considered the first three of these in previous chapters and will come back to them when we consider particular expert systems. Before that, let us look in a little more detail at the last two.

6.4.1 Explanation facility

It is not acceptable for an expert system to make decisions without being able to provide an explanation for the basis of those decisions. Clients using an expert system need to be convinced of the validity of the conclusion drawn before applying it to their domain. They also need to be convinced that the solution is appropriate and applicable in their circumstances. Engineers building the expert system also need to be able to examine the reasoning behind decisions in order to assess and evaluate the mechanisms being used. It is not possible to know if the system is working as intended (even if it produces the expected answer) if an explanation is not provided. So explanation is a vital part of expert system technology.

There are a number of ways of generating an explanation, the most common being to derive it from the goal tree that has been traversed. Here the explanation facility keeps track of the subgoals solved by the system, and reports the rules that were used to reach that point. For example, imagine the following very simple system for diagnosing skin problems in dogs.

Rule 1: IF the dog is scratching its ears
AND the ears are waxy
THEN the ears should be cleaned

Rule 2: IF the dog is scratching its coat
AND if insects can be seen in the coat
AND if the insects are grey
THEN the dog should be treated for lice

Rule 3: IF the dog is scratching its coat
AND if insects can be seen in the coat
AND if the insects are black
THEN the dog should be treated for fleas

Rule 4: IF the dog is scratching its coat
AND there is hair loss
AND there is inflammation
THEN the dog should be treated for eczema

Imagine we have a dog that is scratching and has insects in its coat. A typical consultation would begin with a request for information, in an attempt to match the conditions of the first rule "is the dog scratching its ears?", to which the response would be no. The system would then attempt to match the conditions of rule 2, asking "is the dog scratching its coat?" (yes), "can you see insects in the coat?" (yes), "are the insects grey?". If we respond yes to this question the system will inform us that our dog needs delousing. At this point if we asked for an explanation the following style of response would be given:

It follows from rule 2 that

If the dog is scratching

And if insects can be seen

And if the insects are grey

Then the dog should be treated for lice.

This traces the reasoning used through the consultation so that any errors can be identified and justification can be given to the client if required. However, as you can see, the explanation given is simply a restatement of the rules used, and as such is limited.

In addition to questions such as "how did you reach that conclusion?" the user may require explanatory feedback during a consultation, particularly to clarify what information the system requires. A common request is "why do you want to know that?" when the system asks for a piece of information. In this case the usual response is to provide a trace up to the rule currently being considered and a restatement of that rule. Imagine that in our horror at discovering crawling insects on our dog we hadn't noted the colour – we might ask to know why the system needs this information. The response would be of the form

You said the dog is scratching

and that there are insects.

If the insects are grey

then the dog should be treated for lice.

Notice that it does not present the alternative rule, rule 3, which deals with black insects. This would be useful but assumes look-ahead to other rules in the system to see which other rules may be matched.

This form of explanation facility is far from ideal, both in terms of the way that it provides the explanation and the information to which it has access. In particular it tends to regurgitate the reasoning in terms of rules and goals, which may be appropriate to the knowledge engineer but is less suitable for the user. Ideally, an explanation facility should be able to direct the explanation towards the skill level or understanding of the user. In addition, it should be able to differentiate between the domain knowledge that it uses and control knowledge, such as that used to control the search. Explanations for users are best described in terms of the domain; those for engineers in terms of control mechanisms.

In addition, rule tracing only makes sense for backward reasoning systems, since in forward reasoning it is not known, at a particular point, where the line of reasoning is going.

For these reasons researchers have looked for alternative mechanisms for providing explanations. One approach is to maintain a representation of the problem-solving process used in reaching the solution as well as the domain knowledge. This provides a context for the explanation: the user knows not only which rules have been fired but what hypothesis was being considered.

The XPLAIN system (Swartout 1983) takes this approach further and links the process of explanation with that of designing the expert system. The system

125

defines a domain model (including facts about the domain of interest) and domain principles that are heuristics and operators – meta-rules. This represents the strategy used in the system. An automatic programmer then uses these to generate the system. This approach ensures explanation is considered at the early specification stage, and allows the automatic programmer to use one piece of knowledge in several ways (problem solving, strategy, explanation). Approaches such as this recognize the need for meta-knowledge in providing explanation facilities. In order to do this successfully, expert systems must be designed for explanation.

6.4.2 Dialogue component

The dialogue component is closely linked to the explanation component, as one side of the dialogue involves the user questioning the system at any point in the consultation in the ways we have considered. However, the system must also be able to question the user in order to establish the existence of evidence. The dialogue component has two functions. First, it determines which question to ask next (using meta-rules and the reasoning mechanism to establish what information is required to fire particular rules). Secondly, it ensures that unnecessary questions are not asked, by keeping a record of previous questions. For example, it is not helpful to request the model of a car when the user has already said that he or she doesn't know its make.

The dialogue could be one of three styles:

- system controlled, where the system drives the dialogue through questioning the user

- mixed control, where both user and system can direct the consultation

- user controlled, where the user drives the consultation by providing information to the system.

Most expert systems use the first of these, the rest the second. This is because the system needs to be able to elicit information from the user when it is needed to advance the consultation. If the user controlled the dialogue, the system might not get all the information required. Ideally a mixed dialogue should be provided, allowing the system to request further information and the user to ask for "why?" and "how?" explanations at any point.

6.5 Examples of four expert systems

To illustrate how the components that we have looked at fit together we will consider four early expert systems. Although these systems are not the most up-to-date, they were systems that were ground breaking when they were built, and they have all been successful in their domains. As such they rank among the "classics" of expert systems, and therefore merit a closer look. In each case we will summarize the features of the expert system in terms of the five key components we have identified. This will help you to see how different expert systems can be constructed for different problems. In each case, consider the problem that the expert system was designed to solve, and why the particular components chosen are suited to that task.

6.5.1 Example 1: MYCIN

MYCIN is an expert system for diagnosing and recommending treatment of bacterial infections of the blood (such as meningitis and bacteremia) (Shortliffe 1976). It was developed at Stanford University in California in the 1970s, and has become a template for many similar rule-based systems. It is intended to support clinicians in the early diagnosis and treatment of meningitis, which can be fatal if not treated in time. However, the laboratory tests for these conditions take several days to complete, so doctors (and therefore MYCIN) have to make decisions with incomplete information. A consultation with MYCIN begins with requests for routine information such as age, medical history and so on, progressing to more specific questions as required.

- *knowledge representation.* Production rules (implemented in LISP).

- *reasoning.* Backward chaining, goal-driven reasoning. MYCIN uses certainty factors to reason with uncertain information.

- *heuristics.* When the general category of infection has been established, MYCIN examines each candidate diagnosis in a depth first manner. Heuristics are used to limit the search, including checking all premises of a possible rule to see if any are known to be false.

- *dialogue/explanation.* The dialogue is computer controlled, with MYCIN driving the consultation through asking questions. Explanations are generated through tracing back through the rules that have been fired. Both "how?" and "why?" explanations are supported.

6.5.2 Example 2: PROSPECTOR

PROSPECTOR is an expert system to evaluate geological sites for potential mineral deposits, again developed at Stanford in the late 1970s (Duda et al. 1979). Given a set of observations on the site's attributes (provided by the user), PROSPECTOR provides a list of minerals, along with probabilities of them being present. In 1984 it was instrumental in discovering a molybdenum deposit worth 100 million dollars!

- *knowledge representation.* Rules, semantic network.

- *reasoning.* Predominantly forward chaining (data-driven), with some backward chaining. Bayesian reasoning is used to deal with uncertainty.

- *heuristics.* Depth first search is focused using the probabilities of each hypothesis.

- *dialogue/explanation.* The dialogue uses mixed control. The user volunteers information at the start of the consultation, and PROSPECTOR can request additional information when required. Explanations are generated by tracing back through the rules that have been fired.

6.5.3 Example 3: DENDRAL

DENDRAL is one of the earliest expert systems, developed at Stanford during the late 1960s (Lindsay et al. 1980). It infers the molecular structure of organic compounds from chemical formulae and mass spectrography data. It is not a "stand-alone" expert, more an expert's assistant, since it relies on the input of the human expert to guide its decision making. However, it has been successful enough in this capacity to discover results that have been published as original research.

- *knowledge representation.* Production rules and algorithms for generating graph structures, supplemented by expert user's knowledge.

- *reasoning.* Forward chaining (data-driven).

- *heuristics.* DENDRAL uses a variation on depth first search called generate and test, where all hypotheses are generated and then tested against the available evidence. Heuristic knowledge from the users (chemists) is also used to constrain the search.

- *dialogue/explanation.* The dialogue uses mixed control. The user can supply information and the system can request information as required.

6.5.4   Example 4: XCON

XCON is a commercial expert system developed by Digital Electronics Corporation to configure VAX computer systems to comply with customer orders (Barker & O'Connor 1989). The problem is one of planning and design: there are up to 100 components in any system and XCON must decide how they can best be spatially arranged to meet the specification. The design also has to meet constraints placed by the functionality of the system, and physical constraints.

- *knowledge representation*. Production rules.

- *reasoning*. Forward chaining (data-driven). Since it is possible to specify rules exactly no uncertainty is present.

- *heuristics*. The main configuration task is split into subtasks which are always examined in a predetermined order. Constraint satisfaction is used to inform the search for a solution to a subtask.

- *dialogue/explanation*. The dialogue is less important than in the previous situations since the customer's requirements can be specified at the beginning and the system contains all the information it needs regarding other constraints.

These examples illustrate how the different techniques we have considered in previous chapters can be combined to produce a useful solution, and how different problems require different solutions. We will now look at the practical aspects of building an expert system.

6.6   Building an expert system

We have looked at some of the applications for which expert systems have proved successful, and what components an expert system will have. But how would we go about building one? First, we need to be certain that expert system technology is appropriate to solve the problem that we have in mind. If the problem falls into one of the categories we have already mentioned, such as diagnosis, planning, design or advice giving, then it has passed the first test. The second consideration is whether the problem can be adequately solved using conventional technology. For example, can it be solved statistically or algorithmically? If the answer to this is no, we need to ask whether the problem justifies the expense and effort required to produce an expert system solution. This usually means that the expert system is expected to save costs in the long term, perhaps by making an operation more efficient or making knowledge more widely available. The problem should also be clearly defined and of reasonable size, since expert system technology cannot handle general or common-sense knowledge.

So we have examined our candidate problem and decided that an expert system would be an appropriate solution; what next? Assuming that we have considered our domain of interest carefully and defined the boundaries of the expert system, our first and most crucial stage is *knowledge acquisition*. Knowledge acquisition is the process of getting information out of the head of the expert or from the chosen source and into the form required by the expert system. We can identify two phases of this process: knowledge elicitation, where the knowledge is extracted from the expert, and knowledge representation, where the knowledge is put into the expert system. We considered the latter in Chapter 1. Here we will look briefly at knowledge elicitation.

6.6.1 Knowledge elicitation

The knowledge engineer (the title often given to the person developing the expert system) is probably not an expert in the domain of interest. The engineer's first task is therefore to become familiar with the domain through talking to domain experts and reading relevant background material. Once the engineer has a basic level of understanding of the domain he or she can begin knowledge elicitation. There are a number of techniques used to facilitate this. It is the job of the knowledge engineer to spot gaps in the knowledge that is being offered and fill them.

The problem of knowledge elicitation is not a trivial one. To help you to understand the magnitude of the problem, think of a subject on which you would consider yourself expert. Imagine having to formalize all this information without error or omission. Think about some behaviour in which you are skilled (a good example is driving a car): can you formalize all the actions and knowledge required to perform the necessary actions? Alternatively, imagine questioning someone on a topic on which they are expert and you are not. How do you know when information is missing? This is where concrete examples can be useful since it is easier to spot a conceptual leap in an explanation of a specific example than it is in more general explanations.

Techniques for knowledge elicitation

The interview can capture qualitative information, which is the crux of knowledge elicitation, and therefore provides the key mechanism for acquiring knowledge. There are a number of different types of interview, each of which can be useful for eliciting different types of information. We will consider a number of variants on the interview: the unstructured interview; the structured interview; focused discussion; role reversal and think aloud.

  – *unstructured interviews.* The unstructured interview is open and exploratory: no fixed questions are prepared and the interviewee is allowed to cover topics as he or she sees fit. It can be used to set the scene and gather contextual information at the start of the knowledge elicitation process. Probes, prompts and seed questions can be used to encourage the interviewee to provide relevant information. A probe encourages the expert to provide further information without indicating what that information should be. Examples of such questions are "tell me more about that", "and then?", and "yes?". Prompts are more directed and can help return the interview to a relevant topic that is incomplete. Seed questions are helpful in starting an unstructured interview. A general seed question might be: "Imagine you went into a bookshop and saw the book you wished you'd had when you first started working in the field. What would it have in it?" (Johnson & Johnson 1987).

– *structured interviews*. In structured interviews a framework for the interview is determined in advance. They can involve the use of check-lists or questionnaires to ensure focus is maintained. Strictly structured interviews allow the elicitor to compare answers between experts whereas less strict, perhaps more accurately termed semi-structured interviews combine a focus on detail with some freedom to explore areas of interest.

Appropriate questions can be difficult to devise without some understanding of the domain. Unstructured interviews are often used initially, followed by structured interviews and more focused techniques.

– *focused discussions*. A focused discussion is centred around a particular problem or scenario. This may be a case study, a critical incident or a specific solution. Case analysis considers a case study that might occur in the domain or one that has occurred. The expert explains how it would be or was solved, either verbally or by demonstration. Critical incident analysis is a variant of this that looks at unusual and probably serious incidents, such as error situations.

In critiquing, the expert is asked to comment on someone else's solution to a problem or design. The expert is asked to review the design or problem solution and identify omissions or errors. This can be helpful as a way of cross-referencing the information provided by different experts, and also provides validation checks, since each solution or piece of information is reviewed by another expert.

– *role reversal*. Role reversal techniques place the elicitor in the expert's role and vice versa. There are two main types: teach-back interviews and Twenty Questions. In teach-back interviews the elicitor "teaches" the expert on a subject that has already been discussed. This checks the elicitor's understanding and allows the expert to amend the knowledge if necessary. In Twenty Questions, the elicitor chooses a topic from a predetermined set and the expert asks questions about the topic in order to determine which one has been selected. The elicitor can answer yes or no. The questions asked reflect the expert's knowledge of the topic and therefore provide information about the domain.

- *think-aloud.* Think-aloud is used to elicit information about specific tasks. The expert is asked to think aloud while carrying out the task. Similarly, the post-task walk-through involves debriefing the expert after the task has been completed. Both techniques are better than simple observation, as they provide information on expert strategy as well as behaviour.

Tool support for knowledge elicitation

There are a number of tools to support knowledge acquisition, and some expert system shells provide this support. For example, the expert system shell MacS-MARTS includes an example-based component that allows the domain expert to input information in terms of primary factors, questions and advice (instead of rules), and the system generates a knowledge base from these. This knowledge base can then be validated by the expert. Another system, Teiresias (Davis 1982) (after the Greek sage), was designed alongside EMYCIN (van Melle et al. 1981) (an expert system shell based on MYCIN) to help the expert enter knowledge. The expert critiques the performance of the system on a small set of rules and some problems. This focuses the knowledge elicitation process on the specific problems.

6.6.2 Representing the knowledge

When the knowledge engineer has become familiar with the domain and elicited some knowledge, it is necessary to decide on an appropriate representation for the knowledge, choosing, for example, to use a frame-based or network-based scheme. The engineer also needs to decide on appropriate reasoning and search strategies. At this point the engineer is able to begin prototyping the expert system, normally using an expert system shell or a high-level AI language.

Expert system shells

An expert system shell abstracts features of one or more expert systems. For example, EMYCIN is an expert system shell derived from the MYCIN system. The shell comprises the inference and explanation facilities of an existing expert system without the domain-specific knowledge. This allows non-programmers to add their own knowledge on a problem of similar structure but to re-use the reasoning mechanisms. A different shell is required for each type of problem, for example to support data-driven or goal-driven reasoning, but one shell can be used for many different domains.

Expert system shells are very useful if the match between the problem and the shell is good, but they are inflexible. They work best in diagnostic and advice-style problems rather than design or constraint satisfaction, and are readily available for most computer platforms. This makes building an expert system using a shell relatively cheap.

High-level programming languages

High-level programming languages, designed for AI, provide a fast, flexible mechanism for developing expert systems. They conceal their implementation details, allowing the developer to concentrate on the application. They also provide inbuilt mechanisms for representation and control. Different languages support different paradigms, for example PROLOG supports logic, LISP is a functional programming language, OPS5 is a production system language.

The language we are using for the examples in this book is PROLOG. It provides a database that can represent rules, procedures and facts and can implement pattern matching, control (via depth first searching and backward chaining) and structured representations. It can be used to build simple expert systems, or to build a more complex expert system shell.

However, high-level languages do demand certain programming skills in the user, particularly to develop more complex systems, so they are less suitable for the "do-it-yourself" expert system developer. Some environments have been developed that support more than one AI programming language, such as POPLOG which incorporates LISP and PROLOG. These provide even more flexibility and some programming support, but still require programming skills.

Selecting a tool

There are a number of things to bear in mind when choosing a tool to build an expert system. First, select a tool which has only the features you need. This will reduce the cost and increase the speed (both in terms of performance and development). Secondly, let the problem dictate the tool to use, where possible, not the available software. This is particularly important with expert system shells, where choosing a shell with the wrong reasoning strategy for the problem will create more difficulties than it solves. Think about the problem in the abstract first and plan your design. Consider your problem against the following abstract problem types:

- problems with a small solution space and reliable data

- problems with unreliable or uncertain data

- problems where the solution space is large but where you can reduce it, say using heuristics

- problems where the solution space is large but not reducible.

Each of these would need a different approach. Look also at example systems (such as the four we have touched on). Try to find one that is solving a similar problem to yours and look at its structure. Only when you have decided on the structure and techniques that are best for your problem should you look for an appropriate tool. Finally, choose a tool with built-in explanation facilities and debugging if possible. These are easier to use and test and will save time in implementation.

6.7 Limitations of expert systems

We have looked at expert systems, what they are used for and how to build one. But what are the current limitations of expert system technology that might affect our exploitation of them? We have already come across a number of limitations in our discussion, but we will reconsider them here.

First, there is the problem of knowledge acquisition: it is not an easy task to develop complete, consistent and correct knowledge bases. Experts are generally poor at expressing their knowledge, and non-expert (in the domain) knowledge engineers may not know what they are looking for. Some tool support is available, and using a structured approach can alleviate the problem, but it remains a bottleneck in expert system design.

A second problem is the verification of the knowledge stored. The knowledge may be internally consistent but inaccurate, due to either expert error or misunderstanding at the acquisition stage. Validation of data is usually done informally, on the basis of performance of the system, but this makes it more difficult to isolate the cause of an observed error. Knowledge elicitation techniques such as critiquing, where the domain expert assesses the knowledge base in stages as it is developed, help to alleviate this problem, although the verification is still subjective.

Thirdly, expert systems are highly domain dependent and are therefore brittle. They cannot fall back on general or common-sense knowledge or generalize their knowledge to unexpected cases. A new expert system is therefore required for each problem (although the shells can be re-used) and the solution is limited in scope.

An additional problem with brittleness is that the user may not know the limitations of the system. For example, in a PROLOG-based system a goal may be proved false if the system has knowledge that it is false or if the system does not have knowledge that it is true. So the user may not know whether the goal is in fact false or whether the knowledge base is incomplete.

Finally, expert systems lack meta-knowledge, that is knowledge about their own operations, so they cannot reason about their limitations or the effect of these on the decisions that are made. They cannot decide to use a different reasoning or search strategy if it is more appropriate or provide more informative explanations.

6.8   Hybrid expert systems

One possible solution to some of the limitations of expert systems is to combine the knowledge-based technology of expert systems with technologies that learn from examples, such as neural networks and inductive learning. These classify instances of an object or event according to their closeness to previously trained examples, and therefore do not require explicit knowledge representation (see Ch. 11 and Ch. 4 for more details). However, they tend to be "black-box" techniques, which are poor at providing explanations for their decisions.

It has been suggested that these techniques may help in a number of areas. We have also mentioned MacSMARTS, which uses inductive learning to alleviate the knowledge elicitation problem. Other suggestions are to use the techniques to deal with uncertainty since they are more tolerant of error and incompleteness than knowledge-based systems. This would result in a "hybrid" expert system using both methods in parallel. Another area in which they could be helpful is pruning search spaces, since they could be trained to recognize successful search paths.

However, this is still very much a research area and there is some suspicion on either side as to the value of the other approach.

6.9   Summary

In this chapter we looked at the main applications of expert systems and the components that we would expect to see in an expert system. We then examined the structure of four classic expert systems in order to illustrate how different types of problem can be solved. We considered the stages in building an expert system, concentrating on knowledge acquisition and choosing appropriate tools. Finally, we considered some of the limitations of current expert system technology and some possible solutions for the future.

6.10   Exercises

1. You are asked to advise on the use of expert systems for the following tasks. Outline appropriate reasoning methods and other key expert system features for each application.

   - a system to advise on financial investment (to reduce enquiries to a bank's human advisor)
   - a medical diagnosis system to help doctors

– a kitchen design system to be used by salesmen.

2. Working in small groups and using the information below (extending it where necessary)

– formalize the knowledge as a set of rules (of the form IF evidence THEN hypothesis)

– calculate certainty factors (see Ch. 2) for each hypothesis given the evidence (estimate measures of belief and disbelief from the statements made)

– use an expert system shell to implement this knowledge.

There are a number of reasons why a car might overheat. If the radiator is empty it will certaily overheat. If it is half full this may cause overheating but is quite likely not to. If the fan belt is broken or missing the car will again certainly overheat. If it is too tight it may cause this problem but not always. Another possible cause is a broken or jammed thermostat, or too much or too little oil. If the engine is not tuned properly it may also overheat but this is less likely. Finally, the water pump may be broken. If none of these things is the cause, the temperature gauge might be faulty (the car is not overheating at all). Also the weather and the age of the car should be considered (older cars are more likely to overheat). A combination of any of the above factors would increase the likelihood of overheating.

6.11   Recommended further reading

Jackson, P. 1990. *An introduction to expert systems*, 2nd edn. Wokingham: Addison Wesley.
Detailed coverage of many of the topics introduced here as well as other aspects of expert systems. An excellent next step for anyone wanting to know more about the subject.

Medsker, L. & J. Liebowitz 1994. *Design and development of expert systems and neural networks*. New York: Macmillan.
A book that attempts to provide a balanced view of the role of traditional and connectionist techniques in the practical development of expert systems.

Goonatilake, S. & S. Khebbal (eds) 1995. *Intelligent hybrid systems*. Chichester: John Wiley.
A collection of papers detailing some of the research in using hybrid techniques in expert systems and knowledge acquisition.

Kidd, A. (ed.) 1989. *Knowledge acquisition for expert systems: a practical handbook*. New York: Plenum Press.
A collection of papers discussing a range of knowlege elicitation techniques. A worthwhile read for anyone wanting to gather information to build an expert system.

Chapter Seven

Natural language understanding

7.1 Overview

Natural language understanding is one of the most popular applications of artificial intelligence portrayed in fiction and the media. The idea of being able to control computers by talking to them in our own language is very attractive. But natural language is ambiguous, which makes natural language understanding particularly difficult. In this chapter we examine the stages of natural language understanding – syntactic analysis, semantic analysis and pragmatic analysis – and some of the techniques that are used to make sense of this ambiguity.

7.2 What is natural language understanding?

Whenever computers are represented in science fiction, futuristic literature or film, they invariably have the ability to communicate with their human users in natural language. By "natural language", we mean a language for human communication such as English, French, Swahili, or Urdu, as opposed to a formal "created" language (for example, a programming language or Morse code). Unlike computers in films, which understand spoken language, we will concern ourselves primarily with understanding written language, rather than speech, and on analysis rather than language generation. As we shall see, this will present enough challenges for one chapter! Understanding speech shares the same difficulties, but has additional problems with deciphering the sound signal and identifying word parts.

7.3 Why do we need natural language understanding?

Before we consider how natural language understanding can be achieved, we should be clear about the benefits that it can bring. There are a number of areas that can be helped by the use of natural language. The first is human–computer interaction, by the provision of natural language interfaces for the user. This would allow the user to communicate with computer applications in their own language, rather than in a command language or using menus. There are advantages and disadvantages to this: it is a natural form of communication that requires no specialized training, but it is inefficient for expert users and less precise than a command language. It may certainly be helpful in applications that are used by casual users (for example, tourist information) or for novice users.

A second area is information management, where natural language processing could enable automatic management and processing of information, by interpreting its content. If the system could understand the meaning of a document it could, for example, store it with other similar documents.

A third possibility is to provide an intuitive means of database access. At present most databases can be accessed through a query language. Some of these are very complex, demanding considerable expertise to generate even relatively common queries. Others are based on forms and menus, providing a simpler access mechanism. However, these still require the user to have some understanding of the structure of the database. The user, on the other hand, is usually more familiar with the content of the database, or at least its domain. By allowing the user to ask for information using natural language, queries can be framed in terms of the content and domain rather than the structure. We will look at a simple example of database query using natural language later in the chapter.

7.4 Why is natural language understanding difficult?

The primary problem with natural language processing is the ambiguity of language. There are a number of levels at which ambiguity may occur in natural language (of course a single sentence may include several of these levels). First, a sentence or phrase may be ambiguous at a *syntactic* level. Syntax relates to the structure of the language, the way the words are put together. Some word sequences make valid sentences in a given language, some do not. However, some sentence structures have more than one correct interpretation. These are syntactically ambiguous. Secondly, a sentence may be ambiguous at a *lexical* level. The lexical level is the word level, and ambiguity here occurs when a word can have more than one meaning. Thirdly, a sentence may be ambiguous at a *referential* level. This is concerned with what the sentence (or a part of the sentence) refers to. Ambiguity occurs when it is not clear what the sentence is referring to or where it may legally refer to more than one thing. Fourthly, a sentence can be ambiguous at a *semantic level*, that is, at the point of the meaning of the sentence. Sometimes a sentence is ambiguous at this level: it has two different meanings. Indeed this characteristic is exploited in humour, with the use of double entendre and inuendo. Finally, a sentence may be ambiguous at a *pragmatic* level, that is at the level of interpretation within its context. The same word or phrase may have different interpretations depending on the context in which it occurs. To make things even more complicated some sentences involve ambiguity at more than one of these levels. Consider the following sentences; how many of them are ambiguous and how?

1. I hit the man with the hammer.

2. I went to the bank.

3. He saw her duck.

4. Fred hit Joe because he liked Harry.

5. I went to the doctor yesterday.

6. I waited for a long time at the bank.

7. There is a drought because it hasn't rained for a long time.

8. Dinosaurs have been extinct for a long time.

How did you do? In fact all the sentences above have some form of ambiguity. Let's look at them more closely.

- *I hit the man with the hammer.* Was the hammer the weapon used or was it in the hand of the victim? This sentence contains syntactic ambiguity: there are two perfectly legitimate ways of interpreting the sentence structure.

- *I went to the bank.* Did I visit a financial institution or go to the river bank? This sentence is ambiguous at a lexical level: the word "bank" has two meanings, either of which fits in this sentence.

- *He saw her duck.* Did he see her dip down to avoid something or the web-footed bird owned by her? This one is ambiguous at a lexical and a semantic level. The word "duck" has two meanings and the sentence can be interpreted in two completely different ways.

- *Fred hit Joe because he liked Harry.* Who is it that likes Harry? This is an example of referential ambiguity. Who does the pronoun "he" refer to, Fred or Joe? It is not clear from this sentence structure.

- *I went to the doctor yesterday.* When exactly was yesterday? This demonstrates pragmatic ambiguity. In some situations this may be clear but not in all. Does yesterday refer literally to the day preceding today or does it

139

refer to another yesterday (imagine I am reading this sentence a week after it was written, for example). The meaning depends on the context.

- *I waited for a long time at the bank.*

- *There is a drought because it hasn't rained for a long time.*

- *Dinosaurs have been extinct for a long time.* The last three sentences can be considered together. What does the phrase *for a long time* mean? In each sentence it clearly refers to a different amount of time. This again is pragmatic ambiguity. We can only interpret the phrase through our understanding of the sentence context.

In addition to these major sources of ambiguity, language is problematic because it is imprecise, incomplete, inaccurate, and continually changing. Think about the conversations you have with your friends. The words you use may not always be quite right to express the meaning you intend, you may not always finish a sentence, you may use analogies and comparisons to express ideas. As humans we are adept at coping with these things, to the extent that we can usually understand each other if we speak the same language, even if words are missed out or misused. We usually have enough knowledge in common to disambiguate the words and interpret them correctly in context. We can also cope quickly with new words. This is borne out by the speed with which slang and street words can be incorporated into everyday usage. All of this presents an extremely difficult problem for the computer.

7.5   An early attempt at natural language understanding: SHRDLU

We met SHRDLU briefly in the Introduction. If you recall, SHRDLU is the natural language processing system developed by Winograd at MIT in the early 1970s (Winograd 1972). It is used for controlling a robot in a restricted "blocks" domain. The robot's world consists of a number of blocks of various shapes, sizes and colours, which it can manipulate as instructed or answer questions about. All instructions and questions are given in natural language and even though the robot's domain is so limited, it still encounters the problems we have mentioned. Consider for example the following instructions:

Find a block that is taller than the one you are holding and place it in the box

How many blocks are on top of the green block?

Put the red pyramid on the block in the box

Does the shortest thing the tallest pyramid's support supports support anything green?

What problems did you spot? Again each instruction contains ambiguity of some kind. We'll leave it to you to figure them out! (The answers are given at the end of the chapter in case you get stuck.)

However, SHRDLU was successful because it could be given complete knowledge about its world and ambiguity could be reduced (it only recognizes one meaning of "block" for instance and there is no need for contextual understanding since the context is given). It is therefore no use as a general natural language processor. However, it did provide insight into how syntactic and semantic processing can be achieved. We will look at techniques for this and the other stages of natural language understanding next.

7.6 How does natural language understanding work?

So given that, unlike SHRDLU, we are not able to provide complete world knowledge to our natural language processor, how can we go about interpreting language? There are three primary stages in natural language processing: syntactic analysis, semantic analysis and pragmatic analysis. Sentences can be well formed or ill formed syntactically, semantically and pragmatically. Take the following responses to the question: *Do you know where the park is?*

- *The park is across the road.* This is syntactically, semantically, and pragmatically well formed, that is, it is a correctly structured, meaningful sentence which is an appropriate response to the question.

- *The park is across the elephant.* This is syntactically well formed but semantically ill formed. The sentence is correctly structured but our knowledge of parks and elephants and their characteristics shows it is meaningless.

- *The park across the road is.* This is syntactically ill formed. It is not a legal sentence structure.

- *Yes.* This is pragmatically ill formed: it misses the intention of the questioner.

At each stage in processing, the system will determine whether a sentence is well formed. These three stages are not necessarily always separate or sequential. However, it is convenient to consider them as such.

Syntactic analysis determines whether the sentence is a legal sentence of the language, or generates legal sentences, using a grammar and lexicon, and, if so, returns a *parse tree* for the sentence (representing its structure). This is the process of *parsing*. Take a simple sentence, "The dog sat on the rug." It has a number of constituent parts: nouns ("dog" and "rug"), a verb ("sat"), determiners ("the") and a preposition ("on"). We can also see that it has a definite structure: noun followed by verb followed by preposition followed by noun (with a determiner associated with each noun). We could formalize this observation:

sentence = determiner noun verb preposition determiner noun

Such a definition could then be tested on other sentences. What about "The man ran over the hill."? This too fits our definition of a sentence. Looking at these two sentences, we can see certain patterns emerging. For instance, the determiner "the" always seems to be attached to a noun. We could therefore simplify our definition of a sentence by defining a sentence component called noun_phrase

noun_phrase = determiner noun

Our sentence definition would then become

sentence = noun_phrase verb preposition noun_phrase

This is the principle of syntactic grammars. The grammar is built up by examining legal sentence structures and a lexicon is produced identifying the constituent type of each word. In our case our lexicon would include

dog : noun

the : determiner

rug : noun

sat : verb

and so on. If a legal sentence is not parsed by the grammar then the grammar must be extended to include that sentence definition as well. Although our grammar looks much like a standard English grammar, it is not. Rather, we create a grammar that exactly specifies legal constructions of our language. In practice such grammars do bear some resemblance to conventional grammar, in that the symbols that are chosen to represent sentence constituents often reflect conventional word types, but do not confuse this with any grammar you learned at school!

Semantic analysis takes the parse tree for the sentence and interprets it according to the possible meanings of its constituent parts. A representation of semantics may include information about different meanings of words and their characteristics. For example, take the sentence "The necklace has a diamond on it." Our syntactic analysis of this would require another definition of sentence than the one we gave above:

sentence = noun_phrase verb noun_phrase prepositional_phrase

prepositional_phrase = preposition pronoun

This gives us the structure of the sentence, but the meaning is still unclear. This is because the word diamond has a number of meanings. It can refer to a precious stone, a geometric shape, even a baseball field. The semantic analysis would consider each meaning and match the most appropriate one according to its characteristics. A necklace is jewellery and the first meaning is the one most closely associated with jewellery, so it is the most likely interpretation.

Finally, in pragmatic analysis, the sentence is interpreted in terms of its context and intention.

For example, a sentence may have meanings provided by its context or social expectations that are over and above the semantic meaning. In order to understand the intention of sentences it is important to consider these. To illustrate, consider the sentence "He gave her a diamond ring." Semantically this means that a male person passed possession of a piece of hand jewellery made with precious stones over to a female person. However, there are additional likely implications of this sentence. Diamond rings are often (though of course not exclusively) given to indicate engagement, for example, so the sentence could mean the couple got engaged. Such additional, hidden meanings are the domain of pragmatic analysis.

7.7 Syntactic analysis

Syntactic analysis is concerned with the structure of the sentence. Its role is to verify whether a given sentence is a valid construction within the language, and to provide a representation of its structure, or to generate legal sentences. There are a number of ways in which this can be done.

Perhaps the simplest option is to use some form of pattern matching. Templates of possible sentence patterns are stored, with variables to allow matching to specific sentences. For example, the template

< the ** rides ** >

(where ** matches anything) fits lots of different sentences, such as *the show-jumper rides a clear round* or *the girl rides her mountain bike*. These sentences have similar syntax (both are basically noun_phrase verb noun_phrase), so does this mean that template matching works? Not really. What about the sentence *the theme park rides are terrifying*? This also matches the template but is clearly a very different sentence structure to the first two. For a start, in the first two sentences "rides" is a verb, whereas here it is a noun. This highlights the fundamental flaw in template matching. It has no representation of word types, which essentially means it cannot ensure that words are correctly sequenced and put together.

Template matching is the method used in ELIZA (Weizenbaum 1966), which, as we saw in the Introduction, fails to cope with ambiguity and so can accept (and generate) garbage. These are problems inherent in the approach: it is too simplistic to deal with a language of any complexity. However, it is a simple approach that may be useful in very constrained environments (whether such a restricted use of language could be called "natural" is another issue).

A more viable approach to syntactic analysis is sentence parsing. Here the input sentence is converted into a hierarchical structure indicating the sentence constituents. Parsing systems have two main components:

1. *a grammar*: a declarative representation of the syntactic facts about the language

2. *a parser*: a procedure to compare the input sentence with the grammar.

Parsing may be *top down*, in which case it starts with the symbol for a sentence and tries to map possible rules to the input (or target) sentence, or *bottom up*, where it starts with the input sentence and works towards the sentence symbol, considering all the possible representations of the input sentence. The choice of which type of parsing to use is similar to that for top-down or bottom-up reasoning; it depends on factors such as the amount of branching each will require and the availability of heuristics for evaluating progress. In practice, a combination is sometimes used. There are a number of parsing methods. These include grammars, transition networks, context-sensitive grammars and augmented transition networks. As we shall see, each has its benefits and drawbacks.

7.7.1 Grammars

We have already met grammars informally. A grammar is a specification of the legal structures of a language. It is essentially a set of rewrite rules that allow any element matching the left-hand side of the rule to be replaced by the right-hand side. So for example,

$$A \rightarrow B$$

allows the string XAX to be rewritten XBX. Unlike template matching, it explicitly shows how words of different types can be combined, and defines the type of any given word. In this section we will examine grammars more closely, and demonstrate how they work through an example.

A grammar has three basic components: *terminal symbols, non-terminal symbols* and *rules*. Terminal symbols are the actual words that make up the language (this part of the grammar is called the *lexicon*). So "cat", "dog", "chase" are all terminal symbols. Non-terminal symbols are special symbols designating structures of the language. There are three types:

- *lexical categories*, which are the grammatical categories of words, such as noun or verb

- *syntactic categories*, which are the permissible combinations of lexical categories, for instance "noun_phrase", "verb_phrase"

- a special symbol representing a sentence (the *start_symbol*).

The third component of the grammar is the rules, which govern the valid combinations of the words in the language. Rules are sometimes called *phrase structure rules*. A rule is usually of the form

S → NP VP

where S represents the sentence, NP a noun_phrase and VP a verb_phrase. This rule states that a noun_phrase followed by a verb_phrase is a valid sentence.

The grammar can generate all syntactically valid sentences in the language and can be implemented in a number of ways, for example as a production system implemented in PROLOG. We will look at how a grammar is generated and how it parses sentences by considering a detailed example.

7.7.2 An example: generating a grammar fragment

Imagine we want to produce a grammar for database queries on an employee database. We have examples of possible queries. We can generate a grammar fragment by analyzing each query sentence. If the sentence can be parsed by the grammar we have, we do nothing. If it can't, we can add rules and words to the grammar to deal with the new sentence. For example, take the queries

Who belongs to a union?

Does Sam Smith work in the IT Department?

In the case of the first sentence, *Who belongs to a union?*, we would start with the sentence symbol (S) and generate a rule to match the sentence in the example. To do this we need to identify the sentence constituents (the non-terminal symbols). Remember that the choice of these does not depend on any grammar of English we may have learned at school. We can choose any symbols, as long as they are used consistently. We designate the symbol RelP to indicate a relative pronoun, such as "who", "what" (a lexical category), and the symbol VP to designate a verb_phrase (a syntactic category). We then require rules to show how our lexical categories can be constructed. In this case VP has the structure V (verb) PP (prepositional phrase), which can be further decomposed as P, a preposition, followed by NP, a noun_phrase. Finally the NP category is defined as Det (determiner) followed by N (noun). The terminal symbols are associated with a lexical category to show how they can fit together in a sentence. We end up with the grammar fragment in Figure 7.1.

This will successfully parse our sentence, as shown in the parse tree in Figure 7.2, which represents the hierarchical breakdown of the sentence. The root of the tree is the sentence symbol. Each branch of the tree represents a non-terminal symbol, either a syntactic category or a lexical category. The leaves of the tree are the terminal symbols.

However, our grammar is still very limited. To extend the grammar, we need to analyze many sentences in this way, until we end up with a very large grammar

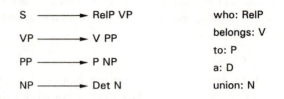

Figure 7.1 Initial grammar fragment.

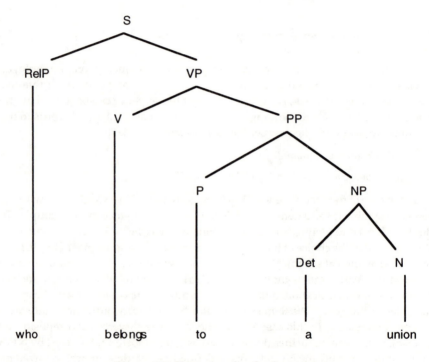

Figure 7.2 Parse tree for the first sentence.

S ⟶ Aux V NP NP

NP ⟶ PN

NP ⟶ Det PN

does: AuxV
Sam Smith: PN
work: V
in: P
the: Det
IT Department: PN

Figure 7.3 Further grammar rules.

and lexicon. As we analyze more sentences, the grammar becomes more complete and, we hope, less work is involved in adding to it.

We will analyze just one more sentence. Our second query was *Does Sam Smith work in the IT Department?* First, we check whether our grammar can parse this sentence successfully. If you recall, our only definition of a sentence so far is

S → RelP VP

Taking the VP part first, *work in the IT Department* does meet our definition of a word phrase, if we interpret *IT Department* loosely as a noun. However, *Does Sam Smith* is certainly not a RelP. We therefore need another definition of a sentence. In this case a sentence is an auxiliary verb (AuxV) followed by an NP followed by a VP. Since Sam Smith is a proper noun we also need an additional definition of NP, and for good measure we will call *IT Department* a proper noun as well, giving us a third definition of NP. The additional grammar rules are shown in Figure 7.3.

Note that we do not need to add a rule to define VP since our previous rule fits the structure of this sentence as well. A parse tree for this sentence using this grammar is shown in Figure 7.4.

Grammars such as this are powerful tools for natural language understanding. They can also be used to generate legal sentences, constructing them from the sentence symbol down, using appropriate terminal symbols from the lexicon. Of course, sentence generation is not solely a matter of syntax; it is important that the sentence also makes sense. Therefore semantic analysis is also important. We shall consider this shortly. First we will look briefly at another method of parsing, the *transition network*.

7.7.3 Transition networks

The *transition network* is a method of parsing that represents the grammar as a set of finite state machines. A finite state machine is a model of computational behaviour where each node represents an internal state of the system and the arcs are the means of moving between the states. In the case of parsing natural

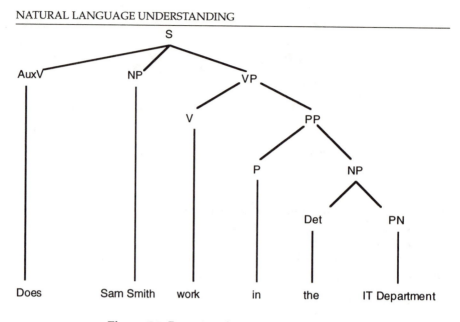

Figure 7.4 Parse tree for the second sentence.

language, the arcs in the networks represent either a terminal or a non-terminal symbol. Rules in the grammar correspond to a path through a network. Each non-terminal is represented by a different network. To illustrate this we will represent the grammar fragment that we created earlier using transition networks. All rules are represented but to save space only some lexical categories are included. Others would be represented in the same way.

In Figure 7.5 each network represents the rules for one non-terminal as paths from the initial state (I) to the final state (F). So, whereas we had three rules for NP in our grammar, here we have a single transition network, with three possible paths through it representing the three rules. To move from one state to the next through the network the parser tests the label on the arc. If it is a terminal symbol, the parser will check whether it matches the next word in the input sentence. If it is a non-terminal symbol, the parser moves to the network for that symbol and attempts to find a path through that. If it finds a path through that network it returns to the higher-level network and continues. If the parser fails to find a path at any point it backtracks and attempts another path. If it succeeds in finding a path, the sentence is a valid one. So to parse our sentence *Who belongs to a union?* the parser would start at the sentence network and find that the first part of a sentence is RelP. It would therefore go to the RelP network and test the first word in the input sentence "who" against the terminal symbol on the arc. These match, so that network has been traversed successfully and the parser returns to the sentence network able to cross the arc RelP. Parsing of the sentence continues in this fashion until the top-level sentence network is successfully traversed. The full navigation of the network for this sentence is shown in Figure 7.6.

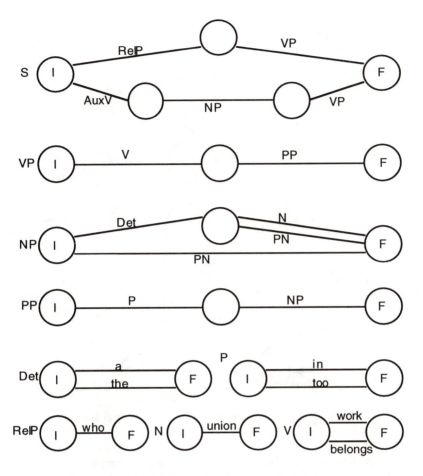

Figure 7.5 Transition network.

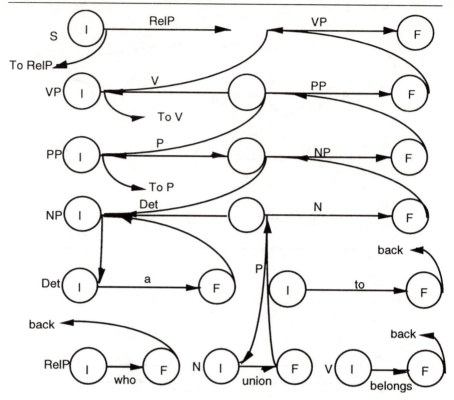

Figure 7.6 Navigation through transition network.

The transition network allows each non-terminal to be represented in a single network rather than by numerous rules, making this approach more concise than grammars. However, as you can see from the network for just two sentences, the approach is not really tenable for large languages since the networks would become unworkable. Another disadvantage over grammars is that the transition network does not produce a parse tree for sentences and tracing the path through the network can be unclear for complex sentences. However, the transition network is an example of a simple parsing algorithm that forms the basis of more powerful tools, such as augmented transition networks, which we will consider in Section 7.7.6.

7.7.4 Context-sensitive grammars

The grammars considered so far are context-free grammars. They allow a single non-terminal on the left-hand side of the rule. The rule may be applied to any instance of that symbol, regardless of context. So the rule

   A → B

will match an occurrence of A whether it occurs in the string ABC or in ZAB. The context-free grammar cannot restrict this to only instances where A occurs surrounded by Z and B. In order to interpret the symbol in context, a context-sensitive grammar is required. This allows more than one symbol on the left-hand side, and insists that the right-hand side is at least as long as the left-hand side. So in a context-sensitive grammar, we can have rules of the form

   ZAB → ZBB

Context-free grammars are not sufficient to represent natural language syntax. For example, they cannot distinguish between plural and singular nouns or verbs. So in a context-free grammar, if we have a set of simple definitions

   S → NP VP

   NP → Det N

   VP → V

and the following lexicon

   dog : N

   guide : V

   the : Det

   dogs : N

   guides : V

   a : Det

we would be able to generate the sentences *the dog guides* and *the dogs guide*, both legal English sentences. However, we would also be able to generate sentences such as *a dogs guides*, which is clearly not an acceptable sentence.

By incorporating the context of agreement into the left-hand side of the rule we can provide a grammar which can resolve this kind of problem.

An example is shown in Figure 7.7.

The use of the symbols "Sing" and "Plur", to indicate agreement, does not allow generation of sentences that violate consistency rules. For example, using the grammar in Figure 7.7 we can derive the sentence "a dog guides" but not "a dogs guides". The derivation of the former is shown using the following substitutions:

   S

   NP VP

   Det AGR N VP

S	⟶ NP VP
NP	⟶ Det AGR N
AGR	⟶ Sing
AGR	⟶ Plur
Sing VP	⟶ Sing V
Plur VP	⟶ Plur V
dog Sing:	Sing N
dogs Plur:	Plur N
a Sing:	Det Sing
the Sing:	Det Sing
the Plur:	Det Plur
guides:	Sing V
guide:	Plur V

Figure 7.7 Grammar fragment for context-sensitive grammar.

Det Sing N VP

a Sing N VP

a dog Sing VP

a dog Sing V

a dog guides

Unfortunately context sensitivity increases the size of the grammar considerably, making it a complex method for a language of any size. Feature sets and augmented transition networks are alternative approaches to solving the context problem.

7.7.5 Feature sets

Another approach to incorporating context in syntactic processing is the use of feature sets. Feature sets provide a mechanism for subclassifying syntactic categories (noun, verb, etc.) in terms of contextual properties such as number agreement and verb tense. The descriptions of the syntactic categories are framed in terms of constraints. There are many variations of feature sets, but here we shall use one approach to illustrate the general principle – that of Pereira and

Warren's Direct Clause Grammar (Pereira & Warren 1980). In this grammar each syntactic category has an associated feature set, together with constraints that indicate what context is allowable. So, for example,

$$S \rightarrow NP \ (agreement =?a) \ VP \ (agreement =?b): a = b$$

Feature sets are a relatively efficient mechanism for representing syntactic context. However, we have still not progressed to understanding any semantics of the sentence. Augmented transition networks provide an approach that begins to bridge the gap between syntactic and semantic processing.

7.7.6 Augmented transition networks

The *augmented transition network* provides context without an unacceptable increase in complexity (Woods 1970). It is a transition network that allows procedures to be attached to arcs to test for matching context. All terminals and non-terminals have frame-like structures associated with them that contain their contextual information. To traverse an arc, the parser tests whatever contextual features are required against these stored attributes. For example, a test on the V arc may be to check number (i.e. plural or singular). The structure for the word *guides* would contain, among other things, an indication that the word is singular. The sentence is only parsed successfully if all the contextual checks are consistent. Augmented transition networks can be used to provide semantic information as well as syntactic, since information about meaning can also be stored in the structures. They are therefore a bridge between syntactic analysis and the next stage in the process, semantic analysis.

7.8 Semantic analysis

Syntactic analysis shows us that a sentence is correctly constructed according to the rules of the language. However, it does not check whether the sentence is meaningful, or give information about its meaning. For this we need to perform semantic analysis. Semantic analysis enables us to determine the meaning of the sentence, which may vary depending on context. So, for example, a system for understanding children's stories and a natural language interface may assign different meanings to the same words. Take the word "run", for example. In a children's story this is likely to refer to quick movement, while in a natural language interface it is more likely to be an instruction to execute a program. There are two levels at which semantic analysis can operate: the lexical level and the sentence level.

Lexical processing involves looking up the meaning of the word in the lexicon.

However, many words have several meanings within the same lexical category (for example, the noun "square" may refer to a geometrical shape or an area of a town). In addition, the same word may have further meanings under different lexical categories: "square" can also be an adjective meaning "not trendy", or a verb meaning "reconcile". The latter cases can be disambiguated syntactically but the former rely on reference to known properties of the different meanings. Ultimately, words are understood in the context of the sentences in which they occur. Therefore lexical processing alone is inadequate. Sentence-level processing on the other hand does take context into account. There are a number of approaches to sentence-level processing. We will look briefly at two: semantic grammars and case grammars.

7.8.1   Semantic grammars

As we have seen, syntactic grammars enable us to parse sentences according to their structure and, in the case of context-sensitive grammars, such attributes as number and tense. However, syntactic grammars provide no representation of the meaning of the sentence, so it is still possible to parse nonsense if it is written in correctly constructed sentences. In a semantic grammar (Burton 1976), the symbols and rules have semantic as well as syntactic significance. Semantic actions can also be associated with a rule, so that a grammar can be used to translate a natural language sentence into a command or query. Let us take another look at our database query system.

An example: a database query interpreter revisited

Recall the problem we are trying to address. We want to produce a natural language database query system for an employee database that understands questions such as *Who belongs to a union?* and *Does Sam Smith work in the IT Department?* We have already seen how to generate a syntactic grammar to deal with these sentences but we really need to derive a grammar that takes into account not only the syntax of the sentences but their meaning. In the context of a query interpreter, meaning is related to the form of the query that we will make to the database in response to the question. So what we would like is a grammar that will not only parse our sentence, but interpret its meaning and convert it into a database query. This is exactly what we can do with a semantic grammar.

In the following grammar, a query is built up as part of the semantic analysis of the sentence: when a rule is matched, the query template associated with it (shown in square brackets) is instantiated. The grammar is generated as follows. First, sentence structures are identified. Our sentences represent two types of question: the first is looking for information (names of union members), the second for a yes/no answer. So we define two legal sentence structures, the first seeking information and preceded by the word "who", the second seeking a yes/no response, preceded by the word "does". The action associated with these rules is to set up a query which will be whatever is the result of parsing the INFO or YN structures. Having done this we need to determine the structure of the main query parts. We will concentrate on the INFO category to simplify matters but the YN category is generated in the same way. Words are categorized in terms of their meaning to the query (rather than, for example, their syntactic category). Therefore, the words "belong to" and "work in" are semantically equivalent, because they require the same query (but with different information) to answer. Both are concerned with who is in what organization. Similarly, "union" and "department" are also classed as semantically equivalent: they are both examples of a type of organization. Obviously, such an interpretation is context dependent. If, instead of a query interpreter, we wanted our natural language processing system to understand a political manifesto, then the semantic categories would be very different. INFO is therefore a structure that consists of an AFFIL_VB (another category) followed by an ORG. Its associated action is to return the query that results from parsing AFFIL_VB. The rest of the grammar is built up in the same way down to the terminals, which return the values matched from the input sentence. The full grammar is shown in Figure 7.8.

Using this grammar we can get the parses

query: is_in(PERSON, org(NAME, union))

query: is_in(Sam Smith, org(IT, Department))

for the above sentences respectively. Parse trees for these sentences are shown in Figures 7.9 and 7.10. These show how the query is built up at every stage in the parse. Instantiation of the query components works from the bottom of the tree and moves up.

7.8.2   Case grammars

Semantic grammars are designed to give a structural and semantic parse of the sentence. Grammars can get very big as a result. Case grammars represent the semantics in the first instance, ignoring the syntactic, so reducing the size of the grammar (Fillmore 1968). For example, a sentence such as *Joe wrote the letter* would be represented as

wrote (agent(Joe), object(letter))

This indicates that Joe was the active participant, the agent, who performed the action "wrote" on the object "letter". The passive version *The letter was written by Joe* would be represented in the same way, since the meaning of the sentences is identical.

Case grammars rely on *cases*, which describe relationships between verbs and their arguments. A number of cases are available to build case grammar

S	⟶	who INFO	[query: INFO]
S	⟶	does YN	[query: YN]
INFO	⟶	AFFIL_VB ORG	[AFFIL_VB]
YN	⟶	PERSON AFFIL_VB	[AFFIL_VB]
ORG	⟶	Det NAMETYPE	[org (NAME, TYPE)]
ORG	⟶	Det TYPE	[org (NAME, TYPE)]
Department:	TYPE		[value]
Union:	TYPE		[value]
IT:	NAME		[value]
Sam Smith:	PERSON		[value]
belongs to:	AFFIL_VB		[is_in(PERSON, ORG)]
work in:	AFFIL_VB		[is_in(PERSON, ORG)]
the:	Det		
a:	Det		

Figure 7.8 Semantic grammar fragment.

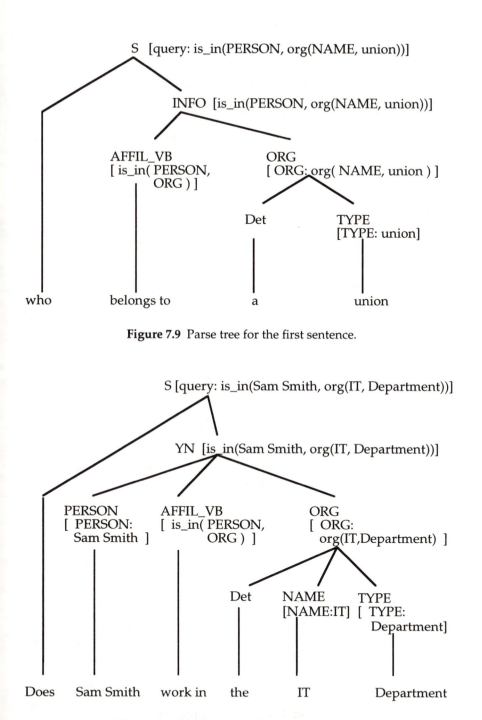

Figure 7.9 Parse tree for the first sentence.

Figure 7.10 Parse tree for the second sentence.

representations. The following list is not exhaustive. Can you think of other cases?

- *agent*: the person or thing performing the action.

- *object*: the person or thing to which something is done.

- *instrument*: the person or thing which allows an agent to perform an action.

- *time*: the time at which an action occurs.

- *beneficiary*: the person or thing benefiting from an action.

- *goal*: the place reached by the action.

So, for example, the sentence *At 1 pm, Paul hit the gong with the hammer for lunch* would be parsed as

hit(time(1pm), agent(Paul), object(gong), instrument(hammer),
 goal(lunch))

If we changed the sentence to *At 1 pm, Paul hit the gong with the hammer for his father*, the case representation would be

hit(time(1pm), agent(Paul), object(gong), instrument(hammer),
 beneficiary(his father))

The case structures can be used to derive syntactic structures, by using rules to map from the semantic components that are present to the syntactic structures that are expected to contain these components. However, case grammars do not provide a full semantic representation, since the resulting parse will still contain English words that must be understood.

7.9   Pragmatic analysis

The third stage in understanding natural language is pragmatic analysis. As we saw earlier, language can often only be interpreted in context. The context that must be taken into account may include both the surrounding sentences (to allow the correct understanding of ambiguous words and references) and the receiver's expectations, so that the sentence is appropriate for the situation in which it occurs. There are many relationships that can exist between sentences and phrases that have to be taken into account in pragmatic analysis. For example:

- A pronoun may refer back to a noun in a previous sentence that relates to the same object. *John had an ice cream. Joe wanted to share it.*

- A phrase may reference something that is a component of an object referred to previously. *She looked at the house. The front door was open.*

- A phrase may refer to something that is a component of an activity referred to previously. *Jo went on holiday. She took the early train.*

- A phrase may refer to agents who were involved in an action referred to previously. *My car was stolen yesterday. They abandoned it two miles away.*

- A phrase may refer to a result of an event referred to previously. *There have been serious floods. The army was called out today.*

- A phrase may refer to a subgoal of a plan referred to previously. *She wanted a new car. She decided to get a new job.*

- A phrase may implicitly intend some action. *This room is cold (expects an action to warm the room).*

One approach to performing this pragmatic analysis is the use of scripts (Schank & Abelson 1977). We met scripts in Chapter 1. In scripts, the expectations of a particular event or situation are recorded, and can be used to fill in gaps and help to interpret stories. The main problem with scripts is that much of the information that we use in understanding the context of language is not specific to a particular situation, but generally applicable. However, scripts have proved useful in interpreting simple stories.

7.9.1 Speech acts

When we use language our intention is often to achieve a specific goal that is reached by a set of actions. The acts that we perform with language are called *speech acts* (Searle 1969). Sentences can be classified by type. For example, the statement "I am cold" is a declarative sentence. It states a fact. On the other hand, the sentence "Are you cold?" is interrogative: it asks a question. A third sentence category is the imperative: "Shut the window". This makes a demand. One way to use speech acts in pragmatic analysis is to assume that the sentence type indicates the intention of the sentence. Therefore, a declarative sentence makes an assertion, an interrogative sentence asks a question and an imperative sentence issues a command.

This is a simplistic approach, which fails in situations where the desired action is implied. For example, the sentence "I am hungry" may be simply an assertion or it may be a request to hurry up with the dinner. Similarly, many commands are phrased as questions ("Can you tell me what time it is?"). However, most commercial natural language processing systems ignore such complexity and use speech acts in the manner described above.

Such an approach can be useful in natural language interfaces since assertions, questions and commands map clearly onto system actions. So if I am interacting with a database, an assertion results in the updating of the data held, a question results in a search and a command results in some operation being performed.

7.10 Summary

In this chapter we have looked at the issue of ambiguity, which makes natural language understanding so difficult. We have considered the key stages of natural language understanding: syntactic analysis, semantic analysis and pragmatic analysis. We have looked at grammars and transition networks as techniques for syntactic analysis; semantic and case grammars for semantic analysis; and scripts and speech acts for pragmatic analysis.

7.11 Exercises

1. For each of the sentences below generate the following:

   - a syntactic grammar and parse tree
   - a transition network
   - a semantic grammar and parse tree
   - a case grammar

   What additional features would you represent if you were generating context-sensitive grammars for these sentences?

   - My program was deleted by Brian
   - I need a print-out of my program file
   - The system administrator removed my files
   - I want to create a new document file

2. Identify the ambiguity in each of the following sentences and indicate how it could be resolved.

   - She was not sure if she had taken the drink
   - Joe broke his glasses
   - I saw the boy with the telescope
   - They left to go on holiday this morning

3. Devise a script for visiting the doctor, and indicate how this would be used to interpret the statement: "Alison went to the surgery. After seeing the doctor she left."

7.12 Recommended further reading

Allen, J. 1995. *Natural language understanding,* 2nd edn. Redwood, CA.: Benjamin Cummings.

A comprehensive text book covering all aspects of natural language understanding; a good next stage from here.

Winograd, T. & F. Flores 1987. *Understanding computers and cognition.* Norwood, NJ: Addison-Wesley, Ablex Corporation.

Includes a discussion of speech act theory and other aspects of natural language understanding.

7.13 Solution to SHRDLU problem

1. Find a block that is taller than the one you are holding and place it in the box. This is referential ambiguity. What does the word "it" refer to?

2. How many blocks are on top of the green block? This is perhaps more tricky but it involves semantic ambiguity. Does "on top of" mean directly on top of or above (that is, it could be on top of a block that is on top of the green block)?

3. Put the red pyramid on the block in the box. This is syntactic ambiguity. Is it the block that is in the box or the red pyramid that is being put into the box?

4. Does the shortest thing the tallest pyramid's support supports support anything green? This is lexical: there are two uses of the word "support"!

Chapter Eight

Computer vision

8.1 Overview

Computer vision is one way for a computer system to reach beyond the data it is given and find out about the real world. There are many important applications, from robotics to airport security. However, it is a difficult process. This chapter starts with an overview of the typical phases of processing in computer vision. Subsequent sections (8.3–8.7) then follow through these phases in turn. At each point deeper knowledge is inferred from the raw image. Finally, in Section 8.8, we look at the special problems and opportunities that arise when we have moving images or input from several cameras.

In this chapter we shall assume that the cameras are *passive* – we interpret what we are given. In Chapter 9 we shall look at *active vision*, where the camera can move or adjust itself to improve its understanding of a scene.

8.2 Introduction

8.2.1 Why computer vision is difficult

The human visual system makes scene interpretation seem easy. We can look out of a window and can make sense of what is in fact a very complex scene. This process is very difficult for a machine. As with natural language interpretation, it is a problem of ambiguity. The orientation and position of an object changes its appearance, as does different lighting or colour. In addition, objects are often partially hidden by other objects.

In order to interpret an image, we need both low-level information, such as texture and shading, and high-level information, such as context and world knowledge. The former allows us to identify the object, the latter to interpret it according to our expectations.

8.2.2 Phases of computer vision

Because of these multiple levels of conformation, most computer vision is based on a hierarchy of processes, starting with the raw image and working towards a high-level model of the world. Each stage builds on the features extracted at the stage below. Typical stages are (see Fig. 8.1):

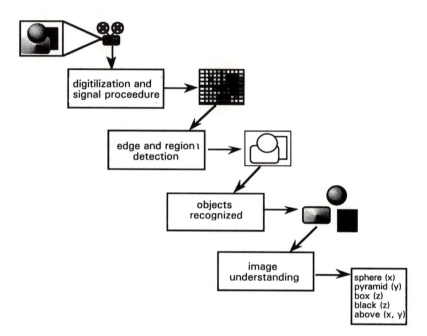

Figure 8.1 Phases of computer vision.

- *digitization*: the analogue video signal is converted into a digital image.

- *signal processing*: low-level processing of the digital image in order to enhance significant features.

- *edge and region detection*: finding low-level features in the digital image.

- *three-dimensional or two-dimensional object recognition*: building lines and regions into objects.

- *image understanding*: making sufficient sense of the image to use it.

Note, however, that not all applications go through all the stages. The higher levels of processing are more complicated and time consuming. In any real situation one would want to get away with as low a level of processing as possible.

The rest of this chapter will follow these levels of processing, and we will note where applications exist at each level.

8.3   Digitization and signal processing

The aim of computer vision is to understand some scene in the outside world. This may be captured using a video camera, but may come from a scanner (for example, optical character recognition). Indeed, for experimenting with computer vision it will be easier to digitize photographs than to work with real-time video. Also, it is not necessary that images come from visible light. For example, satellite data may use infrared sensing. For the purposes of exposition, we will assume that we are capturing a visible image with a video camera. This image will need to be digitized so that it can be processed by a computer and also "cleaned up" by signal processing software. The next section will discuss signal processing further in the context of edge detection.

8.3.1   Digitizing images

For use in computer vision, the image must be represented in a form that the machine can read. The analogue video image is converted (by a video digitizer) into a digital image. The digital image is basically a stream of numbers, each corresponding to a small region of the image, a pixel. The number is a measure of the light intensity of the pixel, and is called a grey level. The range of possible grey levels is called a grey scale (hence grey-scale images). If the grey scale consists of just two levels (black or white) the image is a binary image.

Figure 8.2 shows an image (ii) and its digitized form (i). There are ten grey levels from 0–white to 9–black. More typically there will be 16 or 256 grey levels rather than ten and often 0 is black (no light). However, the digits 0–9 fit better into the picture. Also, in order to print it, the image (ii) is already digitized and we are simply looking at a coarser level of digitization.

Most of the algorithms used in computer vision work on simple grey-scale images. However, sometimes colour images are used. In this case, there are usually three or four values stored for each pixel, corresponding to either primary colours (red, blue and green) or some other colour representation system.

Look again at Figure 8.2. Notice how the right-hand edge of the black rectangle translates into a series of medium grey levels. This is because the pixels each include some of the black rectangle and some of the white background. What was a sharp edge has become fuzzy.

As well as this blurring of edges, other effects conspire to make the grey-scale image inaccurate. Some cameras may not generate parallel lines of pixels, the pixels may be rectangular rather than square (the *aspect ratio*) or the relationship

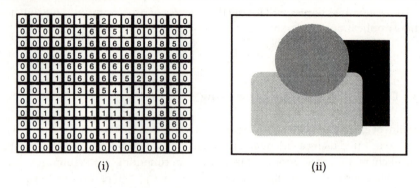

Figure 8.2 Digitized image.

between darkness and grey scale recorded may not be linear. However, the most persistent problem is noise: inaccurate readings of individual pixels due to electronic fluctuations, dust on the lens or even a foggy day!

8.3.2 Thresholding

Given a grey-scale image, the simplest thing we can do is to threshold it; that is, select all pixels whose greyness exceed some value. This may select key significant features from the image.

In Figure 8.3, we see an image (i) thresholded at three different levels of greyness. The first (ii) has the lowest threshold, accepting anything that is not pure white. The pixels of all the objects in the image are selected with this threshold. The next threshold (iii) accepts only the darker grey of the circle and the black of the rectangle. Finally, the highest threshold (iv) accepts only pure black pixels and hence only those of the obscured rectangle are selected.

This can be used as a simple way to recognize objects. For example, (Loughlin 1993) shows how faults in electrical plugs can be detected using multiple threshold levels. At some levels the wires are selected, allowing one to check that the wiring is correct; at others the presence of the fuse can be verified. In an industrial setting one may be able to select lighting levels carefully in order to make this possible.

One can also use thresholding to obtain a simple edge detection. One simply follows round the edge of a thresholded image. One can do this without actually performing the thresholding as one can simply follow pixels where the grey changes from the desired value. This is called contour following.

However, more generally, images resist this level of interpretation. Consider Figure 8.4. To the human eye, this also consists of three objects. However, see what two levels of thresholding, (ii) and (iii), do to the image. The combination

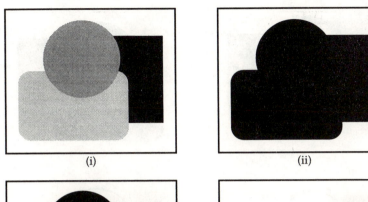

(i)

(ii)

(iii)

(iv)

Figure 8.3 Thresholding.

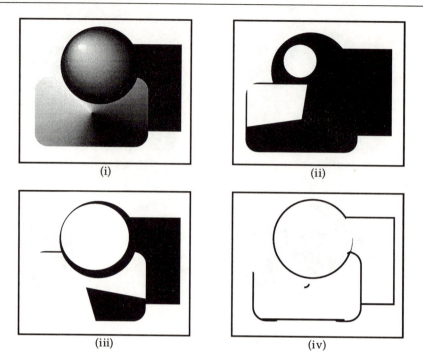

(i)

(ii)

(iii)

(iv)

Figure 8.4 A difficult image to threshold.

of light and shadows means that the regions picked out by thresholding show areas of individual objects instead of distinguishing the objects. Indeed, even to the human eye, the only way we know that the sphere is not connected to the black rectangular area is because of the intervening pyramid.

Contour following would give the boundary of one of these images – not really a good start for image understanding. The more robust approaches in the next section will instead use the rate of change in intensity – slope rather than height – to detect edges. However, even that will struggle on this image. The last image (iv) in Figure 8.4 shows edges obtained by looking for sharp contrasts in greyness. See how the dark side of the sphere has merged into the black rectangle, and how the light shining on the pyramid has lost part of its boundary. There is even a little blob in the middle where the light side of the pyramid meets the dark at the point.

In fact, as a human rather than a machine, you will have inferred quite a lot from the image. You will see it as a three-dimensional image where the sphere is above the pyramid and both lie above a dark rectangle. You will recognize that the light is shining somewhere from the top left. You will also notice from the shape of the figures and the nature of the shading that this is no photograph, but

168

a generated image. The algorithms we will discuss later in this chapter will get significantly beyond thresholding, but nowhere near your level of sophistication!

8.3.3 Digital filters

We have noted some of the problems of noise, blurring and lighting effects that make image interpretation difficult. Various signal processing techniques can be applied to the image in order to remove some of the effects of noise or enhance other features, such as edges. The application of such techniques is also called digital filtering. This is by analogy with physical filters, which enable you to remove unwanted materials, or to find desired material. Thresholding is a simple form of digital filter, but whereas thresholding processes each pixel independently, more sophisticated filters also use neighbouring pixels. Some filters go beyond this and potentially each pixel's filtered value is dependent on the whole image. However, all the filters we will consider operate on a finite window – a fixed-size group of pixels surrounding the current pixel.

Linear filters

Many filters are linear. These work by having a series of weights for each pixel in the window. For any point in the image, the surrounding pixels are multiplied by the relevant weights and added together to give the final filtered pixel value.

In Figure 8.5 we see the effect of applying a filter with a 3×3 window. The filter weights are shown at the top right. The initial image grey levels are at the top left. For a particular pixel the nine pixel values in the window are extracted. These are then multiplied by the corresponding weights, giving in this case the new value 1. This value is placed in the appropriate position in the new filtered image (bottom left).

The pixels around the edge of the filtered image have been left blank. This is because one cannot position a window of pixels 3×3 centred on the edge pixels. So, either the filtered image must be smaller than the initial image, or some special action is taken at the edges.

Notice also that some of the filtered pixels have negative values associated with them. Obviously this can only arise if some of the weights are negative. This is not a problem for subsequent computer processing, but the values after this particular filter cannot easily be interpreted as grey levels.

A related problem is that the values in the final image may be bigger than the original range of values. For example, with the above weights, a zero pixel surrounded by nines would give rise to a filtered value of 36. Again, this is not too great a problem, but if the result is too large or too small (negative) then it may be too large to store – an overflow problem. Usually, the weights will be scaled to avoid this. So, in the example above, the result of applying the filter would be divided by 8 in order to bring the output values within a similar range to the input grey scales. The coefficients are often chosen to add up to a power of 2, as dividing can then be achieved using bit shifts, which are far faster.

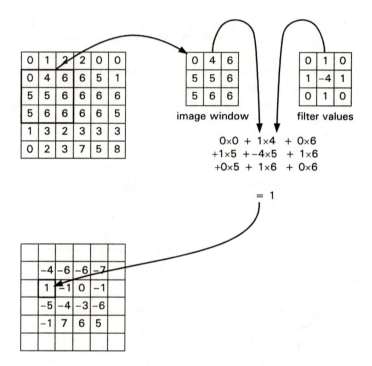

Figure 8.5 Applying a digital filter.

Smoothing

The simplest type of filter is for smoothing an image. That is, surrounding pixels are averaged to give the new value of a pixel. Figure 8.6 shows a simple 2 × 2 smoothing filter applied to an image. The filter window is drawn in the middle, and its pivot cell (the one which overlays the pixel to which the window is applied) is at the top left. The filter values are all ones, and so it simply adds the pixel and its three neighbours to the left and below and averages the four (note the ÷4). The image clearly consists of two regions, one to the left with high (7 or 8) grey-scale values and one to the right with low (0 or 1) values. However, the image also has some noise in it. Two of the pixels on the left have low values and one on

170

the right a high value. Applying the filter has all but removed these anomalies, leaving the two regions far more uniform, and hence suitable for thresholding or other further analysis.

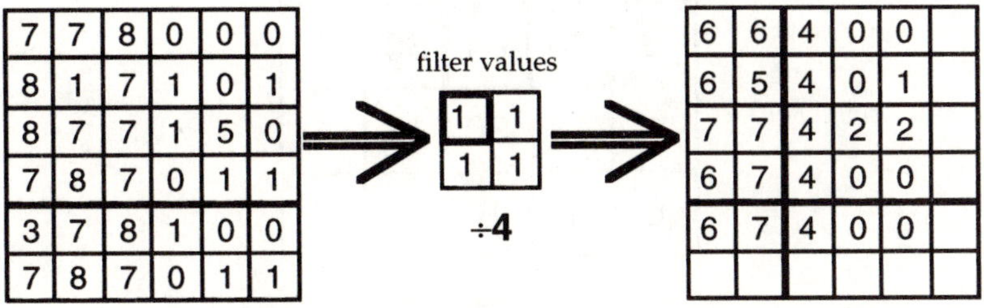

7	7	8	0	0	0
8	1	7	1	0	1
8	7	7	1	5	0
7	8	7	0	1	1
3	7	8	1	0	0
7	8	7	0	1	1

filter values

1	1
1	1

÷4

6	6	4	0	0
6	5	4	0	1
7	7	4	2	2
6	7	4	0	0
6	7	4	0	0

Figure 8.6 Applying a 2 × 2 smoothing filter.

Because only a few pixels are averaged with the 2 × 2 filter, it is still susceptible to noise. Applying the filter would only reduce the magnitude by a factor of 4. Larger windows are used if there is more noise, or if later analysis requires a cleaner image. A larger filter will often have an uneven distribution of weights, giving more importance to pixels near the chosen one and less to those far away.

There are disadvantages to smoothing, especially when using large filters. Notice in Figure 8.6 that the boundary between the two regions has become blurred. There is a line of pixels that are at an average value between the high and low regions. Thus, the edge can become harder to trace. Furthermore, fine features such as thin lines may disappear altogether. There is no easy answer to this problem – the desire to remove noise is in conflict with the desire to retain sharp images. In the end, how do you distinguish a small but significant feature from noise?

Gaussian filters

The Gaussian filter is a special smoothing filter based on the bell-shaped Gaussian curve, well known in statistics as the "normal" distribution. One imagines a window of infinite size, where the weight, $w(x, y)$, assigned to the pixel at position x, y from the centre is

$$w(x, y) = \frac{1}{\sqrt{\pi \sigma^2}} \exp[-(x^2 + y^2)/2\sigma^2]$$

The constant σ is a measure of the spread of the window – how much the image will be smeared by the filter. A small value of σ will mean that the weights in the filter will be small for distant pixels, whereas a large value allows more distant pixels to affect the new value of the current pixel. If noise affects groups of pixels together then one would choose a large value of σ.

0	1	3	1	0
1	13	30	13	1
3	30	64	30	3
1	13	30	13	1
0	1	3	1	0

Figure 8.7 Gaussian filter with $\sigma = 0.8$.

Although the window for a Gaussian filter is theoretically infinite, the weights become small rapidly and so, depending on the value of σ, one can ignore those outside a certain area and so make a finite windowed version. For example, Figure 8.7 shows a Gaussian filter with a 5×5 window. Notice how it is symmetric and how the weights decrease towards the edge. This filter has weights totalling 256, but this took some effort! The theoretical weights are not integers, and the rounding errors mean that in general the sum of weights will not be a nice number.

One big advantage of Gaussian filters is that the parameter σ can be set to any value yielding finer or coarser smoothing. Simple smoothing methods tend only to have versions getting "bigger" at fixed intervals (3×3, 5×5, etc.). The Gaussian with $\sigma = 0.7$ would also fit on a 5×5 window, but would be weighted more towards the centre (less smoothing).

Practical considerations

We have already discussed problems of overflow when computing filtered images, and in general there are various computational factors that influence the choice of filter. Indeed, the cost of image processing is so high that it is often better to use a simple method rather than an optimal one. It's no good an industrial robot recognizing a nut ten seconds after it has passed by on the conveyor belt.

Images are large. A 512×512 image with 256 grey levels consumes 256 kilobytes of memory. This is expensive in terms of storage, but also those 262 144 pixels take a long time to process one by one. A linear filter with a 2×2 window takes four multiplications per pixel, a 3×3 window takes nine and 5×5 takes 25! Also, a simple filter with coefficients of ± 1 or powers of 2 can be calculated by simple adds and shifts, further reducing the cost. So, the simple 2×2 smoothing filter in Figure 8.6, although crude, only takes 1 million additions, whereas the Gaussian filter in Figure 8.7 takes over 6 million multiplications. One solution is to use special hardware, *DSP* (*Digital Signal Processing*) chips or parallel processing. Indeed, your brain works in something like this fashion, with large areas committed to specific tasks such as line detection. It processes the whole image at once, rather than sequentially point by point. Whether or not this is available, care in the choice of processing method is essential.

The large amounts of storage required make it imperative that algorithms do not generate lots of intermediate images (unless you have masses of memory!). One way to achieve this is to overwrite the original image as it is filtered. But beware – look again at the 3 × 3 filter in Figure 8.5. If the image is processed from the top left downwards, then by the time a pixel is processed those pixels above and to the left of it will have been overwritten. With some very simple filters (such as the averagin filter in Fig. 8.6) this is not a problem, but in general one must be careful to avoid overwriting pixels that will be needed. It is possible with care! An alternative way to avoid intermediate storage is to work out the effects of multiple steps and to compute them in one step. We see an example of this in the next section, in the calculation of the Laplacian-of-Gaussian filter.

8.4 Edge detection

Edge detection is central to most computer vision. There is also substantial evidence that edges form a key part of human visual understanding. An obvious example is the ease with which people can recognize sketches and cartoons. A few lines are able to invoke the full two- or three-dimensional image. Edge detection consists of two subprocesses. First of all, potential edge pixels are identified by looking at their grey level compared with surrounding pixels. Then these individual edge pixels are traced to form the edge lines. Some of the edges may form closed curves, while others will terminate or form a junction with another edge. Some of the pixels detected by the first stage may not be able to join up with others to form true edges. These may correspond to features too small to recognize properly, or simply be the result of noise.

8.4.1 Identifying edge pixels

The grey-level image is an array of numbers (grey levels) representing the intensity value of the pixels. It can be viewed as a description of a hilly landscape where the numbers are altitudes. So a high number represents a peak and a low number a valley. Edge detection involves identifying ridges, valleys and cliffs. These are the edges in the image. We can use gradient operators to perform edge detection by identifying areas with high gradients. A high gradient (that is, a sudden change in intensity) indicates an edge. There are a number of different gradient operators in use.

173

Gradient operators

If you subtract a pixel's grey level from the one immediately to its right, you get a simple measure of the horizontal gradient of the image. This two-point filter is shown in Figure 8.8(i), together with two alternatives: a four-point filter (ii), which uses a 2×2 window, and a six-point filter (iii), which uses a 3×3 window. The vertical version of the six-point filter is also shown (iv).

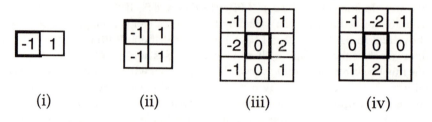

Figure 8.8 Different gradient filters.

The effects of the six-point filters are shown in Figure 8.9. The image shows the corner of a rectangular region in the bottom right-hand corner. Notice how the horizontal gradient operator picks out the left edge of the region and the vertical operator picks out the upper edge. Both operators would detect a diagonal edge, but less efficiently than one in their preferred direction. So, in Figure 8.10, the pixel values are large, but the filtered values at the edge are smaller and more smeared.

These operators can be useful if edges at a particular orientation are important, in which case one can simply threshold the filtered image and treat pixels with large gradients as edges. However, neither operator on its own detects both horizontal and vertical edges.

Robert's operator

Robert's operator uses a 2×2 window. For each position (x, y), a gradient function, $G(x, y)$, is calculated by

$$G(x, y) = |f(x, y) - f(x + 1, y - 1)| + |f(x + 1, y) - f(x, y - 1)|$$

where $f(x, y)$ is the intensity of the pixel at that position. Notice that this is not a simple linear filter, as it involves calculating the absolute value of the difference between diagonally opposite pixels. This is necessary in order to detect lines in all directions.

The results of the gradient function can be compared with a predetermined threshold to detect a local edge. Consider the various examples in Figure 8.11(i–iv):

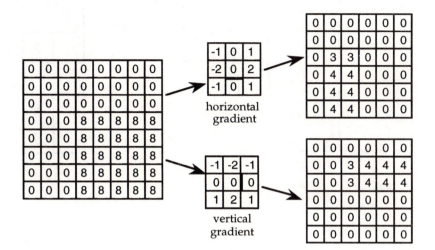

Figure 8.9 Applying gradient filters.

9	9	9	9	9	9	9	9
0	9	9	9	9	9	9	9
0	0	9	9	9	9	9	9
0	0	0	9	9	9	9	9
0	0	0	0	9	9	9	9
0	0	0	0	0	9	9	9
0	0	0	0	0	0	9	9
0	0	0	0	0	0	0	9

⟹

-1	0	1
-2	0	2
-1	0	1

⟹

3	1	0	0	0	0
3	3	1	0	0	0
1	3	3	1	0	0
0	1	3	3	1	0
0	0	1	3	3	1
0	0	0	1	3	3

Figure 8.10 Gradient filter on a diagonal edge.

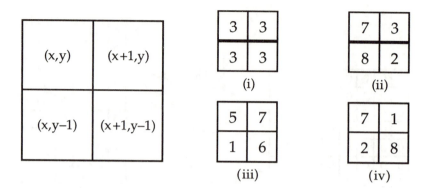

Figure 8.11 Robert's operator.

(i) G = $|3 - 3| + |3 - 3|$ = $|0| + |0|$ = 0
(ii) G = $|7 - 2| + |3 - 8|$ = $|5| + |-5|$ = 10
(iii) G = $|5 - 6| + |7 - 1|$ = $|-1| + |6|$ = 7
(iv) G = $|7 - 8| + |1 - 2|$ = $|-1| + |-1|$ = 2

A threshold of 5 would detect (ii) and (iii) as edges, but not (i) or (iv). Let's look at each example. The first is a constant grey level: there are no edges and none are detected whatever threshold is chosen. The second is a very clear edge running up the image, and it gets the highest gradient of the four examples. The third example also has quite a strong gradient. It appears to represent an edge running diagonally across the image. The final example has dramatic changes in intensity, but a low gradient. This is because there is little overall slope in the image. It represents a sort of ridge going across the picture. This might be a line a single pixel wide, but not an edge between regions.

Robert's operator has the advantage of simplicity, but suffers from being very localized and therefore easily affected by noise. For example, (ii) got a high gradient reading and would have been detected as a potential edge, but this is largely based on the bottom right pixel. If this one pixel were wrong, perhaps as a result of random noise, a spurious edge would be detected.

Sobel's operator

Sobel uses a slightly larger 3×3 window, which makes it somewhat less affected by noise. Figure 8.12 labels the grey levels of the nine pixels. The gradient function is calculated as

$$G = |(c + 2f + i) - (a + 2d + g)| + |(g + 2h + i) - (a + 2b + c)|$$

Again, this can be thresholded to give potential edge points.

a	b	c
d	e	f
g	h	i

where
$$
\begin{aligned}
a &= f(x-1,y+1)\\
b &= f(x,y+1)\\
c &= f(x+1,y+1)\\
d &= f(x-1,y)\\
e &= f(x,y)\\
f &= f(x+1,y)\\
g &= f(x-1,y-1)\\
h &= f(x,y-1)\\
i &= f(x+1,y-1)
\end{aligned}
$$

Figure 8.12 Sobel's operator.

Notice that the grey level at the pixel itself, e, is not used: the surrounding pixels give all the information. We can see the operator as composed of two terms, a horizontal and a vertical gradient:

$$
\begin{aligned}
H &= (c+2f+i) - (a+2d+g)\\
V &= (g+2h+i) - (a+2b+c)\\
G &= |H| + |V|
\end{aligned}
$$

The first term, H, compares the three pixels to the right of e with those to the left. The second, V, compares those below the pixel with those above. In fact, if you look back at the six-point gradient filters in Figure 8.8, you will see that V and H are precisely the absolute values of the outputs of those filters. An edge running across the image will have a large value of V, one running up the image a large value of H. So, once we have decided that a pixel represents an edge point, we can give the edge an orientation using the ratio between H and V. Although we could follow edges simply by looking for adjacent edge pixels, it is better to use edge directions (as we shall see later).

Note that it is also possible to give an orientation with Robert's operator, as the two terms in it correspond to a northwesterly and northeasterly gradient respectively. However, this estimate of direction would be even more subject to noise.

Note also that Sobel's operator uses each pixel value twice, either multiplying it by two (the side pixels: f, d, h and b) or including it in both terms (the corner pixels: a, c, g and i). However, an error in one of the corner pixels might cancel out, whereas one in the side pixels would always affect the result. For this reason, some prefer a modified version of Sobel's operator:

$$
G = |(c+f+i) - (a+d+g)| + |(g+h+i) - (a+b+c)|
$$

On the other hand, there are theoretical reasons for preferring the original operator, so the choice of operator in a particular application is rather a matter of taste!

Laplacian operator

An alternative to measuring the gradient is to use the Laplacian operator. This is a mathematical measure (written ∇) of the change in gradient. Its mathematical definition is in terms of the second differential in the x and y direction (where the first differential is the gradient):

$$\nabla f = \frac{d^2 f}{dy^2} + \frac{d^2}{dy^2}$$

However, for digital image processing, linear filters are used which approximate to the true Laplacian. Approximations are shown in Figure 8.13 for a 2×2 grid and a 3×3 grid.

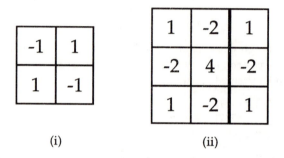

(i)   (ii)

Figure 8.13 Approximations to the Laplacian.

To see how they work, we will use a one-dimensional equivalent to the Laplacian which filters a one-dimensional series of grey levels using the weights $(1, -2, 1)$. The effect of this is shown in Figure 8.14. Notice how the edge between the nines and ones is converted into little peaks and troughs. The actual edge detection then involves looking for zero crossings, places where the Laplacian's values change between positive and negative.

Notice that in Figure 8.14 the boundary between the nines and the ones is a 5. The one-dimensional image is slightly blurred. When Robert's or Sobel's operators encounter such an edge they are likely to register several possible edge pixels either side of the actual edge. The Laplacian will register a single pixel in the middle of the blurred edge.

The Laplacian also has the advantage that it is a linear filter and can thus be easily manipulated with other filters. A frequent combination is to use a Gaussian filter to smooth the image, and then follow this with a Laplacian. Because both are linear filters, they can be combined into a single filter called the Laplacian-of-Gaussian (LOG) filter.

Note that the Laplacian does not give any indication of orientation. If this is required then some additional method must be used once an edge has been detected.

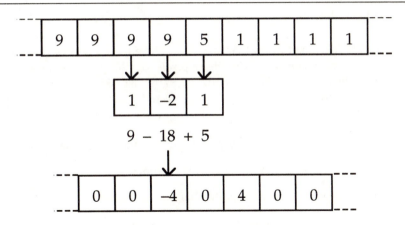

Figure 8.14 Using the Laplacian.

Successive refinement and Marr's primal sketch

We saw earlier that images are very large and hence calculations over the whole image take a long time. One way to avoid this is to operate initially on coarse versions of the image and then successively use more detailed images to examine potentially interesting features. For example, we could divide a 512×512 image into 8×8 cells and then calculate the average grey level over the cell. Treating each cell as a big "pixel", we get a much smaller 64×64 image. Edge detection is then applied to this image using one of the methods suggested above. If one of the cells is registered as an edge then the pixels comprising it are investigated individually. Assuming that only a small proportion of the cells are potential edges then the savings in computation are enormous – the only time we have to visit all the pixels is when the cell averages are computed. This method of successive refinement can be applied to other parts of the image processing process, such as edge following and region detection (discussed later).

One representation of images, Marr's primal sketch (Marr 1982), uses similar methods to detect features at different levels of detail, but for a very different reason. Instead of averaging over cells, Laplacian-of-Gaussian filters are used with different standard deviations, where small standard deviations correspond to fine detail. Recall that Gaussians use large windows, so this is definitely not a cost-cutting route to image processing! The concept of different levels of detail is central to the model. The primal sketch is divided into edges, terminations (ends of edges), bars (regions between parallel edges) and blobs (small isolated regions). In particular, blobs are regions of pixels that register as edges (zero crossings of the Laplacian) at fine resolution, but disappear at high resolution. Look at the room and then screw up your eyes. If you can see it when your eyes are open, but not when they are screwed up, then it is a blob.

8.4.2   Edge following

We have now identified pixels that may lie on the edges of objects. We are not there yet! The next step is to string those pixels together to make lines, that is, to identify which groups of pixels make up particular edges. The basic rule of thumb is that if two suspected edges are connected then they form a single line. However, this needs to be modified slightly for three reasons:

– because of noise, shadows, and so on, some edges will contain gaps

– noise may cause spurious pixels to be candidate edges

– edges may end at junctions with other lines.

The first means that we may have to look more than one pixel ahead to find the next edge point. The other two mean that we have to use the edge orientation information in order to reject spurious edges or detect junctions.

A basic edge-following algorithm is then as follows:

1. Choose any suspected edge pixel that has not already been used.

2. Choose one direction to follow first.

3. Look for an adjoining pixel in the right general direction.

4. If the orientation of the pixel is not too different then accept it.

5. If there is no adjoining pixel scan those one or two pixels away.

6. If an acceptable pixel has been found repeat from 3.

7. If no acceptable pixel is found repeat the process for the other direction.

The pixels found during a pass of this algorithm are regarded as forming a single edge. The whole process is repeated until all edge pixels have been considered.

A few of the steps in this algorithm need unpacking slightly. First, in step 2, a line has two ends, so one has to choose which to follow first. As both will eventually be traced, the choice is unimportant and some default, say towards the right, can be chosen. Remember, though, that the orientation of the edge is at 90° to the line of maximum slope. At step 3, one only bothers to look for pixels that are in the general direction of the edge. For example, if the orientation is northeast, one would look at the pixels to the top right, right and top. Similarly at step 5, one only looks slightly further in the relevant directions. Figure 8.15 shows a typical order in which pixels are scanned. You have to look at quite a wide swath of pixels, as even a straight line is quite jagged when digitized and also the edge may bend. Note that the figure includes the additional pixels searched at step 5. The threshold used to decide whether two edge pixels have

edge orientation
in this octant

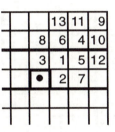

search in this order

Figure 8.15 Following edges.

a "close enough" orientation will depend somewhat on the sort of images, noise levels, and so on. However, a typical rule might be to accept if the orientations lie within 60° of one another.

The output of this algorithm is a collection of edges, each of which consists of a set of pixels. The end points of each edge segment will also have been detected at step 7. If the end point is isolated then it is a termination; if several lie together, or if it lies on another edge, then the end point is at a junction. This resulting set of edges and junctions will be used by Waltz's algorithm in the next section to infer three-dimensional properties of the image.

However, before passing these data on to more knowledge-rich parts of the process, some additional cleaning up is possible. For example, very short edges may be discarded as they are likely either to be noise, or to be unimportant in the final image (for example, texture effects). Also, one can look for edges that terminate close to one another. If they are collinear and there are no intervening edges then one may join them up to form a longer edge. Also, if two edges with different orientation terminate close together, or an edge terminates near the middle of another edge, then this can be regarded as a junction. One problem with too much guessing at lower levels is that it may confuse higher levels (the source of optical illusions in humans). One solution is to annotate edges and junctions with certainty figures. Higher levels of processing can then use *Bayesian*-style inferencing and accept or reject these guesses depending on higher-level semantic information. However, for the purposes of exposition, we will assume that the output of this level of analysis is perfect.

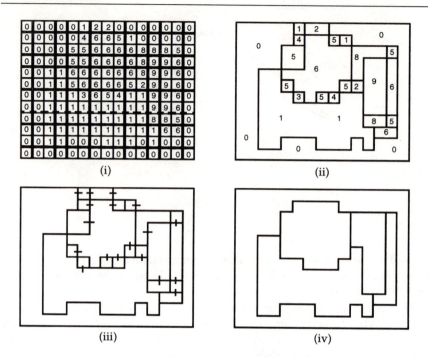

Figure 8.16 Region merging.

8.5 Region detection

In the previous section we likened edge detection to understanding a cartoon. In contrast, an oil painting will not have lines drawn at the edges, but will consist of areas of different colours. An alternative to edge detection is to concentrate on the regions composing the image. We considered this briefly when we discussed thresholding, but will now look at a more sophisticated algorithm.

8.5.1 Region growing

A region can be regarded as a connected group of pixels whose intensity is almost the same. Region detection (or segmentation) aims to identify the main shapes in an image. This can be done by identifying clusters of similar intensities. The main process is as follows:

- group identical pixels into regions

182

– examine the boundaries between these regions – if the difference is lower than a threshold, merge the regions.

The result is the main regions of the image.

This process is demonstrated in Figure 8.16. The first image (i) shows the original grey levels. Identical pixels are merged giving the initial regions in (ii). The boundaries between these are examined and in (iii) those where the intensity is less than 3 are marked for merging. The remainder, those where the difference in intensity is more than 2, are retained, giving the final regions in (i).

8.5.2 The problem of texture

Texture can cause problems with all types of image analysis, but region growing has some special problems. If the image is unprocessed then a textured surface will have pixels of many different intensities. This may lead to many small island regions within each large region. Alternatively, the texture may "feather" the edges of the regions so that different regions get merged. The obvious response is to smooth the image so that textures become greys. However, if the feathering is bad, then sufficient smoothing to remove the texture will also blur the edge sufficiently that the regions will be merged anyway. In a controlled environment, where lighting levels can be adjusted, one may be able to adjust the various parameters (level of smoothing, threshold for merging) so that recognition is possible, but where such control is not easily possible region merging may fail completely.

8.5.3 Representing regions – quad-trees

In the previous section we represented regions by simply drawing lines round them on the page. In a computer program it is not that straightforward! The simplest representation would be to keep a list of all the pixels in each region. However, this would take an enormous amount of storage. There are various alternatives to reduce this overhead. One popular representation is quad-trees. These make use of the fact that images often have large areas with the same value – precisely the case with regions. We will describe the algorithm in terms of storing a binary image and then show how it can be used for recording regions.

Start off with a square image where the width in pixels is some power of 2. Examine the image. Is it all black or white? If so, stop. If not, then divide the image into four quarters and look at each quarter. If any quarter is all black or white, then leave it alone, but if any quarter is mixed, then split it into quarters. This continues until either each region is of one colour, or else one gets to individual pixels – which must be one colour by definition. This process is illustrated in

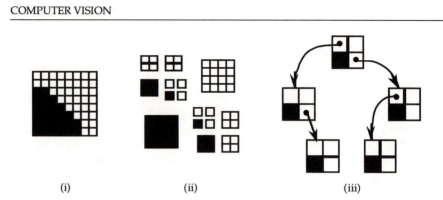

Figure 8.17 Quad-tree representation of image.

Figure 8.17. The first part (i) shows the original image, perhaps part of a black circle. This is then divided and subdivided into quarters in (ii). Finally, in (iii) we see how this can be stored in the computer as a tree data structure. See how the 64 pixels of the image are stored in five tree nodes. Of course the tree nodes are more complicated than simple bitmaps and so for this size of image a quad-tree is a little over the top, but for larger images the saving can be enormous.

This can be used to record regions in two ways. Each region can be stored as a quad-tree where a black means that the pixel is part of the region. Alternatively, one can use a multi-coloured version of a quad-tree where each region is coded as a different colour. In either case, regions can easily be merged using the quad-tree representation.

8.5.4   Computational problems

Region growing is very computationally expensive, involving many passes over the digitized image. Operating on reduced representations such as quad-trees can reduce the number of operations, but at the expense of more complicated data structures. For this reason, (Vernon 1991) suggests that region growing is not generally applicable in industrial contexts. Instead, edge detection methods are preferred. The contrast is easy to see – a 100 × 100 pixel square has 10 000 interior pixels, but only 400 on the boundary! However, against this one should note that region growing is easily amenable to parallel processing and so the balance between different techniques may change.

8.6 Reconstructing objects

8.6.1 Inferring three-dimensional features

Edge and region detection identify parts of an image. We need to establish the objects that the parts depict. We can use constraint satisfaction algorithms to determine what possible objects can be constructed from the lines given. First, we need to label the lines in the image to distinguish between concave edges, convex edges and obscuring edges. An obscuring edge occurs where a part of one object lies in front of another object or in front of a different part of the same object. The convention is to use a "+" to label a convex edge, a "−" for a concave edge and an arrow for an obscuring edge. The arrow has the object the edge is "attached" to on its right and the obscured object on its left. Figure 8.18 shows an object with the lines in the image suitably labelled.

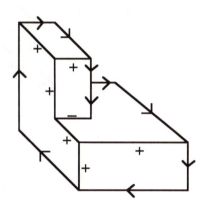

Figure 8.18 Scene with edges labelled.

How do we decide which labels to use for each line? Lines meet each other at vertices. If we assume that certain degenerate cases do not occur, then we need only worry about trihedral vertices (in which exactly three lines meet at a vertex). There are four types of such vertices, called L, T, fork (or Y) and arrow (or W). There are 208 possible labellings using the four labels available, but happily only 18 of these are physically possible (see Figs 8.19–8.22). We can therefore use these to constrain our line labelling. Waltz proposed a method for line labelling using these constraints.

Waltz's algorithm

Waltz's algorithm (Waltz 1975) basically starts at the outside edges of the objects and works inward using the constraints. The outside edges must always be

185

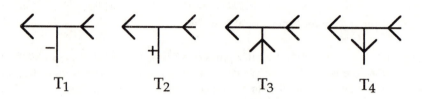

Figure 8.19 Possible trihedral vertices – T junctions.

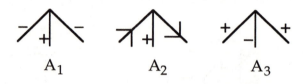

Figure 8.20 Possible trihedral vertices – arrows.

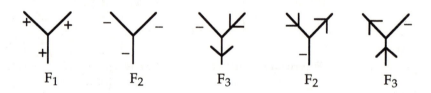

Figure 8.21 Possible trihedral vertices – forks.

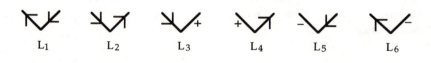

Figure 8.22 Possible trihedral vertices – L junctions.

obscuring edges (where it is the background that is obscured). Therefore, these can always be labelled with clockwise arrows. The algorithm has the following stages:

1. Label the lines at the boundary of the scene.

2. Find vertices where the currently labelled lines are sufficient to determine the type of the vertex.

3. Label the rest of the lines from those vertices accordingly.

Steps 2 and 3 are repeated either until there are no unlabelled lines (success), or until there are no remaining vertices which are completely determined (failure).

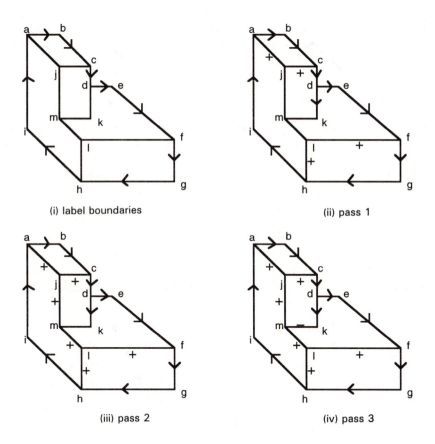

(i) label boundaries

(ii) pass 1

(iii) pass 2

(iv) pass 3

Figure 8.23 Applying Waltz's algorithm.

We will follow through the steps of this algorithm attempting to label the object in Figure 8.18. We start by naming the vertices and labelling the boundary lines. This gives the labelling in Figure 8.23(i).

187

We now perform the first pass of steps 2 and 3. Notice how a, c , f and h are arrow vertices with the two side arms labelled as boundaries (">"). Only type A_6 matches this, so the remaining line attached to each of these vertices must be convex ("+"). Similarly, the T vertex d must be of type T_4; hence the line d–k is a boundary. Vertices e and i are already fully labelled, so add no new information. The results of this pass are shown in (ii).

On the second pass of steps 2 and 3 we concentrate on vertices j, k and l. Unfortunately, vertex k is not determined yet; it might be of type L_1 or L_5 and we have to wait until we have more information. However, vertices j and l are more helpful: they are forks with one concave line. We see that if one line to a fork is concave it must be of type F_1 and so all the lines from it are concave. These are marked in (iii).

As we start the third pass, we see that k is still not determined, but m is an arrow with two concave arms. It is therefore of type A_3 and the remaining edge is concave. This also finally determines that k is of type L_5. The fully labelled object (iv) now agrees with the original labelling in Figure 8.18.

Problems with labelling

Waltz's algorithm will always find the unique correct labelling if one exists. However, there are scenes for which there are multiple labellings, or for which no labelling can be found. Figure 8.24 shows a scene with an ambiguous labelling. The first labelling corresponds to the upper block being attached to the lower one. In the second labelling the upper block is "floating" above the lower one. If there were a third block between the other two we would be able to distinguish the two, but with no further information we cannot do so. With this scene, Waltz's algorithm would come to an impasse at stage 2, when it would have unlabelled vertices remaining, but none that are determined from the labelled edges. At this stage, you could make a guess about edge labelling, but whereas the straightforward algorithm never needs to backtrack, you might need to change your guesses as you search for a consistent labelling.

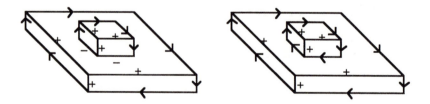

Figure 8.24 Scene with ambiguous labelling.

Figure 8.25(i) shows the other problem, a scene that cannot be labelled consistently. In this case Waltz's algorithm would get stuck at step 3. Two different vertices would each try to label the same edge differently. The problem edge is the central diagonal. Reasoning from the lower arm, the algorithm thinks it is convex, but reasoning from the other two arms it thinks it is concave. To be fair, the algorithm is having exactly the same problem as you have with this image. It is locally sensible, but there is no reasonable interpretation of the whole scene.

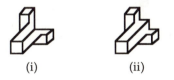

(i)   (ii)

Figure 8.25 Improper scene.

Given only the set of vertex labellings from Figures 8.19–8.22, there are also sensible scenes that cannot be labelled. A pyramid that has four faces meeting at the top cannot be labelled using trihedral vertices. Even worse, a piece of folded cloth may have a cusp, where a fold line disappears completely. These problems can be solved by extending the set of vertex types, but as one takes into account more complex vertices and edges, the number of cases does increase dramatically.

Note also that the algorithm starts with the premise that lines and vertices have been identified correctly. Given what you know about edge detection, you will see that this is not necessarily a very robust assumption. If the edge detection is not perfect, then one might need to use uncertain reasoning while building up objects. Consider Figure 8.25 (ii) – a valid scene that can be labelled consistently. However, if the image is slightly noisy at the top right vertex it might be uncertain whether it is a T, an arrow or a Y vertex. If it chose the last of these, it would have the same problems as with the first, inconsistent figure. If the edge detection algorithm instead gave probabilities, one could use these with *Bayesian reasoning* to get the most likely labelling.

However, the search process would be somewhat more complicated than Waltz's algorithm!

8.6.2   Using properties of regions

Edge detection simply uses lines of rapid change, but discards the properties of the regions between the lines. However, there is a lot of information in these regions that can be used to understand the image or to identify objects in the image. For example, in Figure 8.26, it is likely that the regions labelled A and B are part of the same object partly obscured by the darker object. We might have guessed this from the alignment of the two regions, but the fact that they are the same colour reinforces this conclusion.

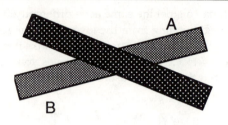

Figure 8.26 Two objects or three?

Also, the position and nature of highlights and shadows can help to determine the position and orientation of objects. If we have concluded that an edge joins two parts of the same object, then we can use the relative brightness of the two faces to determine which is facing the light. Of course, this depends on the assumption that the faces are all of similar colour and shade. Such heuristics are often right, but can sometimes lead us to misinterpret an image – which is precisely why we can see a two-dimensional picture as if it had depth.

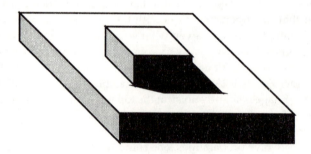

Figure 8.27 Shadows and highlights.

Once we know the position of the light source (or sources), we can work out which regions represent possible shadows of other objects and hence connect them to the face to which they belong. For example, in Figure 8.27, we can see from the different shadings that the light is coming from above, behind and slightly to the left. It is then obvious that the black region is the shadow of the upper box and so is part of the top face of the lower box.

Shadows and lighting can also help us to disambiguate images. If one object casts a shadow on another then it must lie between that object and the light. Also, the shape of a shadow may be able to tell us about the distance of objects from one another and whether they are touching. Recall in Figure 8.24 how the edges had no unambiguous labelling. However, looking at the shadow in Figure 8.27 it is clear that the upper box is in contact with the lower one.

Lighting effects can also help us to interpret curved objects. For example, in Figure 8.4 at the beginning of this chapter, the sphere gets darker and darker until it becomes indistinguishable from the black rectangle in the background. However, we have no trouble identifying it as a sphere as we infer a boundary based on the rate of change of colour. A similar rule can be built into an image analysis program.

8.7 Identifying objects

Finally, having extracted various features from an image, we need to establish what the various objects are. The output of this will be some sort of symbolic representation at the semantic level. We will discuss three ways of doing this that operate on different sorts of lower-level representation.

8.7.1 Using bitmaps

The simplest form of object identification is just to take the bitmap, suitably thresholded, and match it against various templates of known objects. One can simply count the number of pixels that disagree and use this as a measure of fit. The best match is chosen, and so long as its match exceeds a certain threshold it is accepted.

template

match 60%

match 60%

Figure 8.28 Simple template matching.

This form of matching can work well where one can be sure that shapes are not occluded and where lighting levels can be chosen to ensure clean thresholded images. However, in many situations the match will be partial, either because of noise, or because the object is partly obscured by another object. Simply reducing the threshold for acceptability will not work. Consider the two images in Figure 8.28. They have a similar amount of pixels in common, but the first is clearly a triangle like the template whereas the latter is not.

Neural network techniques (see Ch. 11) can be used to deal with noisy pattern

191

matching. Several different types could be used, but most work by taking a series of examples of images of the different objects and "learning" how to recognize them. Depending on the particular technique, the examples may be of perfect or of noisy images. After training, when the network is presented with an image it identifies the object it thinks it matches, sometimes with an indication of certainty. Neural networks can often give accurate results even when there is a large amount of noise, but without some of the unacceptable spurious matches from crude template matching. One reason for this is that many nets effectively match significant features (such as the corners and edges of the triangle). This is not because they have any particular knowledge built in, but simply because of the low-level way that they learn.

One problem with both template matching and neural networks is that they are looking for the object at a particular place in the image. They have problems when the object is at a different location or orientation than the examples with which they are taught. One solution is to use lots of examples at different orientations. For template matching this increases the cost dramatically (one test for each orientation). For neural nets, the way in which the patterns are stored reduces this cost to some extent, but if too many patterns are taught without increasing the size of the network, the accuracy will eventually decay.

An alternative approach is to move the object so that it is in the expected location. In an industrial situation this can often be achieved by using arrangements of chutes and barriers that force the object into a particular position and orientation. Where this is not possible, an equivalent process can be carried out on the image. If one is able to identify which region of the image represents an object, then this can be moved so that it lies at the bottom left-hand corner of the image, and then matched in this standard position. This process is called normalization. A few stray pixels at the bottom or left of the object can upset this process, but alternative normalization methods are less susceptible to noise, for example moving the centre of gravity of the object to the centre of the image.

Similar methods can be used to standardize the orientation and size of the object (the size may be different if it is closer or farther away than the examples). The general idea is to find a co-ordinate system relative to the object and then use this to transform the object into the standard co-ordinate system used for the matching. A typical algorithm works like this:

1. Select a standard point on the object (say its centre of gravity).

2. Choose the direction in which the object is "widest"; make this the x axis.

3. Take the axis orthogonal to the x axis as the y axis.

4. Scale the two axes so that the object "fits" within the unit square.

The definitions of "widest" and also "fits" from steps 2 and 4 can use the simple extent of the object, but are more often based on measures which are less noise sensitive. The process is illustrated in Figure 8.29. The resulting x and y axes are called an object-centred co-ordinate system. Obviously all the example images must be transformed in a similar fashion so that they match!

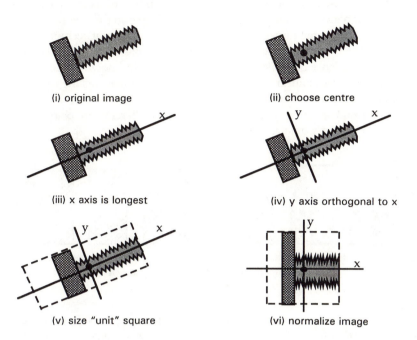

Figure 8.29 Choosing an object-centred co-ordinate system.

8.7.2 Using summary statistics

An even simpler approach than template matching is to use simple statistics about the objects in the image, such as the length and width of the object (possibly in the object-centred system), the number of pixels with various values, and so on. For example, if one were trying to separate nuts and bolts on a production line, then those objects with an aspect ratio (ratio of length to width) greater than some critical value would be classified as nuts. Another example would be a line producing washers where you are trying to reject those that have not had their centres properly removed. Those objects with too many pixels would be rejected as defects.

8.7.3 Using outlines

We saw when discussing template matching that issues of location, orientation and size independence cause some problems. These get far worse when we have to consider three-dimensional rotations. At this point techniques using higher-level features, such as those generated by Waltz's algorithm, become very attractive. In essence one is still template matching, but now the templates are descriptions of the connectivity of various edges. Of course, the same object will have different edges visible depending on its orientation. However, one can generate a small set of representative orientations whereby any object matches one or other after a certain amount of deformation.

Figure 8.30 Different orientations of an object.

Figure 8.30 shows some of the representative orientations of a simple geometric object. The example set of all possible orientations can be generated by hand, or (ideally) automatically using a three-dimensional geometric model of the object. The number of orientations can be reduced dramatically if one can make any assumptions, say that the object's base stays on the ground, or that the camera position is within certain bounds.

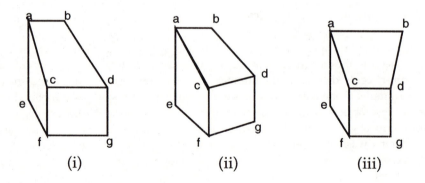

Figure 8.31 Matching an object.

When an object is to be recognized it is matched against the representatives of

194

all known objects. Each vertex and edge in the image object is matched with a corresponding one in the example. If such a correspondence can be found then the match succeeds. The exact positions of the vertices and edges don't matter, but the relative geometric constraints must match. For example, in Figure 8.31, image (ii) matches the template (i). However, (iii) doesn't because vertex d is a fork-type junction rather than an arrow.

The matching process can be more or less precise. As well as the types of junctions, it may use information such as whether certain lines are parallel or vertical. However, adding constraints tends to mean that there are more cases to consider when producing the set of all representative orientations.

Note that this type of method can be used to match more complicated objects. If an object consists of various pieces then the pieces can be individually identified by the above method and then a description of the connectivity of the pieces within the object matched against the known objects. This allows one to detect objects which change their shape, such as people.

8.7.4 Using paths

Finally in this section we look at the special case of handwriting and gesture recognition. Reading human handwriting has long been an aim of AI (as well as many of the authors' friends). This has recently come to fruition, and pen-based computing is now affordable and rapidly becoming ubiquitous. These systems recognize both characters (to enter data) and gestures (such as a scribble to mean "delete"). These systems either demand that the writer uses very stylized letters, or that new writers spend some time training the system. Even when the system is trained the writer must write each character individually. Reliable and flexible writer-independent recognition of connected writing is not yet with us.

One way to approach handwritten text is to take the bitmap generated by the path of the pen and then process it. Some applications demand this approach, for example if you want to interpret proof corrections written onto paper copies and then scanned in. However, for an interactive system this throws away too much useful information. If we trace the path of the pen, we not only have the lines already separated from the background (why bother to detect them again!), but we also know the direction of the strokes and the order in which they were written.

These path data differ from the grey-scale or bitmap images we have considered so far. Instead of a set of intensities at positions, we have a set of positions of the pen at various times. We can match the strokes in the image against those learnt for the particular writer. However, handwritten letters and gestures are never exactly the same and so we must accept some variation. There are various approaches to this.

One way is to look for characteristic shapes of strokes: lines, curves, circles, and so on. Characters and gestures are then described using this "vocabulary".

195

A letter "a" might be described as either "a circle with a line connected to the right" or "a semi-closed curve with a line closing it to the right".

An alternative is to try and match the strokes against examples stored during training. However, not only may the written characters vary, but also the points at which the pen is sampled may differ between the training example and the one to be recognized. One therefore has to "warp" the points on the path and find intermediate points that match most closely the example. The idea is to choose points that were not in the sample, but might have been!

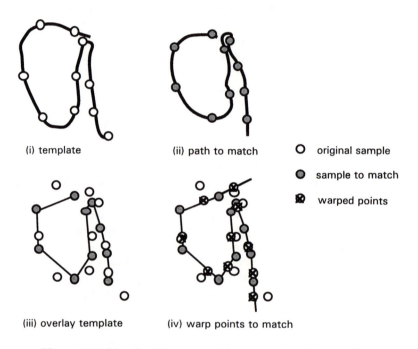

(i) template   (ii) path to match   O   original sample

                                              ◉   sample to match

                                              ✖   warped points

(iii) overlay template   (iv) warp points to match

Figure 8.32 Handwriting recognition – warping the sample.

The process is illustrated in Figure 8.32. The sample points on the original template and the character that needs to be matched are shown in (i) and (ii). The template sample points are overlaid as closely as possible (iii), and then intermediate points (the warp points) are chosen on the lines connecting the sample points. These are chosen so as to be as close to the template points as possible. At the ends of the stroke the warp points must be chosen on the extrapolation of the last lines. Now the warped points are used rather than the originals in deciding whether or not the character really matches the template.

8.8 Multiple images

So far, we have looked at single images. This may be all we have to work on, for example a single photograph of a scene. However, in some circumstances we have several images, which together can be used to interpret a scene. On the one hand, this can make life more difficult (lots of images to process!). On the other hand, we may be able to extract information from the combined images that is not in any single image alone. These multiple images may arise from various sources:

1. Different sensors may be viewing the same scene.

2. Two cameras may be used simultaneously to give stereo vision.

3. We may have continuous video of a changing scene.

4. A fixed camera may be panning (and possibly zooming) over a scene.

5. The camera may be on a moving vehicle or mounting.

The first of these, the combination of different sorts of data (for example, infrared and normal cameras), is called data fusion. It is especially important for remote sensing applications, such as reconstructing images from satellite data. Different sensors may show up different features; hence edges and regions in the two images may not correspond in a one-to-one fashion. If the registration between the sensors is known (that is, one knows how they overlap), then the images can simply be overlaid and the information from each combined. Often this registration process is the most difficult part and the high-level data may be used to aid this process. For example, terrain-following cruise missiles rely on the matching of ground features with digital maps to calculate their course and position.

The last three sources of multiple images have somewhat different characteristics, but are similar enough to discuss together. We will therefore look at stereo vision (Fig. 8.33) and moving images in more detail.

8.8.1 Stereo vision

Look out into the room and hold a finger in front of your face. Now close each eye in turn. Your finger appears to move back and forth across the room. Because your eyes are at different positions they see slightly different views of the world. This is especially important in determining depth. If you have not tried it before, here's another simple experiment. Hold a pencil in one hand and try to touch the tip of the finger of your other hand with the point of the pencil. No problem? Try it with one eye closed. The properties of stereo vision are one of the clues our eyes use to determine how far away things are.

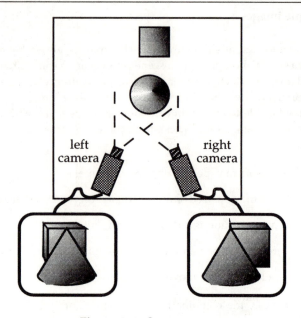

Figure 8.33 Stereo vision.

One way to determine depth is to use triangulation in a similar way to a surveyor. Assuming you have been able to identify the same feature in both images, you can work out the angle between the two and hence the distance (see Fig. 8.34). To use this method to give exact distances, you need very accurate calibration of the cameras. However, even without such accuracy, one can use this method to obtain relative distances (which is probably what your eye is doing with the pen and finger).

In fact, it is not necessary to do any explicit calculations in order to obtain qualitative estimates of relative distance. Notice in Figure 8.33 how the cone moves back and forth relative to the cube. This effect is called parallax. If the amount of movement between the two views is great then we know there is a considerable distance between the two objects.

So far we have assumed that we know which objects are the same in each image. However, this matching of objects between images is a difficult problem in itself. One can attack it at various levels. On the one hand, we can simply look for patterns of pixels that match one another in the grey-scale image. To do this, we work out the correlation (a measure of similarity) between groups of pixels in the two images at small offsets from one another. Where the correlation is large, we assume that there is some feature in common. The size of the offset then tells us the disparity in angle between the two images. Note that this will usually highlight the boundaries of objects, as the faces often have near constant intensity. Alternatively, one can wait until objects have been identified in each

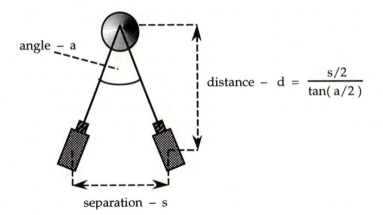

$$\text{distance} - d = \frac{s/2}{\tan(a/2)}$$

Figure 8.34 Triangulation.

image and then match the objects. The low-level approach has the advantage that the information from both images can be used for subsequent analysis. For example, parallax can allow us to label lines ready for Waltz's algorithm and, indeed, is a very good edge indicator in its own right.

8.8.2 Moving pictures

Recall that we listed three types of movement: objects may move in the scene, the camera may pan or zoom, and the camera may be mounted on a moving vehicle. These all lead to similar but slightly different effects. For example, an object moving towards the camera will have a similar effect to zooming the camera, or moving the camera closer to the object. Of course, several or all of the above effects may occur and we may even have stereo cameras and multiple sensors! To simplify the discussion, we will consider principally the case of a single stationary camera.

One special advantage of a stationary camera is that it may be possible to calibrate the camera when the scene is "empty". For example, if the camera is used for surveillance in an airport departure lounge, we can take an image when the lounge is empty. This will contain the fixed furniture, pillars, and so on. Then, when we look at an image of the lounge in use, we will be able to match it with the fixed image, and so identify the additional objects. In fact, it is not quite so easy! Changes in lighting levels, or indeed automatic level control in the camera, mean that one has to perform some adjustment to remove the fixed background.

Whether or not one has removed part of the image, some parts of the image change more rapidly than others. It is these regions of change that correspond to the moving objects. As with stereo vision, one can use local correlation to determine where groups of pixels in the image correspond to the same feature. However, with stereo vision we need only look for change in one direction, parallel to the separation of the "eyes". In contrast, the objects may move in any direction. Furthermore, when an object gets closer or further away, the edges of the object move in different directions as the image of the object expands or contracts. Note also that we can usually only calculate the direction of movement orthogonal to the edge. Any movement parallel to the edge is (at least locally) invisible. Again, in the stereo case, this is only a problem where a long flat object is being viewed.

This all sounds quite complicated. Happily some things are easier! Because we have many images in sequence we can trace known objects. That is, once we have identified an object moving in a particular direction, we have a pretty good idea where to find it in the next image.

It is worth noting for both moving images and stereo vision the magnitude of change that is likely between images. Imagine we are tracking someone walking across the airport lounge. Assume that the person is 10 metres from the camera and walking at a brisk 1.5 m/s. At 15 frames per second the person will move through an angle of 0.01 of a radian (about half a degree) between frames. If the camera has a 60° viewing angle and we are capturing it at a resolution of 512×512 pixels, the person will move five pixels between frames. So, we have to do comparisons at one, two, three, four and five pixel offsets to be able to detect such movements – calculated all over the image 15 times per second! Even then, what about someone moving closer to the camera? Clearly, one has to design the algorithms carefully in order to save some of this work.

8.9 Summary

The processing in a typical computer vision system consists of several phases:

- digitization and signal processing

- edge and region detection

- object recognition

- image understanding

Not all will be present in any one system, as often acceptable results may be obtained with less levels of processing.

The raw image is usually digitized into pixels and may often be thresholded to give a simple black and white image. The image may be affected by noise. Digital filters can be used to smooth the image, which reduces noise, but can also blur edges. Different filters, including Robert's, Sobel's and the Laplacian, can be used to emphasize edges. Large digital filters can be expensive to apply, and so the simplest filter that gives acceptable results is used.

Having identified potential edge pixels, an edge-following algorithm must be used to collect them into lines. Some pixels may at this stage be discarded as noise if they fail to fit into any line. Alternatively, similar pixels can be collected together to form regions. Representing regions can use a lot of space, and quad-trees are one way of efficiently storing regions.

Waltz's algorithm labels edges and vertices in a consistent manner, allowing lines to be built up into objects. However, some images are difficult to label unambiguously, or may have one object split by an occluding object. Additional knowledge such as the use of shadows can help to resolve such ambiguity.

Identifying objects can be difficult because objects may be partly occluded, viewed at different angles or be in different positions from their templates. Techniques based on fuzzy matching of bitmaps, including the use of neural networks, can identify partially obscured objects, and the use of an object-centred co-ordinate system can help to reduce the effects of positioning. In some situations crude identification based on summary statistics may be sufficient. For more complex shapes matching of edges can be used to accommodate different viewing angles, but for paths without obvious vertices, such as handwriting, warping must be used to allow matching.

Multiple images from moving cameras or stereo vision can be used to obtain more information, but can involve more processing time. Stereo vision can be used to calculate the relative distance of objects. Also, by tracking objects between frames of a moving image the object's speed can be calculated.

8.10 Exercises

1. Take the digitized image in Figure 8.2(i). Threshold it at each of the following levels: 1, 5 and 8. Record your results on squared or graph paper, marking each square that exceeds the threshold. In fact, the threshold values above are not random. What does the picture look like thresholded at 6?

2. Again using Figure 8.2(i), apply Sobel's operator and then, choosing an appropriate threshold plot, draw the results.

3. Filters often lose information. To see this experiment with any popular image manipulation application such as Adobe Photoshop. These allow you to apply different kinds of smoothing and sharpening filters to captured images. Unfortunately you are not usually told the exact mathematical filter being applied, but they can give you a good feel for the possibilities of filtering. Compare the results of different filters. Try repeatedly applying smoothing and then sharpening filters to the same image.

4. Apply Waltz's algorithm to the image in Figure 8.35(i). Does it give the labelling you would expect? What happens if you apply Waltz's algorithm to Figure 8.35(ii). Do you have any problems interpreting it?

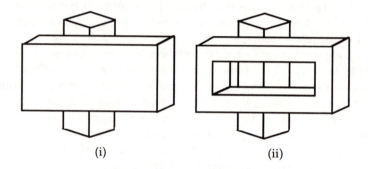

(i)   (ii)

Figure 8.35 For exercise 4.

8.11 Recommended further reading

Fairhurst, M. C. 1988. *Computer vision for robotic systems: an introduction.* Hemel Hempstead: Prentice Hall.

A relatively simple treatment of the subject, giving details of all the main approaches.

Vernon, D. 1991. *Machine vision: automated visual inspection and robot vision.* Hemel Hempstead: Prentice Hall.

A more comprehensive text than the above which includes a case study of robot manipulation.

Nalwa, V. S. 1993. *A guided tour of computer vision.* Reading, Mass.: Addison Wesley.

Another useful text on general computer vision. Features a series of well annotated illustrations which provide a self-contained summary of the subject.

Winston, P. (ed.) 1975. *The psychology of vision.* New York: McGraw-Hill.

A collection of classic papers on early research in computer vision and image understanding.

Chapter Nine

Planning and robotics

9.1 Overview

In order to act in the world, we need to plan what to do. The same is true for computers and robots. Planning has long been an important part of artificial intelligence, and this chapter initially looks at two main aspects: planning actions and planning movements. Planning usually involves manipulating a model of the world in order to decide what actions will bring about the desired effects. However, in the real world we cannot model all the outcomes of our actions, either because the world is too complex, or because of external events over which we have no control, or both. We have already seen aspects of this when discussing games. Local planning deals with those situations where we can only plan so far ahead, but must then respond to the circumstances we observe and the events that occur. In the next chapter we will look at software agents that act in the electronic world where planning is also necessary. However, designing robots that act in the physical world means we have to live within the limitations of reality. We will discuss some of the implications of this for cybernetics research and industrial robotics.

9.2 Introduction

9.2.1 Friend or foe?

Robots have intrigued people since before the word existed. Plans were produced for clockwork and steam-powered men, and moving manikins and automata adorn both fairgrounds and cathedral clock towers. The word "robot" means worker and indeed they have become a major part of modern factory production.

However, popular images of robots are not so prosaic. Humanoid robots hold a particular fascination, with the promise of tireless service and even, like Data in *Star trek* or R2D2 in *Star wars*, friendship. However, there is a dark side as well, and in science fiction robots are often the mortal enemy of humankind (with the added *frisson* of not being mortal!). It is interesting to note that the most dreaded enemies have been those that are only partly robot: Mary Shelley's Frankenstein was constructed from dead flesh and the Daleks have something slimy within. Strangely enough, artificial life (albeit all virtual) has become a respectable area of AI!

For the foreseeable future there is little danger from malevolent robots (although much research in robotics has military funding); accidents and misadventure are far more likely. Isaac Asimov foresaw this with his Laws of Robotics, setting limits on robots' freedom to act. Although real-life robots do not wield ray guns, they often have lasers, and an encounter with a ton of industrial robot, whether "armed" or not, could be unfortunate. In fact, it is likely that the less intelligent the robot, the greater the danger – it will not be able to tell the difference between drilling a hole in an engine block or in your head!

9.2.2   Different kinds of robots

The simplest industrial robots obey a preprogrammed sequence of commands. They have no intelligence whatsoever – although AI might be used in planning their movements. An example of this is spray painting of cars. An operator initially trains the robot by moving an instrumented robot arm to perform the task. The movements are recorded and then the production line robot repeats the movements indefinitely – rote learning. The lack of intelligence becomes obvious when there is any change in the circumstances. If there is a gap in the production line, the robot will happily spray thin air! Although such robots do not include any intelligence, they are very important in industrial applications.

A slightly more complex example would be a drilling machine. The machine needs to detect when a drill bit breaks in order to report the damage to a human operator (as there may be a part-drilled hole, or a piece of drill bit left on the work piece), and load a new bit. This behaviour is pre-programmed, but may involve some planning – perhaps using a different drilling machine when one goes offline.

Finally, we get to robots where the need for AI is obvious. These may be stationary: for example, on a production line where parts come in different orientations (vision needed), perhaps piled on top of one another, and the robot needs to select parts to assemble. Alternatively, they may need to move around in their environment: for example, an automated forklift moving things around a factory.

9.3 Global planning

9.3.1 Planning actions – means–ends analysis

When we have considered state space search with moves between states, we have simply assumed that there is some oracle that gives us the set of possible moves from a given state. In fact, many problems are far more structured than that.

One general class of problems can be attacked by a technique called means–ends analysis. This is based on operators that transform the state of the world. Given a description of the desired state of the world (the end) it works backwards working out operators that will achieve it (the means). This is not done as a single step, but instead works incrementally: in order to apply operators which would achieve the goal state, conditions must apply to the previous state and so the algorithm is applied recursively. Note that this is a special sort of *knowledge-rich search* as discussed in Chapter 3.

States are described in some structured way (for example, by predicates) and moves are performed by the operators. Each operator has a precondition, which constrains the states it can be used in, and a postcondition, which says what will be true when it has finished. In a state described by predicates the postcondition must say both what is additionally true and what ceases to be true in the new state.

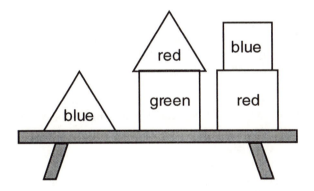

Figure 9.1 Blocks world.

As an example, consider a blocks world similar to that used as the domain of the historic natural language AI program SHRDLU (Winograd 1972). This world consists of blocks of different shapes and colours, which can be piled on top of one another or placed on a table top. An imaginary robot inhabits this world and can pick up and move blocks to try and get to any desired state. The states can be displayed graphically (Fig. 9.1) or described using predicates. Our world has two kinds of shapes, pyramids and boxes, in various colours.

operation	precondition	postcondition
pick_up(A)	on_table(A) $\wedge \neg$ on_top(C,A) $\wedge \neg$ in_hand(X)	in_hand(A) $\wedge \neg$ on_table(A)
put_down(A)	in_hand(A)	on_table(A) $\wedge \neg$ in_hand(A)
pick_off(A,B)	on_top(A,B) $\wedge \neg$ on_top(C,A) $\wedge \neg in\_hand(X)$	in_hand(A) $\wedge \neg$ on_top(A,B)
put_on(A,B)	in_hand(A) $\wedge \neg$ on_top(C,B)	on_top(A,B) $\wedge \neg$ in_hand(A)

Table 9.1 Blocks world operations.

on_table(blue_pyramid)
on_top(red_pyramid,green_box)
on_top(blue_box,red_box)
on_table(green_box)
on_table(red_box)

The predicate "on_top(A,B)" says that block A is on top of block B and "on_table(A)" is self-explanatory. We also require another predicate "in_hand(A)" which says that A is in the robot's (single) hand. There are four operators with the pre- and postconditions shown in Table 9.1.

As an example, we can read the first rule as saying:

> In order to pick up the block A, it must be on the table, must have nothing on top of it and there must be nothing in the robot's hand.

> When it has been picked up, the block A is in the robot's hand and no longer on the table.

Notice how the first operator (pick_up(A)) makes some things true that weren't before (in_hand(A)), and some things false that were previously true (on_table(A)). These are called the add list and the delete list respectively.

In order to simplify the rules, there are two operators to pick things up, one to pick up things from the table "pick_up" and one from other blocks "pick_off".

Now imagine that our goal is to have a pile on the table consisting of the blue triangle on top of the red box. We don't care about any of the other blocks:

on_top(blue_triangle,red_box) $\wedge$ on_table(red_box)

Now the operator information could be used to do a simple depth or breadth first search for this goal state. From the start state we could generate all operators whose precondition was true of the current state, and then search the children in the manner determined by the search. However, this does not effectively use the structural knowledge in this representation. For example, we would examine useless moves like moving the red triangle off the green box.

Means–ends analysis does use this knowledge. It looks at the current state and the goal state and works out the difference between them – not just a numeric measure of distance as used in heuristic search, but an analysis of which things need to be changed. Consider the current state. We see that "on_table(red_box)" is already true, so the difference from the goal state is

on_top(blue_triangle,red_box)

We can then match this difference against the postconditions and look for an operator that reduces the difference. In the example this can be achieved by "put_on(blue_triangle,red_box)". We check its preconditions against the current state. Unfortunately, they are not met. So we make these preconditions a new goal state, calculate the difference and look for a new operator.

This movement from the goal state towards the current state is called *backward chaining*. In this example, it is more efficient than moving from the current state to the goal (*forward chaining*), as the forward branching factor is much larger than the backward branching factor.

If we look at the next stage in this means–ends analysis, we find there are two terms in the new goal state:

in_hand(blue_triangle) $\land \neg$ on_top(C,red_box)

We can either work on both simultaneously or instead work out a way to get to each part separately. For example, we could first work out a way to achieve "in_hand(blue_triangle)":

pick_up(blue_triangle)

and then seek to achieve "$\neg$ on_top(C,red_box)" by

pick_off(blue_box,red_box)

Unfortunately in this case we cannot simply combine these plans, as they interfere with one another. This will not always be the case, and splitting up a problem into subproblems (divide and conquer) is a powerful solution technique. Even where interference is found, it is often more efficient to produce two interfering subplans and then modify them than to work on the whole problem at once.

The process of finding a single sequence of operators that follow one after the other is called *linear planning*. In contrast, *nonlinear planning* builds a partially ordered collection of actions. The actions are each application of operators, and dependencies are recorded between actions. This reduces the amount of *backtracking* required while searching for a plan. However, in the end even nonlinear plans must be reduced to a linear sequence of operators to be performed. This is done by finding a linear ordering that is consistent with the dependencies in the plan.

207

9.3.2   Planning routes – configuration spaces

Suppose the little triangular robot in Figure 9.2(i) wants to get across the room from the place marked start to the one marked finish.   In the room are two obstacles. A straight-line path between the two points will not work – the robot will collide with the obstacles.   One cannot simply find a line that avoids the obstacles because the robot is wide and may not be able to squeeze through every gap. When we plan a path through the obstacles, we must take into account the size and shape of the robot at each point. This makes the planning task quite difficult.

One way to tackle this is using a configuration space. Recall how in Chapter 1 we saw how a change in representation can make a hard problem easier. The configuration space is just such a change of representation. Each object is expanded so that we can regard the robot as a single point and then we can find a simple path across the room.

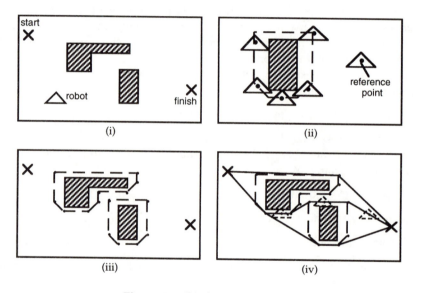

Figure 9.2 Configuration space.

Figure 9.2 shows the stages of route planning using a configuration space. First, a reference point is chosen on the robot (ii). We then imagine moving the robot around each object tracing the path of the reference point. This is shown for a single object in (ii). We then regard these paths as being the boundaries of the expanded objects (iii), and plan a path past these. The shortest path must graze past some of the objects and hence must pass through a series of vertices of the expanded objects. Three such routes are shown in (iv) and some search algorithm, such as A* (Ch. 3), can be used to select the shortest route.

The above algorithm depends on the robot maintaining its orientation. This can lead to it being both optimistic and pessimistic in its chosen paths. We all know that twisting an object round can make it easier to get through an opening. However, some robots may only be able to move forwards. The configuration space solution might include the robot moving sideways, crab-like, and so be impossible. The first problem, finding out whether some combination of movements and rotations can get an object past obstacles, is very difficult. However, we can tackle the second by modifying the configuration space.

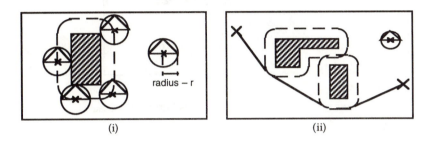

(i)   (ii)

Figure 9.3 Circle-based configuration space.

In Figure 9.3, we see a configuration space based on a circumscribed circle drawn around the robot. The centre of the circle has been chosen so as to make it as small as possible. If the robot can only turn about a particular point, then this should be chosen instead. The circle is then used to generate the expanded obstacles and new paths can be chosen round these. One of these paths is drawn in (ii). Notice how the path between the two objects is not possible in this configuration space. This is because the gap was wide enough for the triangle to navigate sideways, but not point first. The circle-based space is conservative. If you find a path through it, you can definitely do it, but it may disallow some paths that are possible. For example, if the robot were long and narrow, like a truck, it would say that corridors (roads) need to be as wide as the length of the truck!

One way to get round this is to examine the paths based on circles and those based on unexpanded objects. The former is very pessimistic, the latter optimistic. If a promising path exists in the latter, but not the former, one can use more sophisticated methods to check whether the route is possible or not given the particular movements available to the robot.

A similar approach is to generate possible paths based on the narrowest points between obstacles; that is, to concentrate on the gaps rather than the obstructions. Some of these gaps will be so small that they can't possibly be navigated: they can effectively be "filled in" and ignored. Other gaps will be narrow enough that care is needed (say, narrower than the diameter of the circumscribed circle). Finally, some gaps will be so large that they can be considered as rooms – large

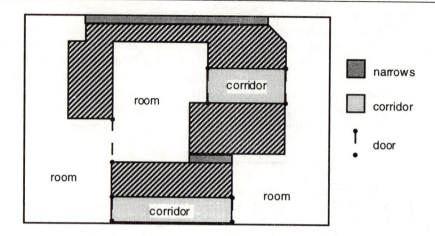

Figure 9.4 Corridors and rooms between obstacles.

enough that free movement is possible. The meetings between these gaps can be thought of as doors between the corridors and rooms. Possible routes criss-cross the rooms going from door to door. One can work out which are navigable and which turns are possible and then use a search algorithm to choose a route. This has the advantage that paths can be constructed to run as far as possible from obstacles and so avoid near misses. It also means that we can use different heuristics for navigating across rooms and down corridors (Fig. 9.4).

9.4 Local planning

9.4.1 Local planning and obstacle avoidance

Get up and walk across the room. Did you use one of the algorithms above? Probably not! Your behaviour will be more like the following:

- Determine approximate direction to take.

- Walk in that direction.

- If an obstacle is encountered walk around it.

Notice how this sort of route planning has two phases: global planning – when you determine the approximate route – and local planning – overcoming obstacles as they occur. The same sort of thing happens at other levels. If you are planning a mountain walk you may plan the route using maps and guides, but you still have to watch where you are going.

In real life, one does not preplan all one's activities. Instead there is a hierarchy of plans at different levels ranging from overall goals of life to automatic reactions. The global level of planning has to know what is reasonable to expect at the local level, but does not have to plan the low-level details. However, there has to be some sort of monitoring to revise global plans should problems occur at the lower level. For example, when hill walking you might find that a path has been washed away and have to replan your route to avoid the unforeseen obstacle.

Planning at multiple levels has computational advantages (several small problems rather than one large one) and is also far more flexible, especially if the environment changes. It is not only useful in route finding, but also in other problems such as assembly tasks.

One way to handle local planning is to give a robot a desired direction of travel, and a set of avoidance rules for obstacles. For example, a rule could be:

1. where possible move towards target
2. if you encounter an obstacle:
    2.1. move back 1 unit
    2.2. move sideways for 5 units
    2.3. resume preferred direction

By "back" and "sideways" we mean that the robot determines (with sensors) in which direction the obstructing object lies and moves first directly away from it (back) and then at 90° to it (sideways). Such a path is illustrated in Figure 9.5.

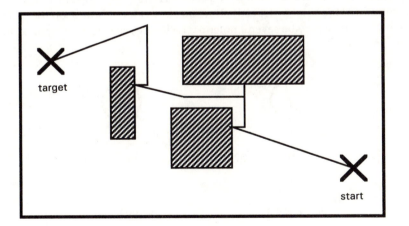

Figure 9.5 Local planning to avoid obstacles.

Notice how this algorithm could get stuck in a deep alcove. If it entered an alcove (concavity) the backward movement at step 2.1 might not be enough to get it out, and so the robot would never escape. It is precisely this behaviour that would have to be detected in order to restart global planning.

In the above example, the robot only noticed the obstacle when it hit it. This may be sufficient in some applications, but more generally some remote sensing would be employed, perhaps vision or sonar. This is particularly important if the obstacles are not stationary. It is no good avoiding a bus after it has hit you! In fact, local avoidance algorithms can be adapted quite easily to handle moving objects. The exact form of the algorithm will depend on the sensors available. Let's assume that the robot can detect objects that are within a certain distance of it and can determine their speed and direction. An avoidance algorithm could be:

1. where possible move towards target
2. when an object is detected and a collision is imminent
    2.1 either (i) move directly away from it (escaping)
         or   (ii) move normal to it (dodging)
    2.2 when the collision has been avoided resume preferred direction

First of all, when an object is detected the robot must determine whether a collision is likely. This depends on the velocity of the object and the current velocity of the robot. It may be that the object will not cross the robot's path, or that the robot can move in front of the object before the object arrives. One way to perform this calculation is to use configuration space techniques to expand the object, and then to subtract the two velocities to give the velocity of the robot relative to the object. If the line in the direction of the relative velocity meets the expanded object then a collision would occur. The distance to the meeting and the magnitude of the velocity (speed) allow one to work out how soon the collision will occur. There may be several potential collisions, so rule 2.1 is applied to the most imminent.

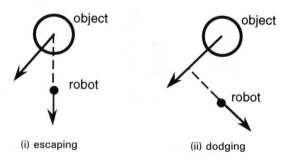

Figure 9.6 Avoiding moving objects.

At step 2.1, two alternative avoidance mechanisms are suggested. These are illustrated in Figure 9.6. The first tries to get away from the oncoming object as fast as possible. It may not be optimal but it is generally a good approximation to the fastest escape. The second is less drastic: avoiding the path of the oncoming object rather than running away. The second is more like stepping back onto the pavement when you see a bus coming rather than running down the road in front of it. It is suggested (Arkin et al. 1993) that (i) is better when a collision is imminent whereas (ii) is better when the collision is some way off (and hence one has more time to avoid it).

Notice how these local algorithms are all more approximate than the global ones (which themselves were inexact). They are reactive and rely on heuristics rather than using prepared plans based on models of the world. The local algorithms must typically execute in real time; hence the need for simplicity. Also these vague algorithms are more likely to be robust when the assumptions they are based on are violated.

9.4.2 Finding out about the world

Global planning algorithms depend on a model of the world. Local algorithms do not build a global model, but they react to local information. However, consider what happens when the local algorithm reaches an impasse, say if the robot enters an alcove. At this stage some more model-based planning is again required. However, it must make use of the additional information gained during the robot's movements. Thus we see that the robot's model of the world is not static but changes as it encounters and senses the environment. This sensing could be deliberate (looking around), or a side effect of locally planned movement.

The robot's knowledge of the world grows as it senses, but is constantly getting out of date. Things move or change and so objects sensed some time ago may not be where they were or even exist at all. The model is therefore uncertain as well as incomplete. We can see these two processes are constantly working against one another: knowledge increases through sensing and decays through ageing.

In Figure 9.7 we see these processes in action. The robot in (i) initially can only see the two moving spheres and the cubes. Its model of the world in (ii) is thus incomplete. The robot then rotates to its right and the cone comes into view. The robot's model of the world is updated accordingly. However, the spheres are moving and so a few moments later the situation is as depicted in (iv). Both spheres have moved and hence the robot's model of the world is now incorrect. Furthermore, one of the spheres has just moved into the robot's range of vision. Is it the same sphere as before?

Obviously the robot's model of the world must include not only the objects' positions, but also their speeds and some estimate as to whether these are likely to stay constant. If watching a game of snooker, the table is likely to stay where it is, the balls will keep moving in the same direction until they hit something, but the players may change their positions and speeds erratically. For a mobile factory floor robot, information about the floor layout and other fixtures (shelves, etc.) can

213

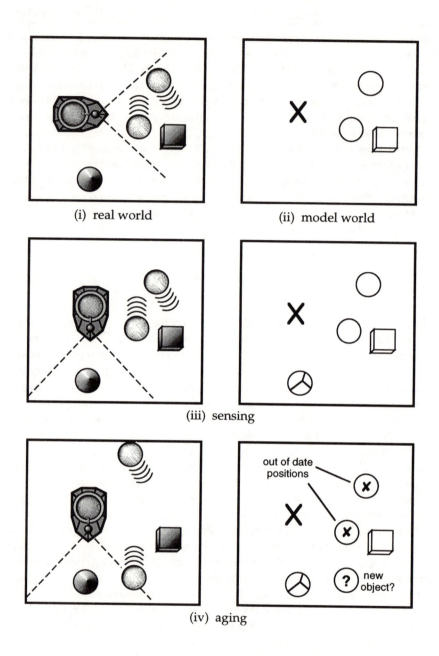

(i) real world

(ii) model world

(iii) sensing

(iv) aging

out of date
positions

new
object?

Figure 9.7 The real world and the model world

be explicitly given and amended when necessary. However, other environments are less predictable. One use of robots is in hazardous environments, perhaps after some nuclear or chemical accident. In such a situation, floor plans are at best tentative: walls or even the floor itself may have collapsed!

The representation within the robot's memory is clearly far more complex than when the environment is fixed and known. The exact choice of representation will depend on a variety of factors, not only the internal AI-related ones (reasoning style, search algorithms, etc.), but also external factors (the types of objects in the environment, the nature and accuracy of sensors). However, we can consider two broad classes of representation: historical and current state.

A historical representation will keep track of what has been observed and when, together with the accuracy of the sensor. At any moment, the robot can estimate the current positions of any objects based on their known past locations. For example, the model of the world at step (iv) in Figure 9.7 could be represented:

time	object id	type	position		velocity	
			(x,y)	error	(x,y)	error
1	#317	ball	(3.3,3.2)	0.1	(−0.5,1.0)	0.2
1	#318	ball	(2.8,2.0)	0.1	(0,−0.5)	0.2
1	#319	box	(3.7,1.7)	0.1	—	0.0
2	#320	cone	(1.5,0.5)	0.1	(0,0)	0.2
3	#321	ball	(2.7,0.7)	0.1	(0.1,−0.8)	0.2

Notice how the position and velocity of each object have accuracy measures. In this case, the error in velocity is greater for most objects, presumably because the sensor is less accurate at measuring velocity. Both the box and the cone have a measured velocity of zero, but the box's error figure for velocity is zero because (in this environment) it is known that boxes never move, whereas the cone is a potentially mobile object that just happens to be (sensed as) stationary.

In the alternative, current state, representation, the robot would keep similar information, but at each time step, it would update the current position of each object based on its last known velocity.

For example, at time 2, the state of ball #318 would be recorded as

object id	type	position		velocity	
		(x,y)	error	(x,y)	error
#318	ball	(2.8,1.5)	0.3	(0,−0.5)	0.2

See how the position of the object has been updated by adding the velocity. However, its error figure has also been increased as the velocity itself is uncertain. Notice that the representation does not keep track of the time the object was observed. This is unnecessary as the passage of time is recorded implicitly in the updated position. The updates in estimated position and velocity might be more complicated. For example, some objects (such as people or other robots) are likely to change velocity spontaneously and for such objects the uncertainty in velocity would increase accordingly.

With the historical representation, one is never committed permanently to an interpretation of the evidence. If at time 3 the robot decided that balls #318 and #321 were the same object, it could still change its mind when at time 4 another ball (even more similar to #318) appeared in view. In contrast, a single model of the world constantly commits the robot to particular interpretations. Once it had decided that the new ball was the same as #318, it would simply update ball #318's position and velocity to reflect the new observation. All memory of the original two observations would be lost.

However, the historical representation is very inefficient. It requires the robot constantly to recalculate the same projections from past data. Also, at some point it will need to forget past observations. The current state representation has some pruning problems – it can't track every object it has ever seen, but is clearly far easier and more efficient to manage.

In practice, a system might involve a combination of a model of the current state for rapid real-time response together with some limited historical information in case it needs to reconsider past judgements. What about you? Which representation do you use as you walk in a busy street or drive a car?

9.5 Limbs, legs and eyes

We have discussed how robots plan how to perform tasks involving picking up and moving objects, how they plan how to move about in the world and how they look at different parts of the world in order to build up their knowledge. Each of these activities involves the control of physical transponders and sensors. The construction of these is a significant engineering problem, especially where the robot is expected to operate in a hostile environment. However, this is general robotics and beyond AI, so we will just consider the issues of control.

9.5.1 Limb control

Consider a simple robot arm as illustrated in Figure 9.8. This has three main degrees of freedom: the arm is mounted on a rotating section of the robot which can be set to any angle θ, the arm can move up and down by an angle ϕ, and can extend by moving the smaller cylinder in and out of the larger by a distance b. In addition, the "hand" at the end can open and close. Other important dimensions are marked on the diagram: the radius of the centre section r, the length of the unextended arm a and the height h of the centre section from the floor.

In order to pick up an object we need to move it to a particular position in space. We can calculate the co-ordinates of the end of the arm using trigonometry:

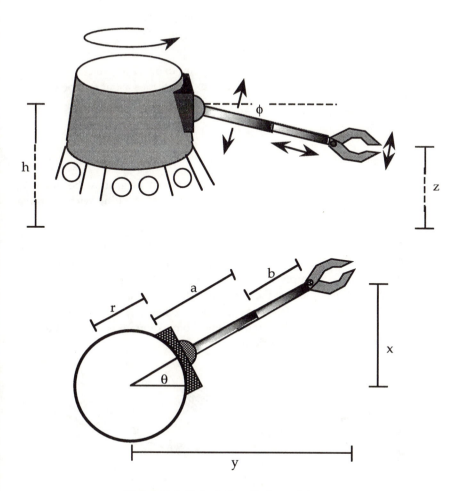

Figure 9.8 Calculating limb positions.

$$\begin{aligned}
x &= [r + (a + b)\cos\phi]\sin\theta \\
y &= [r + (a + b)\cos\phi]\cos\theta \\
z &= h + (a + b)\sin\phi
\end{aligned}$$

Thus, if we have a particular position we want to move to, we can solve these equations to find the right values of θ, ϕ and b. This is messy but not too difficult:

$$\begin{aligned}
\theta &= \arctan(x/y) \\
\phi &= \arctan[(z - h)/(\sqrt{x^2 + y^2} - r)] \\
b &= \sqrt{(\sqrt{x^2 + y^2} - r)^2 + (z - h)^2} - a
\end{aligned}$$

Unfortunately, it gets worse. This is the very simplest an arm can be; you need at least three degrees of freedom to have any chance of reaching within a three-dimensional world. In addition, one often needs some control of the orientation of the hand at the end – some kind of wrist. Let's assume we add some more movement at the wrist. Say we want to pick up a suitcase. The hand must be pointing directly down and opened so that the "fingers" close on the handle. However, it is no good simply turning the wrist at 90° to the arm. We need to take into account the angle ϕ of the arm. Also, the robot on which this diagram is based has two arms, offset from one another (see Fig. 9.9), each with a full ball joint instead of just up and down movement. To make matters worse, the robot will move about and change its orientation.

Figure 9.9 Robot with two limbs.

Working out the final position and orientation of the hand, given all these movements, is a nightmare. Reversing the process to work out the desired movements to get to any position is even worse! The problem can be simplified by breaking the process down into steps using different co-ordinate systems. You start with a position in the world's co-ordinate system. You then take into account the position and orientation of the robot to work out the desired position relative to the robot. If the robot has several joints, you translate the position into co-ordinates relative to each joint in turn, eventually getting the position relative to the hand. Similarly, you can reverse the process to work out the position of the hand in the world. There are special languages for programming industrial robots that include particular constructs for moving between different co-ordinate systems.

Translation between co-ordinate systems does not solve the problem entirely. The equations for calculating the relevant joint angles and extensions for any desired position are still complicated. However, even if one solves the equations exactly the results may not be perfect. Joints have play in them, limbs may flex under strain. When people pick things up, they rely not so much on accurate calculation, but on feedback. We are constantly monitoring and correcting our behaviour. Preplanning everything is called open-loop control, whereas relying on feedback is called closed-loop control. If the environment is very controlled and predictable, say on some production line robots, open-loop control can be effective. However, in general, closed-loop control is far more robust.

For a robot, there are two kinds of feedback: local feedback on a particular joint, which can be used to ensure that the joint is positioned as you want; and global feedback, perhaps through visual sensors, of the relative position of the hand and the target. Local feedback is effectively giving you a more accurate and reliable motor, so does not dramatically affect the style of planning. Global feedback, however, allows more goal-directed behaviour. It is often easier to solve the reverse equations for small movements, and so one can incrementally move the hand towards the desired position.

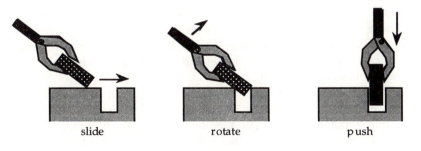

slide   rotate   push

Figure 9.10 Compliant motion.

Of special importance is the pressure feedback when the hand grasps an object or when a held object is being placed. Imagine picking up an egg without such feedback! If such sensors are too expensive, or impractical because of the environment, the robot's hands must be padded or sprung to avoid damage to itself or the work piece. Effective use of this feedback can make positioning of objects far easier. For example, to place a peg in a hole, one can push the peg along the surface until it catches in the hole (see Fig. 9.10), and then rotate it until it slides in. Without pressure feedback the robot would gouge the peg into the surface! This use of feedback to allow things to be naturally slid into place is called compliant motion.

9.5.2 Walking – on one, two or more legs

The robot featured in Figures 9.7 –9.9 moves around skimming the ground using electrostatic levitation. Other robots use wheels or tracks. However, all have a distinct problem with stairs and there has long been an interest in various designs of robots with legs. Pragmatically, this allows the robot to manage in very rough terrain, but also the study of robots with large numbers of legs has given some insight into the way lower animals function. One can identify four styles of robot by counting legs:

one leg – good for trying out ideas but not very practical

two legs – for humanoid robots and animations

four to eight – practical robots for difficult terrain

lots of legs – study of lower animals and distributed control

The earliest attempts at walking robots used detailed physical models of the robots' dynamics. If one knows the masses of all the components that make up the robot and can control the forces that it exerts on the floor, then it is possible to predict how a particular movement of the legs will move the robot as a whole, and hence work out which forces on which joints will make the robot walk in a particular direction. Of course, as in the case of limbs, this involves co-ordinate translations based on all the joint angles and lots of trigonometry.

The robots usually fell over.

In fact humans fall over too, but we are expecting it and can catch ourselves before we go too far. Indeed, one way of thinking about walking is that you are constantly standing on one leg and falling over in the right direction, and then moving the other leg forward to catch yourself before you fall too far. This form of reactive movement is based again on feedback and closed-loop control and is thus far more robust than the use of detailed dynamic models.

The trouble is that even if a model is entirely accurate it is expensive to calculate in real time (if you don't do the calculations fast enough you fall over!) and is difficult to adapt to changing circumstances. Consider what happens when you pick up a heavy object, move your arms so that your centre of gravity moves, or walk out of a building into a high wind. In each case, the dynamics of your body have changed which, for a model, would require extensive recalculations.

In contrast, reactive motion is based on fuzzy rules. For example, some of the rules for standing still might be:

- if you are falling forwards slowly push down on the front of your feet

- if you are falling sideways take a step in the relevant direction.

The rules are not designed to stop you from moving at all (equilibrium), but to keep you constantly moving back towards the desired position (homeostasis).

Detailed physical models still have a part to play in robotic movement. Building robots is expensive and time consuming. Furthermore, trying out new control algorithms on possibly fragile experimental robots is not to be recommended. A detailed model of a robot's dynamics can be used to simulate different designs of robot and the effects of different control algorithms. Indeed, sometimes the simulation is all that is required, and at Georgia Tech's Multimedia Technology Lab such simulations are being used to generate figures for lifelike animations (Hodgins et al. 1995).

9.5.3 Active vision

Computer vision is discussed in detail in Chapter 8. However, the discussion focused on algorithms to interpret an image or set of images that were presented to them – a *fait accompli*. However, where the camera or cameras are fitted on a moving robot, the movements can be planned deliberately to aid the vision process, for example to peek around corners. Similarly, even when cameras are fixed there may be some control of their direction, zoom and focus.

In Chapter 8 we saw how some scenes were difficult to interpret. In Figure 9.11 we see one such scene. The original image on the left is ambiguous. There is no obvious three-dimensional interpretation of the scene. However, if your camera is moved slightly to the left the resulting image is far more easily understood. The confusing cross-junction in the middle has been resolved into two separate fork junctions.

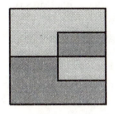
what is it?

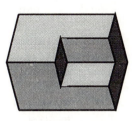
now I see!

Figure 9.11 Resolving ambiguity.

This disambiguation may occur naturally as the result of stereo vision or preprogrammed camera movement, but if the vision system can control the camera, it can deliberately seek the necessary evidence. In fact, Figure 9.11 is rather like those intriguing photographs of everyday objects taken from strange angles. In ordinary life one rarely encounters such effects, as when they occur one automatically moves slightly to obtain a better perspective.

The scenario above used horizontal movement of the camera. Camera heads may allow control over several other degrees of freedom:

- *fixation*: the point at which the camera is "looking"

- *vergence*: the horizontal angle between two cameras in a stereo head, which allows both cameras to fixate on one object

- *cyclotorsion*: the ability to rotate the camera and thus the horizon

- *zoom*: increasing the size of distant images

- *focus*: the distance at which objects are sharp images

- *aperture*: controls the amount of light entering the camera and also the depth of field (what is in focus simultaneously).

All of these can be used to give additional information for image processing, or to make the raw image more easily processed. Controlling the point of fixation allows one to track a moving object, which might otherwise move out of view. This is especially important when it is not easily matched, say a human figure that changes shape as it walks. The angle of vergence when two cameras are fixated on the same object allows easy calculation of distance by triangulation. The matching of objects in the two stereo images is important for this and other stereoscopic effects. However, if the cameras are not perfectly horizontally aligned this can be very difficult. Cyclotorsion allows the cameras to compensate for inaccuracies and any flexing in their supports and so align the horizon in the two images.

The remaining three effects allow one to examine particular objects in detail. Use of zoom can allow one either to scan a large area at low resolution or to examine a particular object in detail, as a small part of the image is spread over all the pixels in the image. Controlling the focus especially allows one to sharpen up the edges in an object of interest, and even obtain an estimate of depth from monocular vision. By adjusting the thresholds for edge detection, the blurred edges will not be registered, hence aiding the separation of an object from its background (called figure–ground separation). This is enhanced if the aperture can be adjusted. Once the object is in focus, the aperture can be opened up to make all other objects more blurred. However, the aperture is probably more important for level control, ensuring that neither too little nor too much light gets to the camera. In many cameras this is automatic, but if the aperture can be controlled by the vision system then it can be adjusted to favour interesting parts of the scene. (NB Our eyes do not allow this degree of high-level control.)

At present, camera heads that allow several or all of these degrees of freedom cost thousands of pounds, and it is not yet clear which of the above effects are most useful.

9.6 Practical robotics

The leading edge of robotics research is designing vehicles that guide themselves over the surface of Mars or micro-robots to travel through human arteries scraping and cleaning, but the majority of robots are far more prosaic. Rather than designing general purpose robots that can operate in unforeseen environments, it is usually better to aim for specific jobs and to control the environment. Indeed, real robots may not look like robots at all. In fact, in the next generation of car electronics the car will drive itself in a skid, and will even be able to steer itself down a road, overtaking where necessary. So you may be inside a robot before you meet one!

9.6.1 Controlling the environment

We have already discussed in Chapter 8 how control of light levels and object positioning can make industrial vision easier and more cost effective. The same applies to other areas of robotics. Suppose you want a robot to move materials around in a warehouse. First of all, you are unlikely to choose a robot with two arms and two legs. A wheeled robot with a forklift is a much more practical arrangement.

What about navigation? A general purpose route planner with sophisticated visual input seems like a neat idea, but why not simply paint white lines on the floor that a trivial image processing system can follow. The only real disadvantage of such a system is that the lines get dirty, but there are various electronic alternatives.

There is a similar tale for manipulation tasks. Just as with manual assembly, a simple redesign of a component may make assembly tasks far easier. For example, consider screwing a bolt into a threaded hole. If the hole is simply drilled into the metal, the screw has to be positioned very accurately in order to ensure it fits properly; a slight inaccuracy to either side will mean that the screw simply spins against the surface of the metal. However, taper the end of the screw slightly and countersink the hole and suddenly the accuracy required reduces dramatically (see Fig. 9.12). Basically, one is designing the system so that *compliant motion* is successful. The greater margin for error means higher reliability and cheaper robots.

There is of course a trade-off between flexibility and economy. It is usually the case that a specialized tool costs less than a general purpose one. But whereas at one stage production lines involved many highly specialized tools, now the move is towards more flexible manufacture. Tools are still specialized, but far more flexible and easily reprogrammed. Successful industrial robotics requires robots that are just general enough to do the range of tasks that they are likely to encounter. However, as more general purpose robots become cheaper and more reliable, the balance of economics may swing even further along the path of generality.

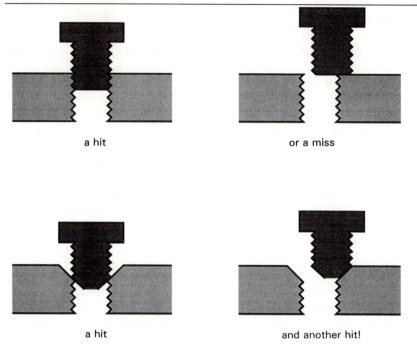

a hit

or a miss

a hit

and another hit!

Figure 9.12 Designing for easy assembly.

9.6.2 Safety and hierarchical control

Industrial robots, like all industrial equipment, are dangerous. They can hurt people, damage their workplace or themselves. However, they act within controlled environments where the issues of safety are at least well established if not universally adhered to. As we begin to consider mobile robots working among other workers, perhaps even in the outside world, the issues of safety become central.

First of all, this re-emphasizes the importance of *feedback* rather than *open-loop control*. Dangerous situations are most likely to arise when the environment changes in an unforeseen way. Furthermore, such situations often require rapid responses; possibly the normal planning cycles may be too slow. We may not even trust the planning totally. As we have seen, the best algorithms usually involve a mixture of heuristics and uncertain reasoning. They do not always guarantee correct behaviour even when programmed correctly, and who really trusts several thousand lines of LISP code!

One solution is to establish a software ring-fence around the normal planning activities. When a dangerous situation is detected a high-level control process takes over and performs some special action. This may be some form of avoidance behaviour or most likely stopping the machine dead. The safety sensors may be based on proximity sensors or based on unexpected resistance to movement. You will almost certainly have encountered such sensors built into lift doors (another robot to get inside of!). The important thing is that the higher levels of control are simple and reliable. We can afford to use clever algorithms at the lower levels so long as we know that we are protected from their malfunction.

9.7 Summary

Real robots do not usually walk about on two legs and fire rayguns. Most are in fixed positions on assembly lines, or moving along marked tracks in warehouses. Many have little "intelligence", but obey preprogrammed actions.

Global planning operates by having a complete model of the world, planning what to do, and only then doing it. Means–ends analysis can be used to plan sequences of actions to achieve a desired end state. This can include knowledge about the positions of objects and physical constraints. Configuration spaces can be used to plan routes where obstacles block the way.

Local planning is more opportunistic. The robot has a general goal, and tries to move towards it reacting to problems as they arise. Routes can be found past obstacles by having a desired direction and then simply changing direction when an obstacle is encountered. Avoidance rules can be added to allow for moving obstacles. While a robot moves about it can find out more about the world (sensing), but also its model of the world may become inaccurate as objects move about (ageing).

Controlling a robot's limbs is not intrinsically difficult, but typically involves a complicated series of translations between co-ordinate systems. Feedback can be used to compensate for slackness and inaccuracy and also allow local planning. It allows closed-loop control, which is more robust than preplanned open-loop control. Pressure feedback is especially useful, as it allows compliant motion to be used to position objects. Many mobile robots use wheels or tracks, but some walk on one, two or more legs. Again, it is usually best not to preplan movements, but instead constantly start to fall over and recover. Active vision uses the movement of the robot or camera adjustments to give more information about a scene and resolve ambiguities.

In practical situations it is often better to design a suitable environment for a simple robot than to use a more complicated one. Simpler robots are usually cheaper, but will be less flexible. Industrial robots can be dangerous and several levels of control may be necessary.

9.8 Exercises

1. Produce an operator table for the Towers of Hanoi problem similar to the blocks world one in Table 9.1. To make it similar to the blocks world think of it as the Tables of Hanoi problem with three tables rather than three towers. Use the same two operations as in Table 9.1, but the "on_table" predicate will have an extra parameter: "on_table(T,R)" where "T" will be a particular table and "R" a ring. You will also need a predicate "bigger_than(R1,R2)" to record which rings are bigger and will have to ensure that you do not put more than one object on top of another.

2. Use your operator table and means–ends analysis to solve the three ring problem given the starting state

   on_table(1,big) ∧ on_top(small,middle) ∧ on_top(middle,big)
   ∧ bigger_than(big,middle) ∧ bigger_than(middle,small)
   ∧ bigger_than(big,small)

   and goal state

   on_table(2,big) ∧ on_top(small,middle) ∧ on_top(middle,big)

3. Consider the shaded rectangle in Figure 9.13. Draw configuration spaces for each of the robot shapes to the right of the rectangle.

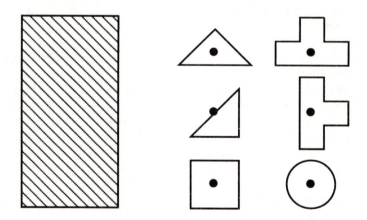

Figure 9.13 For exercise 3.

4. Collect different everyday items, screws, bolts, plugs, lids. Do they exhibit good design for compliant motion – like the screw in the lower illustration of Figure 9.12 or are they more like in the top pictures! (Good class exercise)

9.9 Recommended further reading

A. Newell, A. & H. A. Simon 1963. GPS: a program that simulates human thought. In *Computers and thought*, E. A. Feigenbaum & J. Fieldman (eds), 279–293. New York: McGraw-Hill.

A. Newell, A. & H. A. Simon 1972. *Human problem solving.* Englewood Cliffs, NJ: Prentice-Hall.

GPS, the General Problem Solver, was an early model that used means–ends analysis to emulate aspects of human planning.

Fikes, R. E. & N. J. Nilsson 1971. STRIPS: a new approach to the application of theorem proving to problem solving. *Artificial Intelligence* **2**, 189–208.

STRIPS applied techniques developed in GPS to planning in the blocks world as described in this chapter.

Lozano-Pérez, T. 1983. Spatial planning: a configuration-space approach, *IEEE Transactions on Computers* **71**(7).

Original work on configuration space.

Christensen, H. I., K. W. Bowyer, H. Bunke (eds) 1993. *Active robot vision: camera heads, model based navigation and reactive control.* Singapore: World Scientific.

A collection of articles that deal with both movement (local planning and obstacle avoidance) and vision (the problems and also the leverage that can be obtained by using active vision).

Chapter Ten

Agents

10.1 Overview

In the previous chapter, we considered individual robots planning and acting in the real world. In this chapter, we look at two related areas.

Software agents are autonomous entities that inhabit and act on the electronic world on our behalf. Obviously route planning is not usually necessary for such agents, although they do need some means to choose their actions. The examples we shall consider use a mixture of *ad hoc* rules and machine learning techniques.

In the second half of the chapter, we shall look at what happens when agents (whether electronic or physical) act together. We shall see that they are more than the sum of their parts and can work together to achieve co-operative purposes.

10.2 Software agents

The word robot means worker. As well as working for us in the real world, AI can be used to develop independent entities that work for us in the virtual world of information spaces. These are often called software agents, or simply agents (although the word agent is rather overloaded in AI). These agents can be used to sort your (electronic) mail, perform repetitive tasks, search databases for interesting information, or manage your diary. These are all applications where the agent is "visible" to the user of a system, a sort of helper. The word agent is also often used where a system is split into several co-operating subprograms or agents. We will discuss this case, where the agents are co-operating with one another, in the next section. In this section we'll confine ourselves to agents that interact with and work on behalf of a computer user.

The simplest agents are not really intelligent at all. Imagine you perform the same routine every week to back up your computer files to an optical disk. So, instead of performing the same actions again and again, you write a script that is automatically invoked at the same time each week. This is the simplest kind of software agent. The ability to write such scripts has been around since the earliest operating-system macro languages, and has recently been rediscovered in the world of windowed systems.

In the rest of this section we will consider the reasons for the recent interest in agents and the different sort of events that trigger agents to act. We will then look at email filtering agents, which demonstrate learning, and agents for searching large information spaces.

10.2.1   The rise of the agent

Is the use of the word "agent" just a buzzword or sales gimmick? In fact, there are some recent developments that make the connotations of the word agent appropriate:

– *end-user orientation.* Whereas the writing of scripts in traditional operating systems was confined to the system gurus, the emphasis is now on the ordinary user. The user's control may be exercised using simple scripting languages or by direct demonstration.

– *embodiment.* Most graphical interfaces project a very passive model. The user acts upon objects in the interface. When the application does anything it is as a "tool". However, complex and repetitive tasks do not really fit into this model of the world. It is thus natural to inhabit this virtual world with agents to perform these tasks. Furthermore, to fit within the model-world paradigm, these agents should be visible. So, for example, in Hewlett-Packard's New Wave interface, agents are presented as icons designed to look like a secret agent!

– *lostness.* Most people only use and understand a fraction of the function-ality of a modern application, and even where they know about features it is often far from clear how to combine them to obtain a particular effect. Hence the introduction of the "Wizard" in Microsoft products to guide and help the user. Similar trends can be seen in information spaces. Even traditional hypertexts cause considerable problems and many incorporate various forms of "guide" to show you round. The problem has got far worse with the availability of World Wide Web and other Internet infor-mation sources. There are hundreds of thousands of information sites and countless documents – where do you go to find the information you want? Ask an agent.

– *intelligence.* The scripting languages used for programming agents are now more like natural language (although the same was said of COBOL, which they often resemble!). However, agents are also learning what to do in more intelligent ways. The user may explicitly demonstrate the required behaviour which the agent later copies. Alternatively, the agent may watch the user and learn the user's habits and preferences. It may then use this knowledge when asked to perform a task, or even volunteer help.

Agents that address one or more of these issues are seen by the users of a system to have some level of independence. They are not just part of the system, but act in and on the system on behalf of the user. Where the sense of embodiment is low but aspects of independent activity and/or intelligence are apparent, it is perhaps better to regard the system as exhibiting agency. For example, the wordprocessor being used for this chapter periodically suggests saving the work so far. Another example is in range selection in the Microsoft Excel spreadsheet. When the user invokes the sum operator, the system suggests (in the form of a highlighted selection) the range it thinks the user wants. This is based on simple heuristics, but has the appearance of intelligent behaviour.

10.2.2 Triggering actions

One key difference between a program or macro and an agent is that the former only acts when told to, whereas the latter acts independently. Another way of looking at this is that a program is characterized by *what* it does, whereas an agent is characterized by both *what* it does and *when* it does it.

In addition, because agents have some form of continued existence over time, they usually have a persistent state. Because of the similarities with object-oriented programming, the scripts for actions that an agent performs are often called methods, and the communications between agents are called messages.

A typical life-cycle for an agent will be as follows. It remains in a quiescent state until some event triggers it into action. Depending on the nature of the event it then performs one of its methods. This method will update the internal state of the agent, and also possibly change the state of other things, send messages to other agents or interact with the user.

The event that triggers the method may be caused by various things:

- *user events*. The user may explicitly ask the agent to perform some task. This may result in some instant action on the part of the agent (for example, searching a database), or may simply change the internal state of the agent (for example, setting criteria for sorting incoming mail). Alternatively, the user may engage in some act that the agent is monitoring. For example, an intelligent tutor may notice that a pupil has performed a task in an inefficient or incorrect fashion, and suggest alternatives.

- *system events*. Other events may occur that are not directly caused by the user. For example, email may arrive that the agent sorts into folders. Another example would be where the user has initiated a long-running computation (perhaps compiling a large AI program!). When the computation is finished the agent examines its output, and informs the user if it is not as expected.

- *changes in status*. The agent may constantly monitor parts of the rest of the system and act when certain changes occur. For example, if free disk space falls below a certain level, an agent may compress infrequently used files. In a factory setting, an agent may monitor various processes and warn the operator if the values fall outside acceptable limits.

– *timed events*. The agent may perform repetitive actions at regular intervals or at particular times. For example, an agent may monitor your diary and download necessary files to your laptop computer for the next day's meetings. Timed events may also be used to trigger monitoring activities, such as those discussed under the previous heading. This polling activity should be distinguished from true timed activity.

In addition to triggered actions, an agent may act continuously to gather information. This information may come from the user or from the rest of the system. For example, an agent may monitor the user's interaction with the system and notice frequently repeated actions. Later, when the agent detects the user beginning a complex action sequence, it can offer to complete the task for the user.

10.2.3   Watching and learning

We'll look now at email filtering agents. Studies of the introduction of email into institutions have found that there is little reduction in other forms of communication, but a continued growth in email messages. This is partly because of the ease of replication. The photocopier and the wordprocessor have each made their contribution to junk mail, but neither so effectively as email! It is simply too easy to include a large number of names when sending an email, or to mail to a distribution list of hundreds or thousands of individuals. Sorting the email each morning is now a major task.

Just the job for an agent!

Many email systems now allow the user to set up filters. The email message has specific fields ("To:", "From:", "Subject:", etc.) and the user fills in a template, which is then matched against incoming messages. If the template matches then whatever action the user has specified (say filing the mail in a particular folder) is carried out. For example, a colleague of the authors got fed up with receiving seminar announcements, and so set up a filter to delete all incoming messages that contained the word "seminar". Unfortunately, the agenda of an important meeting included "seminars" as one of its items. The announcement was discarded and the meeting missed!

Filtering may also be carried out by fixed rules. A research email system at Stirling University organized all mail messages into conversations – linked, often branching, streams of messages (Cockburn 1993). If enough people had had compatible mailers these could have been used to ensure that when a message was sent it was added to the appropriate conversation at the recipient's end.

However, email comes from so many disparate sources that this was considered an overrestrictive method. Instead, the system used simple rules to sort incoming messages into conversations. An example rule was

if   the new message (N) is '**From:**' person A
and   the last message (M) sent to person A is in conversation C
then   add N to conversation C linked after message M

There were also rules concerning multiple recipients so that messages from the same person to different distribution lists could be filed successfully. Although the rules were simple they worked most of the time and the cost of a misclassified message was low (it was easy to track all recent messages). Note that this is a general rule – intelligent agents will not always be right, so make sure it doesn't matter when they are wrong.

So, we've seen examples of agents that are told what to do by the user and by the system's designer. A more ambitious kind are those that attempt to work out what to do themselves. Several such agents have been proposed in the literature, but none is yet beyond the experimental stage. The proposed scenario is as follows.

The user interacts with the mail system as normal. Each mail message (or at least its header!) is read and the user performs some action to it, files it in a particular folder, deletes it, or possibly marks it as urgent (if the system supports marking of messages). The agent watches. After a while it has a collection of examples of the form: message$\Rightarrow$action. This is ideal input for machine learning algorithms. The agent can learn patterns in the user's actions and then automatically sort the mail.

Of course, it's not quite that simple! First, it is very important that the user retains a sense of control, especially when the action is to delete a message! There are various ways to achieve this. One way is for the agent to construct filter templates and present these to the user for approval. That is, the job of the learning agent is to simplify the task of creating templates for the agent that does the actual filtering. Another option is for the agent not actually to perform the actions on the messages as they arrive, but simply to add a classification and offer a simple means for the user to accept or reject the agent's offered choice. These issues of control and grace of interaction between agent and user are common to any system that involves learning user actions.

Another problem with learning filtering rules is that the data within email fields are quite complicated. The algorithm needs to be quite knowledgeable about email addresses, since two different addresses may refer to the same person (for example, alan@zeus.hud.ac.uk and A.J.Dix@hud.ac.uk). Also some of the fields may contain lists of addresses or email distribution lists. A simple application of concept learning would give poor results without some of this information being taken into account. Furthermore, the most important information is all in free text fields requiring complex text matching algorithms. These are discussed in the next section.

Although there are difficulties with such agents, the advantages they can bring are clear. It is likely that simple forms of intelligent filtering will be available in mainstream products within the near future.

10.2.4 Searching for information

The amount of information available online is enormous. The problem is finding what you want without wasting time on the even more enormous amount of dross. Agents have been posed as a solution to this problem. The remit of such agents is simple – find interesting information and tell me about it. Satisfying this is less straightforward. Agents can help in three ways:

1. They can **find** where suitable documents are stored.

2. They can **mediate** between the user and different information sources.

3. They can **choose** appropriate documents from a large document set.

The first step is necessary as there are too many information sites to search them all in detail. An agent may find sites by consulting a simple preferences file, perhaps created by hand or built up as a record of sites that the user has visited. A more sophisticated agent may consult a directory of information sites. It will need to match the description of what the sites contain with the interests of the user. This process is similar to the document matching in step 3. Finally, the agent may find sites by following a trail.

Consider a bibliographic search for articles on intelligent agents. The agent looks first at the *Journal of Artificial Intelligence*. It finds some articles of interest (using step 3) and then looks at the articles cited in their reference lists. This will yield potentially interesting articles, but also the journals and conferences where those articles are found are good candidates for searching. A similar process can be followed on the World Wide Web. If you know that a particular document is of interest, the agent can look at the links from that document and search the sites where those documents are found.

Another sort of trail is one based on usage. Suppose that each document server keeps track of who looks at what. Your information agent notices that many of the documents that you read have also been read by another user, so your agent asks the other user's agent about other sites it visits. These are then candidate sites for interesting documents. You are effectively following the other user's path through information space. There are some privacy problems here – it is rather like browsing someone else's bookshelf! However, you can turn the personal element to your advantage: your agent could negotiate with the other user's agent and introduce you – computer dating?

Note that following a trail may lead to both interesting sites and also specific documents.

Once you find an information source you are faced with understanding and navigating a new interface. One of the reasons for the success of the World Wide Web is the common interface to all information. However, this is not shared with other services, and online bibliographic databases are particularly renowned for their obtuse user interfaces. Agents can help you here too. You ask the agent for what you want and it converts this into the required commands for different information services. This is often viewed in terms of multiple agents, one for each type of information service, and these communicate with a single user interface agent. Again, there are problems of control, as online databases often charge quite highly for usage, and it is not clear that an agent, unless very intelligent, can perform as well as an expert user. However, as most users are not experts perhaps this does not matter.

Finally, we have found an information source and can communicate with it, but it contains thousands of documents. How can an agent work out which ones will be of interest? Assume that the agent has access to some collection of documents which you have previously found interesting. One way to use these is to use some form of concept learning and generate a rule for interesting files. This would typically be based on key words or other summary information. For example, the agent might decide that you are interested in all documents with "agent" and "intelligent" in the key word list. However, this sort of precise rule is often not suitable for handling imprecise ideas such as "interesting"; instead more fuzzy forms of matching are often preferred. These are often based on the complete set of words in the abstract of an article or on the whole article itself. The aim is to have some measure of closeness between documents. Then a document is deemed interesting if it is close to one or more of the documents you have previously found interesting. Other measures of similarity may use semantic features of the documents; for example, citations in common for articles, or links between objects in a hypertext.

Let's look at one measure of closeness in detail. Take two documents d_1 and d_2 and generate the complete list of words in each, w_1 and w_2. Let the number of words in each document be n_1 and n_2 and the number that are in both n_{12}. That is, n_1 is the size of w_1 and n_{12} is the size of $w_1 \cap w_2$. Then a measure of *similarity* is

$$similarity(d_1, d_2) = \frac{n_{12}}{n_1 + n_2 - n_{12}}$$

This formula has a value of 1 when the documents have exactly the same words and 0 when they have none in common. Similar, but more complicated, measures take into account various factors. Common words such as "the" and "it" may be ignored or given a low weight in the match; on the other hand, words that occur frequently in both documents may count more highly. Also the word lists may be processed to reduce words to their simplest forms (for example, simplest $\rightarrow$ simple) – called *stemming* – or to equate different words for the same thing using a thesaurus.

235

10.3 Co-operating agents and distributed AI

In the previous section we talked about agents communicating with one another. Also, when we discussed route planning in Chapter 9, we noted that some of the objects one robot might encounter may be other robots. The communication and interaction between agents is an exciting area offering several interrelated benefits:

- Structuring an intelligent system into several communicating but largely independent parts can reduce development costs, increase run-time efficiency and ease maintenance.

- Different parts of the system may reside in physically distinct places. It may be impractical or impossible to perform totally central planning.

- The interactions between agents can give insight into the social interactions between people or between animals. There are also theories of individual cognition which stress the co-operation between semi-independent "agents" within our own minds (Minksy 1985).

The study of interacting intelligent components is called distributed artificial intelligence. When the aim is understanding living creatures it is even called artificial life, although this term also includes other aspects of computer-generated life-forms.

10.3.1 Blackboard architectures

The use of multiple semi-independent knowledge bases is not new, and predates the now ubiquitous use of the word "agent". As we noted, this has obvious software engineering benefits. Each knowledge base can be built, tested and updated individually. Furthermore, when tackling a problem in a particular area, only the relevant knowledge for that area is used. Each knowledge base contains only the knowledge needed for its purpose and may employ representations and reasoning methods appropriate for its particular domain.

However, to solve a common problem, the knowledge bases have to communicate. In an object-oriented architecture this is likely to be via message passing. When a knowledge base/object/agent needs information it sends a message to another to ask for it. When the other one has found the answer it sends a message in reply. This approach can be very powerful, as can be seen in the information-seeking agents described in the last section. However, it has the disadvantage that each object needs to know which other one has the required information or knowledge.

A traditional form of co-operation that avoids this problem is the blackboard architecture. The object-oriented architecture is similar to lots of people working in separate rooms occasionally sending memos to one another. In contrast, the blackboard architecture is rather like a group of people in the same room who are jotting down ideas on a blackboard. As one person writes something down another sees it, perhaps in conjunction with other items on the blackboard, thinks about it and then writes a new idea based on it.

As well as ideas (or solutions), the computer blackboard will also contain unsolved problems. When an agent sees a problem that it can tackle, it solves it and then removes the original problem, posting up the solution. If in trying to solve the problem the agent hits an impasse it can post up a subproblem on the blackboard in the hope that another agent will see the problem and be able to tackle it. Unlike the object-oriented architecture, it does not have to know which agent can solve the subproblem, merely post it to the board. When an agent sees that the subproblem has been solved it can continue to tackle the original problem.

Figure 10.1 shows an example of a blackboard architecture in action. The problem concerns adding up using counting blocks. There are two kinds of blocks, ten-blocks and one-blocks. We have three agents. One agent, the reader, can read numbers and convert them into blocks and vice versa. The second, the grouper, knows how to add up blocks by simply pushing the piles of blocks together. The third, the swopper, knows how to swop a ten-block for ten one-blocks and back again. The initial problem is posed in terms of numbers, "add 13 to 8", and the answer is also required as a written number. The initial representation is shown in the first frame of the figure. The three agents then solve the problem in the following steps:

1. The reader converts the numbers 13 and 8 into the equivalent blocks.

2. The pusher clumps the two together to give an answer in blocks – one ten-block and 11 one-blocks. At this stage the reader might try to convert the answer back into digits, but would fail as there are more than ten one-blocks.

3. However, the swopper can work on the blocks and change ten of the one-blocks into one ten-block, giving two ten-blocks and one one-block.

4. Finally, the reader has a pile of blocks that can be converted into a number, 21, which is the final answer.

Notice how no agent needs to know what the other agents can or can't do. However, it is important that there is a common representation on the blackboard so that the outputs of one agent can be recognized by another.

One disadvantage of a pure blackboard architecture is that there is no central control whatsoever. This can lead to problems. For example, after stage 1, the reader might have looked at the blackboard and thought "Ah, piles of blocks, I'll change them into digits". The system could easily have thrashed about indefinitely changing things back and forth. As a model of cognition this is not

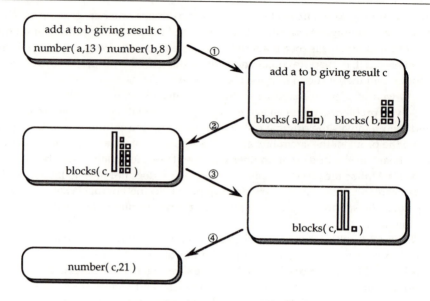

Figure 10.1 Blackboard architecture.

too far from the truth: a frequent error in mathematical proofs is to use a series of equalities, but end up where you began. However, when one becomes practised in a domain, one uses higher-level heuristics. So, for adding with blocks one would learn always to apply the agents in the following order: reader, pusher, swopper and then reader again. A half-way approach between pure blackboard and totally centralized control is to have some sort of co-ordinator agent that activates different agents at different times. The co-ordinator does not need to understand everything on the blackboard, but simply a high-level plan of when to do what.

10.3.2 Distributed control

A production line is producing cream cakes. As the cakes go past, a machine squirts a dollop of cream onto each one. For a few minutes there is a problem on the line and the supply of cakes stops. However, the machine goes on placing a dollop of cream on the line where each cake should have been. This is perfectly understandable, the way machines work. However, if the cream was being put on by a human, the supervisor would be very annoyed to see a hundred dollops of cream on the conveyor belt. People are supposed to use some common sense even in the most repetitive jobs. In a more enlightened factory, the employees may be given more autonomy. Perhaps a group of workers is given targets for the productivity of its particular subprocess and is free to organize its work in whatever fashion it chooses so long as its goals are achieved. Similarly, in an army the commanders make strategic decisions about the deployment of troops and the lines of attack; lower levels of command make tactical decisions; but it is ultimately each soldier who decides precisely when to pull the trigger.

The models of planning we presented in Chapter 9 were largely monolithic. Ultimately the planner knew everything. However, in a large factory such control becomes impractical. Attempting to preplan each machine tool and robot will lead to problems like the cream on the belt. Instead, the central planner must give orders to each tool or robot that it will obey using its own planning systems. This is similar to the issues of hierarchical control we discussed in the context of a single robot, but here we are thinking of many robots co-operating together under some central co-ordinator. Also, unlike the agents co-operating under the blackboard architecture, the major interactions here are physical rather than electronic.

The problem with this form of decentralized control is that the central planner needs to be able to predict global properties from the local properties of agents. Imagine a factory has just two processes: baking and dolloping. Both baker and dolloper have an average throughput of 1800 cakes per hour. So, if both are placed on the same production line, can one assume that the line can produce 1800 cakes per hour? Only if both baker and dolloper can promise a continuous and reliable rate of one cake every two seconds. If the machines sometimes work faster, but sometimes have to pause to refill, then we end up with either the line stopped for a proportion of the time or more dollops on the conveyor belt. Clearly, the central planner would need to have more information about the individual machines. However, it would not need to know about the precise details of each machine. For example, the dolloper might use sophisticated vision processing to determine the positions of the cakes on the line, followed by a planning algorithm to decide the order in which to place a dollop onto the cakes. The planner need know none of this, simply that the machine is capable of putting a dollop on each cake.

10.3.3 Emergent behaviour

In the example of the blackboard architecture, where was the knowledge of adding up? Similarly, in the factory, where was the knowledge of how to make a cream cake? In neither case can we point to any particular agent and say "that one knows". The knowledge and ability is distributed between the agents. So, no one of the adding agents can add up, but together they can. This is called emergent behaviour.

Emergent behaviour is not just a feature of the electronic world, but is present in nature at many levels of life. Consider a swarm of bees building a hive. There is no architect, no plan to follow, but the individual actions of each bee together create a purposeful activity. Similarly, when disease infects your body, there is no central control which says "fight that organism"; instead the various cells and chemical messengers within your body each perform individually in a way that fulfils a common purpose.

The same sort of emergent behaviour is found in humans. This can be seen at a gross level in crowd movements, or in the flow of traffic along a road – lots of individual decisions together giving rise to a global behaviour. On a smaller scale, there is a growing acceptance that the thinking of individuals and groups cannot be isolated in their heads, but is instead distributed between the people and even their environment. This approach is called *distributed cognition* (Hutchins 1990). It is similar to the adding up example. In the building of a skyscraper, where are the thought processes that lead to its construction? In the architect, the engineer, the financier? The answer is in none individually, but in them as a group, and not solely in the people but also in the representations they use, plans, models, even the building itself. In the adding example, the blackboard itself is crucial in the adding task.

Some computational models are built purely to study these emergent behaviours. Groups of agents each act out their own individual, and often very simple, behaviours, but together give rise to complex patterns in the large. Possibly the simplest example is Conway's Game of Life. In Life, the world consists of a rectangular matrix of cells (Fig. 10.2). We consider each cell to be either populated or not. At each step we consider the neighbours of a cell. If an empty cell has three or four of its neighbours populated then the cell is colonized. However, if a populated cell has more than five of its neighbours populated it "dies" through competition. It also dies if fewer than three of its neighbours are populated – loneliness! Most readers will have seen this game animated. Some initial configurations die out completely, others seem to go on indefinitely changing. Some become stable, and others, the gliders, swoop across the screen. These patterns are not coded explicitly into the rules, but emerge from the conjoint behaviour of all the individual cells.

Life is a simple example of a general class of models called *cellular automata*. In general, the state of each cell can be more complicated, not just populated or not, as can the rules. Also the cells need not be in a rectangular mesh, but may have some other topology.

The rules used in cellular automata are usually quite simple and not very intelligent. However, there are other models that give each agent more complex rules, often based on social phenomena. For example, one model has agents wandering over a rectangular playing field, meeting other agents. When they meet, the agents engage in a "prisoner's dilemma"-style interaction. Each agent has a different disposition to "trust" other agents and may reinforce that trust or reduce it depending on the result of the interaction. If the agents are able to choose where to go there is a tendency for trusting agents to group together, building up mutual trust – societies in microcosm.

Another system models robots in a physical environment with obstructions and also simulated locomotion (they are pogoing robots). The individual robots

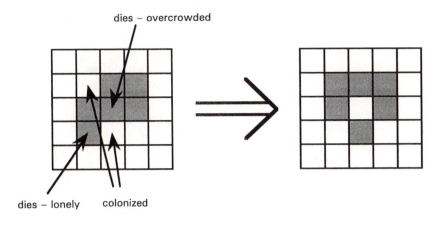

Figure 10.2 Game of Life.

all have a desired direction to travel, but also have rules to avoid bumping into each other or getting too far apart. The robots exhibit flocking behaviour rather like birds. The flock moves in the general direction of travel, but occasionally sweeps one way or another, or a small group may temporarily break away from the main flock. When an obstacle is encountered, the flock divides around it and then, when past the obstacle, the two streams criss-cross and intermingle before merging fully.

These models are not just of theoretical interest. Models of traffic flow on motorways can improve the safety and efficiency of roads and cars. Also, models can tell us about phenomena that cannot be observed directly, for example models of crowd movements in burning buildings. Models have even been formulated of the movements and social structures of hunter-gatherers in prehistoric France, hoping to explain some of the phenomena during the change from nomadic to settled existence. This form of simulation has been called Artificial Society.

10.4 Summary

Software agents are at the heart of several recent and current developments to make software easier to use and to help people find their way through complex information spaces. They act in response to different kinds of events and can gather information to use later. Agents can watch a user's actions, use machine learning algorithms to identify common actions, and then offer to do them for the user. Agents can use knowledge about a user's interests to search for information and may interact with other user's agents in the process. Similarity measures are one technique used for identifying potentially interesting documents.

Co-operating agents can be used to structure an intelligent system, to divide a system between different places or to simulate human co-operation. Blackboard architectures can be used to allow simple agents to solve problems co-operatively. In an industrial setting distributed control can allow groups of simple robots and machinery to work together without a central planner, but some overall direction is usually necessary. The joint actions of many simple agents often give rise to more complex effects, called emergent behaviour. This is observed in humans: a group of people have a shared knowledge and ability that no individual possesses (distributed cognition). Also cellular automata, very simple computational agents, can produce complex, lifelike phenomena. Applications include the simulation of social behaviour and crowd movements.

10.5 Exercises

This is really more of an area for project work than small exercises, but here are some open-ended things to try.

1. Find out about web "crawlers" and "spiders", which rove the Internet looking for useful resources. These are usually not produced commercially and will often refer you to papers which tell you how they work.

2. Similarly, collect examples of "intelligence" in popular applications such as word processors, spreadsheets and drawing packages. Classify the examples you find into those where the intelligence is hidden or working behind the scenes, and those where it is explicitly embodied in some form of agent. Compare your list with other students. Do you agree on what constitutes intelligence and agency?

3. Experiment with different rules similar to the Game of Life. You can start using paper and pencil or draughts on a chess board, but may find it faster to write a program to do it. (It is said that Conway used plates on a tiled kitchen floor!)

10.6 Recommended further reading

Writing on software agents is quite widely dispersed. Papers can be found in conferences and journals on human–computer interaction, the Internet and even sociology, as well as traditional AI sources and proceedings of specialised conferences and workshops on distributed AI such as the annual MAAMAW workshops (Modelling Autonomous Agents in a Multi-Agent World).

Maes, P 1994. Agents that reduce work and information overload. *Communications of the ACM* **37**(7).

Beale, R. & A. Wood 1994. Agent-based interaction. In *People and Computers IX*, G. Cockton, S. W. Draper, G. R. S. Weir (eds), 239–245. Cambridge: Cambridge University Press.
Two articles that survey and discuss the applications of agents in the user interface.

Laurel, B. (ed.) 1990. *The art of human–computer design.* Reading, MA: Addison-Wesley.
Collection with several chapters dedicated to interface agents.

Englemore, R. & T. Morgan (eds) 1988. *Blackboard systems.* Reading, MA: Addison-Wesley.
Collection with contributions on many different blackboard systems.

Minksy, M. 1985. *The society of mind.* New York: Simon and Schuster.
Viewing cognition as interaction.

Chapter Eleven

Models of the mind

11.1 Overview

In this chapter, we consider approaches that have been developed for modelling not only intelligent human activity, but also human cognition. In particular, we discuss production system models which model problem solving and memory activity, and neural networks which attempt to model cognition by mimicking the physical organization of the brain.

11.2 Introduction

So far, we have looked at what might be called engineering applications. The aim has been to use AI techniques to solve a particular problem, such as natural language understanding, or to build an artefact, like an expert system. These systems aim to replicate human behaviour, but are not concerned with whether the way this is done mimics human thought. We will now take a brief look at the other "face" of AI. Many working in AI believe that it should provide a means of modelling the way people think, learn, and make mistakes. Their aim is to understand human intelligence and (ultimately) to reproduce it. In this chapter we will consider some of the approaches taken to modelling the human mind.

11.3 What is the human mind?

To model the human mind we first need to understand what it is like, what it can do, what it can't. A true model of the mind would incorporate the positive and the negative about the human so that what is produced shares our limitations as well as our strengths. Think about the mind for a moment. What qualities does it have? What are its limits? What do you think is its main strength?

The mind has a number of characteristics, some good, some bad. On the positive side we are able to tackle unfamiliar problems and apply our knowledge to produce new solutions. Indeed, we can create original things, from words to machines to music. People are very creative, and, while it is debatable whether anything is truly original (since most ideas are influenced by existing things), we generate considerable variety and make huge leaps through insight and imagination. Another positive aspect of the human mind is its ability to learn. From infancy humans assimilate information and make sense of it, using it to interpret their environment. Our ability to learn degrades as we get older (the speed at which babies and small children learn is remarkable), but we never lose it completely and we can adapt throughout our lives. We can do several things at once, often without any apparent loss of performance (although the less skilled we are at something the more we have to concentrate our attention on it). So experienced drivers have no problem talking to passengers and listening to music while they drive. The capacity of the mind means that we can still function, even if our performance is impaired by fatigue, illness or even partial brain damage. Although we may be less efficient or unable to do some activities, we do not cease to function altogether, and our mind provides inventive solutions to these problems to support us when we face them.

The mind is clearly a remarkable thing. However, it does have its limitations. Compare the performance of a human with that of a computer in arithmetic calculations or remembering the names and ages of all the people who work in an organization, and you will start to see the limits. The human mind works slowly. In the time it takes a human to add up a few numbers, a computer can have summed millions. Human memory is also limited. Our short-term memory capacity (that is, what we can hold in our conscious mind at a time) has been shown to be of the order of 7 ± 2 items, that is a range of 5 to 9 (Miller 1956). Try an experiment to test this. Spend 30 seconds looking at this list of numbers; then, without looking, write down, in order, as many as you can remember.

2 7 12 4 9 3 23 7 1 10 18 16 21

How many could you recall? Unless you have an exceptionally poor or well-trained memory you probably managed between 5 and 9 items. There are of course ways of increasing memory capacity; by relating items together, such as in a phone number, we can remember more. So in fact, our short-term memory capacity is not 7 ± 2 items but 7 ± 2 *chunks* of information. Our long-term memory capacity is another matter. Many believe that this is in principle unlimited, although in practice it is bounded by our ability to recall the information. Again, using cues and association helps us to remember more. Finally, humans make mistakes, even when performing tasks at which we are expert. This is because we have lapses of concentration or get distracted. We are not often precise and thorough.

All in all you can see that the human mind is very different to the computer. The areas that we are good at (creativity, flexibility, learning and so on) computers are notoriously bad at, whereas those areas where we fall down (memory, speed, accuracy) are the strengths of the computer. So how can we make a computer model the human mind? First we should be clear what is meant by a *model*. A model is an approximation or a representation of something else. Think about architectural design. As well as drawing up plans for a new building, an architect will often produce a scale model of it. This is not the building itself, it may not have all the properties of the building (for instance, it is unlikely to be constructed of the same materials), but it will have enough detail to enable the architect to learn something about the real building (perhaps about its appearance or structural limitations).

Models of the mind are proposals for how the human mind works (or how some part of it works). Their aim is to improve our understanding of the mind and, eventually, allow us to reproduce it (or at least an approximation of it). Two main classes of model have been proposed: production system models and connectionist models (neural networks). Note that we have already met both of these, since they are useful tools for engineering AI systems. However, in this chapter, we will concentrate on their role as models of cognition.

11.4 Production system models

Recall our discussion of the production system in Chapter 1. It has three components: a database of current knowledge (the working memory), rules to alter the state of the memory and some method of deciding which rules to apply when. The production system was originally proposed as a method that plausibly reflected human thinking, including short-term memory limitations. However, it was also recognized as a powerful tool for the development of AI applications, such as expert systems, and these pragmatic concerns have rather eclipsed the role of production systems as a model of the mind. However, a number of researchers have continued to work on this and there are several general implementations of models of cognition using production systems. Two of the best known are ACT* (Anderson 1983) and SOAR (Laird et al. 1987). Each is a general model, but more specific applications can be built on top of them. For example, *Programmable User Models* or PUMs (Young & Green 1989), is an application built on top of SOAR, which is designed to simulate the behaviour of a user with a computer or machine interface.

11.4.1 ACT*

ACT* has been developed by Anderson over the past 20 years (Anderson 1983). It comprises a large long-term memory in the form of a semantic net, a small working memory of active items and a production system that operates on the memories. As in humans, only a small part of the long-term memory is active at any time and the condition part of a rule can only match an active element.

The action part of the rule can change memory (say, by activating a new item or deactivating one) or perform some other action. Memory elements can spread activation to their neighbours in the semantic network, mimicking association of ideas. As in human memory, activation decays if an element is not accessed by the rules, so only items that are being used remain in active memory.

ACT* is used to model learning, or the development of skills. It is Anderson's contention that the mind can develop procedures for specialized activities from some basic knowledge, general problem-solving rules and a mechanism for deciding which rules to apply. Consequently skill is acquired in three stages. At first, general purpose rules are used to make sense of facts known about a problem. This is slow and places significant demands on memory. Gradually the learner develops productions or rules specific to the new task and, as skill becomes more developed, these rules are tuned to improve performance.

ACT* provides two general mechanisms to account for each of these transitions. *Proceduralization* is the mechanism to move from general rules to specific rules. Memory access is reduced by removing those parts of the rules that require it and by replacing variables with specific values. *Generalization* is the mechanism that tunes the specific rules to improve performance. Commonalities between specific rules are identified and combined to form a more general rule.

A simple example of ACT* should illustrate this.[1] Imagine you are learning to cook. Initially you may have a general rule to tell you how to determine the cooking time for a dish, together with some explicit examples for particular dishes. You can instantiate the rule by retrieving these cases from memory.

IF cook[type,ingredients,time]

THEN

cook for: time

cook[casserole, [chicken,carrots,potatoes], 2 hours]

cook[casserole, [beef,dumpling,carrots], 2 hours]

cook[cake, [flour,sugar,butter,egg], 45 mins]

Gradually your knowlege becomes proceduralized and you have specific rules for each case:

IF type is casserole

AND ingredients are [chicken,carrots,potatoes]

THEN

cook for: 2 hours

IF type is casserole

AND ingredients are [beef,dumpling,carrots]

THEN

cook for: 2 hours

IF type is cake

AND ingredients are [flour,sugar,butter,egg]

THEN

cook for: 45 mins

Finally you may generalize from these rules to produce general purpose rules which exploit their commonalities:

IF type is casserole

AND ingredients are ANYTHING

THEN

cook for: 2 hours

ACT* has shown impressive results in modelling the learning of arithmetic in children and the utterances of a child learning to speak, indicating that it is quite a powerful general model. However, it is unable to model individual differences in learning or the problem of how incorrect rules are acquired.

11.4.2 SOAR

SOAR is a general model of human problem solving developed by Laird et al. (Laird et al. 1987). In SOAR, long-term memory is represented by production rules, and short-term memory is a buffer containing facts deduced from these rules. Problem solving is modelled as state space traversal (see Ch. 3), and SOAR uses the same approach to problem solving to deal with domain problems and those relating to the process of problem solving. So, given a start state and a goal state, SOAR sets up an initial problem space. It then faces the problem of which rule to choose to move towards the goal. To solve this problem it sets up an auxiliary problem space, and so on. By treating control problems in the same way as domain problems SOAR is able to use either general problem-solving rules or domain-specific rules to deal with all types of problems. If a difficulty is encountered, SOAR sets up an *impasse*, creating a subgoal to resolve the difficulty.

A key characteristic of SOAR is *chunking*. When an operator or sequence of operators has been particularly successful in reaching a goal, SOAR encapsulates this in a "chunk", essentially a new operator that it can use when it meets a similar problem again. The basic operation of SOAR is illustrated in Figure 11.1.

SOAR is a flexible, general purpose architecture but this has its price: it can be resource intensive and slow. However, as an attempt to produce a general cognitive architecture it is of great interest and is the focus of substantial research efforts.

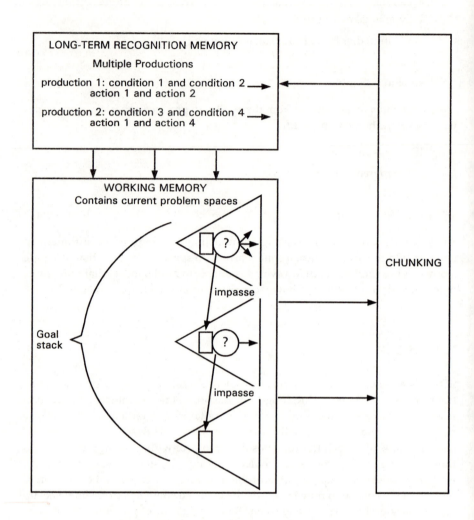

Figure 11.1 Basic SOAR diagram. After Newell (1992).

11.5   Connectionist models of cognition

An alternative model is the connectionist model of cognition (also called *neural networks*). These models are completely different from production system models. Rather than attempting to model the cognitive architecture of the human mind, they focus on the physical architecture of the brain. Supporters of this approach argue that we do not understand enough about cognitive processes to model them effectively. However, we do know how the brain operates at this lower, physical level. The idea is that if we can simulate the way the human brain operates we may achieve some of its power in complex problem solving. The brain consists of billions of small, basic processing units, called neurons. Each is connected to thousands of others, forming a rich network. The basic operations performed by each neuron are simple: summing the inputs received in some way and "reacting" if these exceed a certain level. The connections between neurons can adapt to reinforce those that are successful and to degrade those that are not. The power of the brain, therefore, is not in complex processing units but in the parallel operation of billions of simple units and the ability to adapt the configuration of these. Neural networks attempt to model this architecture, although current networks comprise hundreds rather than billions of neurons.

Connectionist models account for aspects of human thinking such as parallelism, the ability to do more than one thing at once, and graceful degradation, where the mind is able to operate even if impaired by fatigue or damage. Like the brain, a neural network consists of a network of simple processing units, all interconnected. Learning occurs through changes in the connections, and the configuration of connections constitutes the knowledge of the system. Because this knowledge is distributed among the units, the network is fault tolerant and performance degrades only gradually with damage.

Like the production system model, there are several implementations of the connectionist paradigm. We will consider three: the multi-layer perceptron, associative memory, and Kohonen's self-organizing network.

11.5.1   Multi-layer perceptron

The most common connectionist model is the *multi-layer perceptron* (McClelland & Rumelhart 1986). To understand how this works we begin with a single perceptron (a single neuron) as in Figure 11.2 (Minksy & Papert 1969). Each input is multiplied by the weight on its connection, which is set randomly to start with. The weighted inputs are summed by the neuron and compared with a threshold value. The simplest thresholding function is the step function where the response is "on" if the threshold is exceeded and "off" otherwise. The perceptron learns by adjusting the weights to reinforce a correct decision and discourage an incorrect one.

However, the single perceptron has major limitations and can only solve very

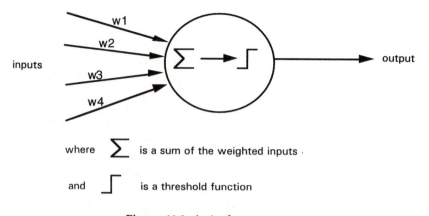

where $\sum$ is a sum of the weighted inputs

and ⌐ is a threshold function

Figure 11.2 A single perceptron.

simple problems. To illustrate this, imagine you have a group of dogs, some of which work as rescue dogs, some as sheep dogs. Your job is to assign them to the correct "class". Thinking about the characteristics of these two groups, you may decide that weight and speed are suitable measures to distinguish them, given that rescue dogs, often St Bernards and Newfoundlands, tend to be larger and slower than sheep dogs (assume that you do not have information about the dogs' breeds). You could plot the weight and speed of each dog on a graph as in Figure 11.3.

Looking at this graph, you can see two definite clusters (which you assume represent your two classes). You can in fact draw a straight line between these clusters and say that any point on one side of the line represents a sheep dog and every point on the other a rescue dog (as in Fig. 11.4). The problem is *linearly separable*.

Unfortunately life is rarely as simple as that. In reality our pattern space is unlikely to be so neat and ordered. We may find when we ask our dogs' owners to identify their dogs' occupations that some of those we identified as sheep dogs are in fact rescue dogs (perhaps search and rescue collies). Similarly, some we thought were rescue dogs may in fact work as flock protection sheep dogs and so be on the larger side. So our graph may really look like Figure 11.5.

It is no longer possible to draw a straight line between the two groups; the problem has become *linearly inseparable*. Our simple perceptron can solve problems that are linearly separable but not those which are *linearly inseparable*, by far the more significant group.

The solution is two-fold: link perceptrons together in layers so that different units can solve small parts of the problem, and combine the results and use a nonlinear thresholding function where the neuron's value is not just 1 or 0 but can take values within a range. The resulting model is the multi-layer perceptron.

The multi-layer perceptron model has three layers: an input layer, an output

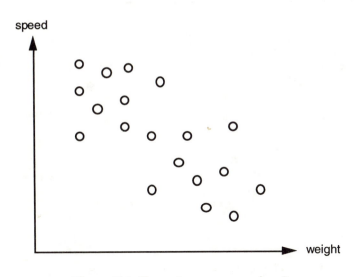

Figure 11.3 Sheep dogs or rescue dogs?

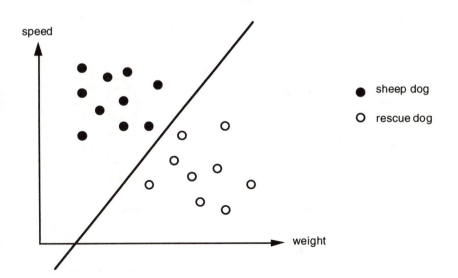

Figure 11.4 A linearly separable problem.

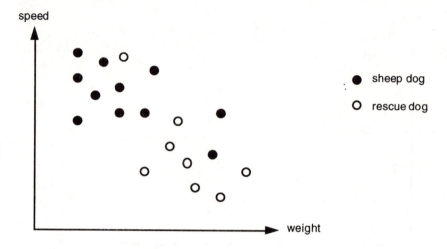

Figure 11.5 The actual pattern space.

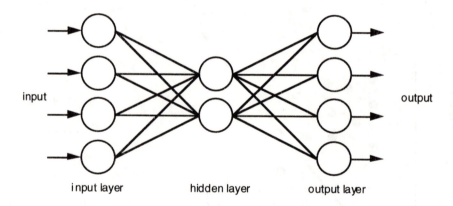

Figure 11.6 A multi-layer perceptron architecture.

layer and a hidden layer that is not directly connected to inputs or outputs (see Fig. 11.6).

The output and hidden layer units act like perceptrons (but with a new thresholding function); the input layer distributes the inputs through the network and so does not threshold. This implementation is able to solve linearly inseparable problems. The network is trained through repeated presentations of expected input and output. It learns by adapting the weights on the inputs to reinforce connections that result in the correct output, until all the outputs are correct. The weights then remain stable and the network is able to work on unseen input.

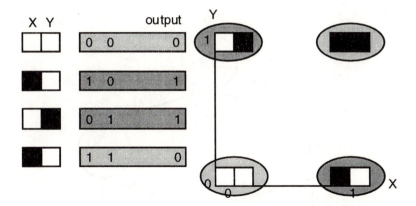

Figure 11.7 XOR problem (diagram after Beale & Jackson (1990)).

A simple example should make this clearer. One problem that is linearly inseparable is the *exclusive OR* or *XOR* function. Given two inputs (X and Y), which can be true or false, the XOR function returns true if either of the inputs is true, but false if both are true or both are false.

X	Y	Output
True	True	False
True	False	True
False	True	True
False	False	False

If we plot this on a graph we will quickly see that it is linearly inseparable. In the graph in Figure 11.7 we represent true as 1 and false as 0.

We therefore need to use a multi-layer perceptron to solve this problem. A simple network which does this is shown in Figure 11.8. It has two input units (for the two inputs X and Y) and one output unit (the output is either 0 or 1). The network also has two hidden units. Work through the network by hand and convince yourself that it does indeed solve the XOR problem (in this case the weights are multiplicative and the threshold function is a simple step function – if the sum is greater than the threshold output 1, otherwise output 0).

Various applications have been built using this implementation, but one in particular is interesting from the point of modelling cognition and human learning. NETtalk (Sejnowski & Rosenberg 1987) is a multi-layer perceptron that has learned to pronounce English text. The network comprises 203 input units, 80 hidden units and 26 output units. The output units represent phonemes, the basic sound unit of the language. The network is presented with text in blocks of seven letters and learns to pronounce the middle letter. It can use the surrounding letters as context to distinguish between different sounds for the same

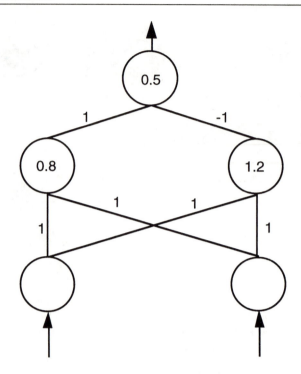

Figure 11.8 A simple multi-layer perceptron to solve the XOR problem.

letter. During the training phase the system appears to mimic the speech sounds of young children. When the weights are random the sounds are meaningless babble. As the network learns it first produces the main sounds of English, finally producing intelligible speech. Listening to a tape recording of NETtalk in training is not unlike listening to a child learning to talk – speeded up of course!

The multi-layer perceptron is the most common and widely used connectionist model, but there are others that model the mind slightly differently. We will consider two of these briefly.

11.5.2   Associative memories

Association of ideas is a familiar concept to us. We may associate a particular piece of music with a person or event, or we may associate a person with an activity. There are many examples in everyday life where we use association to remember things. Indeed, it is fundamental to models of memory such as semantic networks.

Input   Output

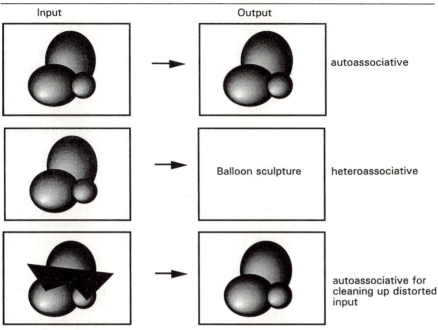

autoassociative

Balloon sculpture   heteroassociative

autoassociative for
cleaning up distorted
input

Figure 11.9 Associative memory.

An associative memory is a neural network that models the associative nature of human memory, by which a particular stimulus triggers a particular response (Kohonen 1990, Aleksander & Stonham 1979). In the associative memory model, an input is stored with the required output, in such a way that when this input (or an incomplete version of it) is presented to the memory the appropriate output is recovered.

There are two types of associative memory: autoassociative, where the input is associated with itself, and heteroassociative, where it is associated with a different output pattern. The former can be used to filter and "clean up" distortion in images, the latter for classification problems. In an autoassociative memory, the network is trained with the same pattern as both input and expected output. When this pattern (or a partial version of it) is presented to the memory, the stored pattern is retrieved. This allows the memory to deal with noise and distortion in patterns, as in Figure 11.9 below.

In a heteroassociative memory, the input pattern is associated with a different output pattern, for example a class identifier. In this case, when the input pattern is encountered again, the class with which it is associated is returned, allowing the network to perform effectively in classification problems.

11.5.3   Kohonen self-organizing networks

The previous methods are called *supervised learning* methods, because they are trained with an input and its corresponding output. Kohonen networks are unsupervised or self-organizing because they cluster the inputs into classes, according to common features (Kohonen 1990). This reflects the ability of the human mind to make sense of unknown situations. Neurons are not arranged in layers but in a flat grid, and all inputs are connected to all nodes. In learning, the nodes are organized into local neighbourhoods that act as feature classifiers. The input is compared with vectors stored at the nodes. If they match, that area of the grid is optimized to represent an average of the training data for that class.

Kohonen's self-organizing network has been used to perform speech recognition, in the form of a phonetic typewriter, a typewriter that could produce text from dictation. The network was used to cluster the phonemes into similar sounds, which could then be manually labelled. The phonetic typewriter is an example of an application that uses both neural and more conventional knowledge-based techniques, the neural network being used to preprocess the input to facilitate use of the knowledge base. This demonstrates an important point about connectionist models: although they were proposed as models of cognition, like production systems, they can also be used for practical AI problem solving. Neural networks are particularly suited to classification and pattern recognition tasks. They are also being used in expert system applications (for example, credit risk assessment), where their ability to learn from examples and generalize to new cases is beneficial. However, their disadvantages should also be acknowledged: they can take a long time to learn and be difficult to update quickly and, perhaps most important, there is no explicit representation of the decision mechanism and therefore no explanation facility.

11.6   Summary

In this chapter we have considered a number of models of the human mind. Production systems model problem solving and memory while neural networks exploit the physical properties of the brain to provide parallelism and fault tolerance.

11.7   Exercises

1. Illustrate how ACT* would represent the process of learning multiplication.

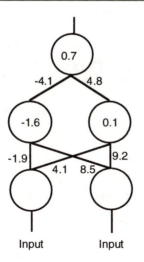

Figure 11.10 Does this network solve the XOR problem?

2. Does the network in Figure 11.10 solve the XOR problem? Show the outputs of the network to support your answer.

3. In the UK dogs are classified into six groups according to breed. Each group contains a number of different breeds. Given two breeds of dog the neural network in Figure 11.11 is required to indicate whether or not they belong to the same group. The two breeds of interest at any time are indicated by setting their input nodes to 1. All other input nodes are set to 0.

   (a) Does the network classify the dogs correctly? (Maremma, Bernese and Border Collie are all members of the working group; Flat Coat Retriever, Pointer and Field Spaniel all belong to the gundog group.)

   (b) How do weights, thresholds and hidden units operate in this problem solution?

11.8   Recommended further reading

Beale, R. & T. Jackson 1990. *An introduction to neural computing*. Bristol: Adam Hilger.
    A readable introduction to neural networks which provides details and algorithms for all the major connectionist models, including those discussed here.

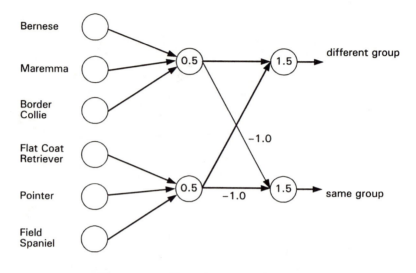

Figure 11.11 Does this network work?

Michon, J. A. & A. Akyurek (eds) 1992. *SOAR: A cognitive architecture in perspective*. Dordrecht: Kluwer.

A collection of papers on SOAR and related research. An excellent survey of the area.

Anderson, J. R. 1983. *The architecture of cognition*. Cambridge, MA: Harvard University Press.

The key work on the ACT* architecture.

11.9 Notes

1. The example is reproduced from the authors' book, *Human–computer interaction*, published by Prentice Hall, with permission.

Chapter Twelve

Epilogue: philosophical and sociological issues

12.1 Overview

Artificial intelligence is not simply a matter of developing appropriate technology. It also raises philosophical, moral and ethical questions that must be addressed. In this chapter we highlight some of these. We look at the Chinese Room argument and its opponents. We consider issues of legal and ethical responsibility, morals and emotions, and the potential social impact of AI.

12.2 Intelligent machines or engineering tools?

"Can machines think?" is a question that has been debated throughout the lifetime of AI. In fact it is a very vague question that begs more questions than it answers. However, the question of whether digital computers will ever be considered intelligent is an important one, since our response to it determines our view of what AI is all about. In this chapter, we will consider some of the arguments in the ongoing debate as well as the implications of seeking machine intelligence. But be warned: our intention is not to direct your choice, simply to map out some of the possibilities. You will have to consider the evidence and make up your own mind!

As we have seen, there is a strand of AI that aims to investigate the nature of intelligence and build intelligent machines. Within this group there are in fact two camps:

- *strong AI*, whose supporters claim that machines can possess cognitive states and can think (or will be able to at some point in the future)

- *weak AI*, whose supporters use computers to test theories of intelligence, and so build models of human intelligence.

A third view of AI is what might be called the pragmatic view: it views AI as a discipline which has provided engineering techniques for solving difficult problems. Whether these techniques indicate intelligence or reflect human cognition is immaterial.

It is the strong AI viewpoint that is most controversial, since it suggests that machines can, or at least will, possess genuine independent intelligence. Fiction and film have taken this notion on board with enthusiasm. But how realistic is it, and what implications does it raise? The first question we need to consider is: what is meant by intelligence?

12.3   What is intelligence?

Intelligence is very difficult to define. Chambers' dictionary describes it as being "endowed with the faculty of reason", but our intuitive notion of intelligence includes more than that. Intelligent agents can plan and adapt plans to respond to changes in circumstance (or anticipated changes); they can recognize what is significant in a situation; they can learn new concepts from old; they can interact and learn from their environment; they can exercise aesthetic appreciation. We might also identify imagination, moral conscience, creativity, and emotion as characteristics associated with intelligence, but while it may not be possible to have these without intelligence, it is possible to have intelligence without these. A psychopath, for example, lacks moral conscience but may be extremely intelligent. So intelligence includes some or all of these characteristics.

So where does such a definition leave us? As we have seen throughout this book, computers are being given the ability to plan, to adapt, to learn, to make decisions, to reason, albeit in a limited form as yet. So perhaps this suggests that machines that simulate human intelligence are ultimately very likely? Many would argue that this is not the case for one crucial reason: machines do not and cannot share the environment in which we live. Weizenbaum (Weizenbaum 1976), for example, claims that the notion that a machine can be modelled on a human is

> artificial intelligence's perverse grand fantasy.

He argues that an organism is defined by the problems it faces. Computers will never face the same problems as humans and therefore cannot simulate human intelligence. Dreyfus (Dreyfus 1979) agrees, arguing that computers do not have bodies and share the human context. They are digital rather than analogue and are therefore fundamentally different from humans. They cannot therefore simulate human intelligence. Others are not so dismissive. Boden (Boden 1987) believes that some aspects of intelligence may be simulated, but not necessarily all:

> The philosophical arguments most commonly directed against artificial intelligence [such as Dreyfus'] are unconvincing.

However, she goes on:

the issues involved are too obscure to allow one ... to insist that all aspects of human thought could in principle be simulated by computational means ... Still less should one assume that complete simulation is possible in practice.

12.4   The computational argument vs. Searle's Chinese Room argument

The theory of strong AI is that human intelligence is computational: we are simply information processing machines and our brain runs "programs". The claim, therefore, is that with the right programs, computers can possess cognitive states and be said to understand and be intelligent. Even if the hardware on which these programs run (the digital computer) differs from that used by the human (the brain), the computer will reflect human cognition. We can use an analogy between natural and artificial flight. In nature, birds have wings made of bone, skin, muscle and feathers, which they flap in order to fly. Early attempts at artificial flight tried to imitate this and failed miserably (humans and birds are constructed very differently). However, by understanding the underlying principles of flight and the laws of thermodynamics, essentially by using a model of flying, we can build machines to fly. They look different from the natural thing and use different materials but reflect the same principles.

Searle criticized the computational view by arguing that a human could run a program and not possess understanding (therefore suggesting that intelligence is more than this) (Searle 1980). He also opposes the behavioural model of the Turing test, since the appearance of intelligence does not indicate actual intelligence. His argument is as follows:

> Imagine a prisoner locked in a room. He understands English but not Chinese. In the room he has pieces of Chinese writing and English rules to say how to manipulate these. An interrogator passes more Chinese writing into the room. The rules say how to give back Chinese symbols in response. Unknown to the prisoner, the writing is a script which the interrogator is asking about. The prisoner uses the rules to answer the questions.

Does the prisoner understand the script? Searle argues that he doesn't: the prisoner has only syntax, not semantics. He has no idea what the scripts are about. In order to understand he needs to know what the symbols mean in the context of the real world. He compares this scenario with another where the prisoner is given scripts and asked questions in his own language. In this case the prisoner does understand since he not only knows how to answer the questions but also what the questions and answers mean. Searle calls this intentionality. Similarly, Searle argues, computers do not have intentionality and therefore cannot be intelligent.

A counter argument to Searle is the Systems Response: the prisoner does not understand Chinese, but is part of a larger system that does (the whole room). The prisoner corresponds to only one level of a full computational system. The functional relationships between the entities make an intelligent system. Searle argued against this by dismissing the notion of a "system": the system is just the man, the symbols, the instructions, and if the man is not demonstrating intelligence, then adding pieces of paper cannot change that. However, this assumes that a system is a physical thing, the combination of its physical constituents, whereas the Systems Response argues that the system is made up of the combined functions of the constituents.

The arguments about machine intelligence will continue. Indeed, we have only scratched the surface of the philosophy of intelligence and artificial intelligence: interested readers are directed to the recommended reading list at the end of the chapter. However, machine intelligence is not simply a philosophical question. It raises important ethical and legal questions that will need to be addressed if it is to become a reality.

12.5   Who is responsible?

The first and, perhaps, most crucial issue raised by the possibility of intelligent, independent machines is responsibility. Who is responsible, both ethically and legally, for their actions? Can a machine be held accountable? This question may be significant sooner than we think. Already an expert system is being used in a UK hospital to decide where resources should be allocated. The expert system predicts which patients have most chance of survival to allow the doctor to decide where treatment should be given. It is a small step from this to the system literally deciding who should live or die. In the case of a wrong decision by an expert system, is the system responsible or the knowledge engineer or the user? And if the system, how can a machine be made accountable? Normal legal methods are not valid here. It is not possible to sue a machine!

12.6   Morals and emotions

We do not normally associate machines with emotion. Indeed it is the ability to perform rationally, logically, without the baggage of emotional response that makes an intelligent machine powerful. Emotion brings uncertainty and irrationality. However, emotion is the mechanism by which we take account of shared human experience in our decisions. We react to situations not only by reason but by emotion. On the one hand, the decision of a machine may be acceptable because it is impersonal and therefore objective. On the other, the emotional empathy tempers decisions that are otherwise too severe. There are two possibilities for machine intelligence. Either we attempt to provide emotion (a necessity if machine intelligence is truly to mirror that of humans) or we preserve objective reasoning. If we do the former, will the occasional emotional decisions of a machine be acceptable to a human? Yet if we do the latter, how will the decisions of the machine be tempered to take into account emotional and moral issues that are important in society?

12.7 Social implications

There have been many debates on the impact of computer technology in general on society and whether increasing computerization will have a dehumanizing effect. These issues are magnified when artificial intelligence is considered. Expert systems have been proposed for many applications, including medicine, counselling and psychotherapy. Such applications raise strong objections from many sides on the grounds that they dehumanize the people who are subjected to them. Weizenbaum, who created ELIZA, believed that it was obscene to use artificial intelligence in clinical situations. Yet it is possible that some prefer the impersonal anonymity of dealing with a machine.

Related to this is the implication of loss of human–human contact. As computers are able to perform more and more of the tasks currently performed by people, there will be less need for human–human contact. This shift from reliance on other people to reliance on machines may cause breakdown in social structures and social responsibility. The prediction that

> it may be possible for intelligent machines of the future to supply
> not only intellectual stimulation or instruction, but also domestic
> and health care, social conversation, entertainment, companionship,
> and even physical gratification (Firschein et al. 1974)

is still as likely to inspire horror as excitement in most.

The dehumanizing potential of artificial intelligence has another aspect: if it is true that we can create intelligent life, then life may cease to have the same value. If artificial intelligence is possible in machines then humans are reduced to little more than machines themselves. The implication of this may change our view of ourselves and those around us.

Artificial intelligence has the potential to empower humans through enhanced learning and performance, and through freeing us from mundane and dangerous tasks. It may provide critical insights into how we ourselves operate. But if this potential is to be realized and accepted the social and ethical aspects as well as the technical must be addressed.

12.8 Summary

In this chapter we have considered whether machine intelligence is possible, looking in particular at the Chinese Room argument and its opponents. We have looked at issues of legal and ethical responsibility, morals and emotions, and the potential social impact of artificial intelligence. It is vital that these questions are tackled if artificial intelligence is to be accepted widely.

12.9 Recommended further reading

Boden, M. (ed.) 1990. *The philosophy of artificial intelligence.* Oxford: Oxford University Press.

A collection of seminal papers on machine intelligence by leaders in the field including Searle and Turing. An excellent and accessible introduction to some of the philosophical issues of AI.

Boden, M. 1987. *Artificial intelligence and natural man,* 2nd edn. London: MIT Press.

Part IV in particular provides a useful survey of the social, psychological and philosophical issues of AI.

Winograd, T. & F. Flores 1987. *Understanding computers and cognition.* Norwood, NJ: Addison-Wesley, Ablex Corporation.

An interesting perspective on the nature of artificial intelligence and human cognition; on what it means to be a machine and to be human.

Bibliography

Aleksander, I. & T. J. Stonham 1979. Guide to pattern recognition using random-access memories. *Proceedings of the IEE: Computers and Digital Techniques* **2**(1), 42–49.

Anderson, J. R. 1983. *The architecture of cognition*. Cambridge, MA: Harvard University Press.

Arkin, R. C., W. M. Carter, D. C. Mackenzie 1993. Active avoidance: escape and dodging behaviors for reactive control. In *Active robot vision: camera heads, model based navigation and reactive control*, H. I. Christensen, K. W. Bowyer, H. Bunke (eds). Singapore: World Scientific.

Barker, V. E. & D. E. O'Connor 1989. Expert systems for configuration at DIGITAL: XCON and beyond. *Communications of the ACM* **32**(3), 298–318.

Beale, R. & T. Jackson 1990. *Neural computing: an introduction*. Bristol: Adam Hilger.

Boden, M. A. 1987. *Artificial intelligence and natural man*, 2nd edn. London: MIT Press.

Burton, R. R. 1976. *Semantic grammar: an engineering technique for constructing natural language understanding systems*. Report No. 3453, Bolt Beranek and Newman, Boston, MA.

Charniak, E. 1972. *Towards a model of children's story comprehension*. Report No. TR-266, AI Laboratory, MIT.

Cockburn, A. J. G. 1993. *Groupware design: principles, prototypes and systems*. PhD thesis, University of Stirling.

Davis, R. 1982. Applications of meta level knowledge to the construction, maintenance and use of large knowledge bases. In *Knowledge-based systems in artificial intelligence*, R. Davis & D. B. Lenat (eds). New York: McGraw-Hill.

Dix, A., J. Finlay, G. Abowd, R. Beale 1993. *Human-computer interaction*. Hemel Hempstead: Prentice Hall.

Doyle, J. 1979. A truth maintenance system. *Artificial Intelligence* **12**(3), 232–272.

Dreyfus, H. 1979. *What computers can't do*, 2nd edn. New York: Harper and Row.

Duda, R. O., J. Gaschnig, P. E. Hart 1979. Model design in the PROSPECTOR consultant system for mineral exploration. In *Expert systems in the micro-electronic age*, D. Michie (ed.). Edinburgh: Edinburgh University Press.

Fillmore, C. 1968. The case for case. In *Universals in linguistic theory*, E. Bach & R. T. Harms (eds). New York: Holt.

Firschein, O., M. A. Fischler, L. S. Coles, J. M. Tenenbaum 1974. Forecasting and assessing the impact of artificial intelligence on society. In *IJCAI-3*, 105–120.

Hall, R. 1989. Computational approaches to analogical reasoning. *Artificial Intelligence* **39**(1), 39–120.

Hodgins, J. K., W. L. Wooten, D. C. Brogan, J. F. O'Brien 1995. Animating human athletics. In *Proceedings of SIGGRAPH95*.

Hutchins, E. 1990. The technology of team navigation. In *Intellectual teamwork: social and technical bases of collaborative work*, J. Gallagher, R. Kraut, C. Egido (eds). Hillsdale, NJ: Lawrence Erlbaum Associates.

Johnson, L. & N. E. Johnson 1987. Knowledge elicitation involving teach-back interviewing. In *Knowledge acquisition for expert systems*, A. Kidd (ed.). London: Plenum Press.

Kilmister, C. W. 1967. *Language, logic and mathematics*. London: English Universities Press.

Kohonen, T. 1990. *Self organisation and associative memory*, 3rd edn. Berlin: Springer-Verlag.

Laird, J. E., A. Newell, P. S. Rosenbloom 1987. SOAR: an architecture for general intelligence. *Artificial Intelligence* **33**(1), 1–64.

Lenat, D. B. & R. V. Guha 1990. *Building large knowledge based systems*. Reading, MA: Addison-Wesley.

Lindsay, R. K., B. G. Buchanan, E. A. Feigenbaum, J. Lederberg 1980. *Applications of artificial intelligence for organic chemistry: the DENDRAL project*. New York: McGraw-Hill.

Loughlin, C. 1993. *Sensors for industrial inspection*. Dordrecht: Kluwer Academic.

Marr, D. 1982. *Vision: a computational investigation into the human representation and processing of visual information*. San Francisco: W. H. Freeman.

McCarthy, J. & P. J. Hayes 1969. Some philosophical problems from the standpoint of artificial intelligence. In *Machine intelligence 4*, B. Meltzer & D. Michie (eds). Edinburgh: Edinburgh University Press.

McClelland, J. L. & D. E. Rumelhart 1986. *Parallel distributed processing*, vol. 1. Cambridge, MA: MIT Press.

Miller, G. A. 1956. The magical number seven, plus or minus two: some limits on our capacity to process information. *Psychological Review* **63**(2), 81–97.

Minksy, M. 1985. *The society of mind*. New York: Simon and Schuster.

Minksy, M. & S. Papert 1969. *Perceptrons*. Cambridge, MA: MIT Press.

Minsky, M. 1975. A framework for representing knowledge. In *The psychology of computer vision*, P. H. Winston (ed.). New York: McGraw-Hill.

Mitchell, T. M. 1978. *Version spaces: an approach to concept learning*. PhD thesis, Stanford University, Stanford, CA.

Newell, A. 1992. Unified theories of cognition and the role of SOAR. In *SOAR: a cognitive architecture in perspective*, J. A. Michon & A. Akyurek (eds), 25–79. Dordrecht: Kluwer.

Newell, A. & H. A. Simon 1972. *Human problem solving*. Englewood Cliffs, NJ: Prentice-Hall.

Newell, A. & H. A. Simon 1976. Computer science as empirical enquiry: symbols and search. *Communications of the ACM* **19**, 113–26.

Pereira, F. C. N. & D. H. D. Warren 1980. Definite clause grammars for language analysis – a survey of the formalism and a comparison with augmented transition networks. *Artificial Intelligence* **13**(3), 231–78.

Quinlan, J. R. 1979. Discovering rules by induction from large collections of examples. In *Expert systems in the micro-electronic age*, D. Michie (ed.), 168–201. Edinburgh: Edinburgh University Press.

Reiter, R. 1978. On closed world data bases. In *Logic and data bases*, H. Gallaire & J. Minker (eds), 55–76. New York: Plenum Press.

Schank, R. C. & R. P. Abelson 1977. *Scripts, plans, goals, and understanding*. Hillsdale, NJ: Lawrence Erlbaum Associates.

Searle, J. R. 1969. *Speech acts*. Cambridge: Cambridge University Press.

Searle, J. R. 1980. Minds, brains and programs. *Behavioural and Brain Sciences* **3**, 417–424.

Sejnowski, T. J. & C. R. Rosenberg 1987. Parallel networks that learn to pronounce English text. *Complex Systems* **1**(1), 145–168.

Shortliffe, E. H. 1976. *Computer-based medical consultations: MYCIN*. New York: Elsevier.

Slate, D. & L. Atkin 1977. Chess 4.5 – the Northwestern University chess program. In *Chess skill in man and machine*, P. W. Frey (ed.). New York: Springer-Verlag.

Swartout, W. R. 1983. XPLAIN: a system for creating and explaining expert consulting programs. *Artificial Intelligence* **21**, 285–325.

Turing, A. M. 1950. Computing machinery and intelligence. *Mind* **59**, 433–460.

van Melle, W., E. H. Shortliffe, B. G. Buchanan 1981. EMYCIN: A domain independent system that aids in constructing knowledge based consultation programs. In *Machine intelligence: infotech state of the art report 9:3*.

Vernon, D. (ed.) 1991. *Computer vision: craft, engineering and science*. Berlin: Springer-Verlag.

Waltz, D. L. 1975. Understanding line drawings of scenes with shadows. In *The psychology of computer vision*, P. Winston (ed.). New York: McGraw-Hill.

Weizenbaum, J. 1966. ELIZA – a computer program for the study of natural language communication between man and machine. *Communications of the ACM* **9**(1), 36–44.

Weizenbaum, J. 1976. *Computer power and human reason: from judgement to calculation*. San Francisco: Freeman.

Winograd, T. 1972. *Understanding natural language*. Reading, MA: Addison-Wesley.

Woods, W. A. 1970. Transition network grammars for natural language analysis. *Communications of the ACM* **13**(10), 591–606.

Young, R. M. & T. R. G. Green 1989. Programmable user models for predictive evaluation of interface designs. In *Proceedings of CHI'89: human factors in computing systems*, K. Bice & C. Lewis (eds), 15–19.

Index